A History of Jazz in Britain 1919-50 was the first truly comprehensive survey of the phenomenon from a purely British perspective. Despite the increase in jazz literature since it was first published, there is no other book to rival it.

Jim Godbolt examines in great detail the arrival of the music with the Original Dixieland Jazz Band in 1919, the struggles towards the establishment of criteria, the big-band era, the disastrous Musicians' Union ban and the extraordinary internecine warfare caused by the advent of bop.

The American trail-blazing artists and bands of the twenties and thirties are all covered: the ODJB itself, the Southern Syncopated Orchestra, Paul Specht's Georgians, Louis Armstrong, Duke Ellington, Paul Whiteman, Ted Lewis, Cab Calloway and many more. Their influence on British musicians is examined, as are contemporary press reports (some quite hilarious, others downright offensive). The specialist magazines, especially the *Melody Maker*, the rhythm clubs, their discographers and pundits are closely scrutinized, and the roots of British trad and bop are traced. In addition, the book tells of the fascinating cloak-and-dagger plots which culminated in the presentation of Sidney Bechet and Coleman Hawkins on British stages in defiance of the Musicians Union ban and of the resulting court fiasco.

All this wealth of conscientiously researched detail is related with the trenchant and pithy humour for which the author is well known in British jazz circles and the result is both an indispensable reference tool for the aficionado and an interesting, sometimes startling, read for the lay observer.

D1634870

Born in Wandsworth, South London, in 1922, Jim Godbolt managed George Webb's Dixielanders from 1946 after demobilisation from the Royal Navy. He ran a band agency with Lyn Dutton and Humphrey Lyttelton in 1951 and formed his own agency in 1952, representing Mick Mulligan's Magnolia Jazz Band, the Sandy Brown–Al Fairweather All-Stars and various pop groups including the Swinging Blue Jeans.

He left the entertainment business in 1971 to concentrate on a career in writing, supporting himself with work as a meter reader, during which time he published an autobiography, *All This and 10%*, later updated to include his hilarious meter-reading experiences as *All This and Many a Dog* (republished in 2007).

In 1979 he founded *Jazz at Ronnie Scott's*, the house magazine of Ronnie Scott's Club and his compilation of features from the magazine, *Ronnie Scott's Jazz Farrago*, was published in 2008. His other books include *A History of Jazz in Britain, 1950–70* and *The World of Jazz in Printed Ephemera and Collectibles*.

A HISTORY OF JAZZ IN

BRITAIN

1919–50

Jim Godbolt

A HISTORY OF

JAZZ IN BRITAIN

1919–50

northway
publications

Northway Publications,
39 Tytherton Road, London N19 4PZ, UK.
www.northwaybooks.com

Edited by Ann and Roger Cotterrell with Chris Parker.

The publishers acknowledge with thanks the kind permission of copyright holders to reprint the photographs used in this book. Permissions have been sought in all cases where the identity of copyright holders is known.

Cover design by Adam Yeldham, Raven Design.

A CIP record for this book is available from the British Library.

First edition,1984, Quartet Books Ltd.
Paperback, 1986.
Revised, 2005, Northway Publications.
Paperback with corrections, 2010.

ISBN 978 0 9557888 1 9

Printed and bound in Great Britain by Cromwell Press Group, Trowbridge, Wiltshire.

Contents

Preface

This book was first published in 1984. When it appeared, my editor at Quartet, Chris Parker, remarked, 'You have written a jazz best seller,' which, of course, did not put it in the same class as *Harry Potter*. But then, jazz is a minority interest.

Unashamedly, I can claim most of the reviews were favourable but, of course, there were exceptions and some of the reviewers couldn't even get the title and contents right.

My book is a history of jazz in Britain, not the history of British jazz. It includes American, French, Belgian and Australian contributions. Also, I would like to emphasize that it was *A* history not *The* history in the period covered, but I acknowledge that there were omissions and mistakes.

One of the reviews I treasure was in the *Observer* by Philip Larkin, who, being a typical jazz buff, rightly pointed to some factual errors. These have been corrected recent editions. However, Mr Larkin rather over-stretched his critique by querying why I didn't include the first jazz concert held at the Royal Festival Hall. The RFH was open in 1951. I could hardly include an event, within the time frame of my volume, at a venue then not opened. Mr Larkin got his come-uppance the following week in the *Observer*, which published a correction in rhyme from a 'Ken Bull', which, in fact, was a misspelling of the correspondent's surname – Bell.

> Philip Larkin must learn the terrors
> Of correcting an author's errors.
> He must not make
> His own mistake
> As he did when, misbegotten,
> He said that Jim Godbolt had forgotten,
> In his jazz history
> To nineteen fifty,
> The concert in the Festival Hall.
> This couldn't have happened then at all

As that place was built to fit in
With the next year's Festival of Britain.
(Excuse the rhyme,
There is no time ...)

A very good friend of mine, discographer-supreme Brian Rust, also pitched in with several corrections including: 'Crown records cost sixpence, not a shilling' and 'you gave Monday 24 June 1933 as the opening date of the No. 1 Rhythm Club. This can't be – 24 June was a Sunday that year.' To many this nit-picking – and I've done my share of it – has a somewhat comical aspect, but it derives from a long tradition of discographical research where correct spellings of personnels, dates of recordings, locations, and matrix numbers were vital.

Peter Clayton writing in the *Sunday Telegraph*, commented that 'Godbolt suffers from galloping nostalgia.' But, since my history started in 1919 and we were well into the twentieth century, where else should I have begun? In Clayton's review he commented that much of the material on the traditional scene would – and I quote – 'come in useful'. There was a typesetter's error in his survey. 'Traditional' became '*traditonal*'. I wrote to Clayton thanking him for introducing me to the word *traditonal* and although I wasn't fully aware of its meaning I would 'find it useful'. I received no reply.

New editions have provided an opportunity for some revisions and updating but, perhaps vainly, I stick largely to my original concept and pronouncements. I regret that I was somewhat dismissive of Nat Gonella's contribution, but that is partly compensated for by the biography of Gonella by Ron Brown with Digby Fairweather, published by Northway in 2005. I barely mentioned George Shearing and made only a passing reference to Billy Munn. I am also sorry that I didn't accord more space to the recordings of Bert Firman as subsequent investigation shows that out of all the British big band leaders of the twenties he allowed more solo space for jazz soloists than any of his contemporaries. Also, I was wrongly dismissive of the Spike Hughes rhythm sections. Re-listening to the hundred tracks that Hughes made for Decca from 1930–32, I marvel at the high standard of musicianship throughout, at a time when there was virtually no jazz movement in this country – no jazz concerts, jazz clubs and very limited amount of literature. Indeed, Hughes was a true trailblazer.

I make a point of drawing attention to the press notices relating to jazz, particularly in the twenties when the music was an unknown quantity and much misrepresented from the press and the pulpit. I also pay tribute to the early journalists who preached the gospel and to the significant part in jazz literature played by the discographers, with particular reference to the unbelievable scholarship of Brian Rust who, happily, is one of the few survivors of those early researchers and still active in the field.

To go with the 2005 edition, I was very fortunate in having the opportunity to produce a four-CD set issued by Proper Records that follows the book's chronology. It comprises a hundred tracks that make a document in sound of the jazz played in this country by local musicians and visitors from abroad, particularly, in the latter regard, the contributions from America that included Muggsy Spanier, Jimmy Dorsey and George Brunies (with Ted Lewis), Louis Armstrong, Duke Ellington, Buck and Bubbles, Art Tatum, Dizzy Gillespie (with Teddy Hill's orchestra), Una Mae Carlisle, Fats Waller, Benny Goodman and Sidney Bechet. My liner notes to the CD set include a selected biblio-gra-phy and a full discography.

Indeed, the history is a rich and varied tapestry and I consider myself fortunate to have witnessed much of this taking place and to have been professionally involved with many of the musicians I cover.

Author's vanity being what it is, the fact of a fourth edition is very comforting. My thanks to Northway Books for persisting with this publication.

Jim Godbolt
London
March 2010

Acknowledgements

I am very much indebted to the large number of individuals who gave me priceless help in the preparation of this book – without such valuable assistance it would never have been completed.

For the first edition:

Regarding printed material, I thank Mike Oldfield, former editor of the *Melody Maker*, for giving me permission to quote extensively from pages of that paper and to peruse its files. Following its inception in 1926 the *MM* – as it was affectionately called – was the jazz buff's bible and most of the history of jazz in Britain for a period of more than five decades is recorded in its pages. I have also drawn upon the *Melody Maker*'s one-time sister paper, *Rhythm*.

I have freely quoted from the first truly specialist magazines, *Swing Music* and *Hot News*, edited by Leonard Hibbs and Eric Ballard respectively. Sadly, both editors have died, but I would like to take this opportunity of paying my posthumous respects to those intrepid pioneers who contributed so much to jazz appreciation in the crucial thirties. Retrospective thanks, as well, to the late Sinclair Traill, founder of *Pick-Up* (in 1947), the forerunner of *Jazz Journal International*, and to the publisher of *Jazz Journal*, Eddie Cook, for permission to quote from the paper. Other editors of specialist magazines to whom I was grateful for permission to quote from their pages were Max Jones and Albert McCarthy (*Jazz Music*). I was also obliged to Albert McCarthy in respect of material from *Jazz Forum* and *Jazz Monthly*, James Asman and Bill Kinnell (*Jazz*), Charles Harvey (*Jazzology*) and Bert Wilcox the proprietor of *Jazz Illustrated*.

I make an extremely humble bow to the reference books, discographical and biographical, that were constantly by my side during the preparation of this volume. These are: *The Illustrated Encyclopedia of Jazz* by Brian Case and Stan Britt, *Who's Who of Jazz* by John Chilton, *The Encyclopedia of Jazz* by Leonard Feather, *Jazz Directory* (six volumes) by

Albert McCarthy, Dave Carey and Ralph Venables, and *Jazz Records 1897–1942* by Brian Rust (two volumes).

Other books that have provided me with vital information are *The Story of the Original Dixieland Jazz Band* by H. O. Brunn, *Music is My Mistress* by Duke Ellington, *Opening Bars* and *Second Movement* by Spike Hughes, *Louis* by Max Jones and John Chilton, *Background of the Blues* by Iain Lang, *Music Ho!* by Constant Lambert, *I Play as I Please* and *The Best of Jazz from Basin Street to Harlem* by Humphrey Lyttelton, *The Dance Band Era* by Albert McCarthy, *All About Jazz* by Stanley Nelson and the early if hardly informative volumes like *The Appeal of Jazz* by R. W. S. Mendl, *So This is Jazz* by Henry Osgood and *Jazz* by Paul Whiteman.

My thanks are due to those who provided me with information, verbal and printed, photographs and other memorabilia, not all of which I could use but the generosity of all concerned was truly appreciated: Jeff Aldam, James Asman (James Asman's Jazz Centre), Bruce Bastin (Harlequin Records), Terry Brown, Philip Buchel, Roy Burchall (*Melody Maker*), Charles Chilton, John Chilton, Tony Crombie, Blanche Curtis, Doug Dobell, Jackie Docherty, Charles Fox, Harry Gold, Joe Green (Ronnie Scott's Club), Rex Harris, Eddie Harvey, Chris Hayes, Harry Hayes, Keith Howell, Spike Hughes, Tony Hughes, John Kendall, Pete King (Ronnie Scott's Club), Harry Klein, Steve Lane, Bill Le Sage, Dr Rainer Lotz, Tony Middleton (Dobell's Record Shop), Gerry Moore, Peter Newbrook (Esquire Records), George Penniket, Brian Peerless, Les Perrin, Steve Race, Don Rendell, Ronnie Scott, Jackie Sharpe, Ray Smith (Ray's Jazz Shop), John Whitehorn (EMI Publishing), Bert Wilcox and especially Alun Morgan, Robin Rathborne and Brian Rust, whose knowledge and files I ruthlessly plundered and whose generosity I shamelessly exploited.

My thanks to George Melly, Brian Rust and Eric Thacker for the poetry in this volume, although their verses are entirely different in character and intent!

I acknowledge the help of Peter Ballard, who made useful revisions on the original manuscript, and of Dennis O'Neill and Chris Parker, my editors at Quartet Books, for their skilled attention to the first edition. My thanks also to Susi Hines and Denise Ward for typing the first edition and making sense of my ham-fisted (or rather two-fingered) typing, and particularly to Ms Hines who helped save this work from being a riot of split infinitives – among other grammatical inexactitudes.

Since no once twisted my arm to embark upon this project I cannot make the writer's now familiar complaint about long and lonely hours crouched over the cold typewriter etc., but during this lengthy chore, many telephonic and personal conversations with the above pleasurably broke the tedium and their generous help warmed the heart of this plodding, often despairing, scribe.

Line illustrations are courtesy of EMI Publishing, *Melody Maker*, Parlophone, Levy's Record Shop, *Hot News*, Albert McCarthy, Max Jones, *Jazz Illustrated*, Decca Records.

Black and white illustrations are courtesy of *Rhythm on Record*, *Record Changer*, *Melody Maker*, Dr Rainer Lotz, Penguin Books, *Era*, Decca Records, *Swing Music*, *Rhythm*, Rex Harris, George Penniket, *Jazz News*, Max Jones, Norman Law, Ed W. Jones, Baltimore Photo, Jackie Sharpe, Bill Le Sage, *Jazz Illustrated*, Philip Lord.

For the 2010 edition:

Additional photos have been made available by Ron Brown and through the assistance of David Nathan of the National Jazz Archive. Others are from my collection and I am grateful to Charles Wilford for the use of his photo on page 165. I am also grateful to Ken Bell for permission to quote his poem.

In addition to the above I wish to acknowledge the invaluable help given to me by Chris Parker, Janet Law, and Ann and Roger Cotterrell in the preparation of this edition.

Introduction

In this book, which I believe was the first attempt at a comprehensive examination of the first three decades of jazz in Britain, I have tried to include mention of as many individuals as possible who have played their part in this saga. My apologies to those who, because of pressure on space or the author's ignorance of their role, have been omitted.

The references to parts of American jazz history were inevitable, as the development of a music, initially played three thousand miles distant, was invariably the inspiration for what followed in Britain and, in some instances, explanations of direct links were, I think, called for.

Regarding race, many of the terms appearing in this book: 'spade', 'negro', 'coloured' and others of a more insulting kind have been retained in many quotes because they describe or reflect the less enlightened racial attitudes of the time and I hope that no offence will be taken at their inclusion.

Although this is not a sociological treatise, certain aspects of British society (eg the Pulpit, Press and the BBC) have been touched upon to indicate the social background against which the playing of jazz and jazz appreciation have evolved in Britain.

I have covered the works of critics, authors, discographers, club organizers and entrepreneurs, as I believe they made a valuable contribution to the evolvement. No art survives without these ancillary activities.

There are extensive quotations from contemporary reports and I believe they evoke a more vivid impression of events and mores of the period than would any historian's retrospective examinations.

I have referred to the lunatic fringe of the jazz world, but do not delude myself that I am guiltless in my past writings and activities. Indeed, during the preparation of this volume many an uncomfortable tremor of embarrassment disturbed me as I recalled adolescent (and post-adolescent!) attitudes I once loudly trumpeted. For instance, I dwell on the sham of 'symphonic' jazz, and how much this nonsense, and favourable reactions to it, delayed appreciation of the real thing and I had to remind myself that when young I was a fervent admirer of Paul Whiteman's futile attempts to 'marry' jazz with the 'classics'. Having this in mind I have tried to avoid mockery of the critical inanities and discographical gaffes of others with the benefit of hindsight. Edgar Jackson's blundering critiques, for instance, have been included princi-pally to demonstrate what an agonized and convoluted business was the beginning of jazz criticism in this country, although some critics of jazz (and some jazz critics!) fully deserve any reproach history can heap on them.

In researching this volume I was frequently struck by the many ironies and paradoxes that attended the history of jazz in Britain and may the reader excuse the number of times I refer to these. Even now, although reasonably familiar with the train of events from 1919, I still marvel at the twists and turns in the skeins of its development, and still feel surprise at the extent to which jazz has entered the psyche of the allegedly cold-blooded Anglo-Saxon.

My own lifespan corresponds roughly with this history and as I have spent some forty enjoyable years in close involvement with many aspects of events I have permitted myself the occasional indulgence of personal reminiscence.

I had two main reasons for not taking this summary beyond 1950. An attempt to embrace events from 1919 to the present day was so daunting a notion that I gave it no more than a cursory thought (with a palpable shudder), and to have covered those years would have meant sacrificing detail. The second reason is that from 1950 the scene was so different from that of the preceding years. The big bands were to collapse; there were to be the coincident phenomena of 'trad' and 'bop' and then 'mainstream', where many of the stylistic opposites came to join hands. For the first time British musicians could earn a living playing jazz. Allied to this was the advent of the long-playing record, which allowed the jazzman to stretch himself fully in one performance, and this invention also gave us compilations of historic 78s. With this came a flood of jazz literature and the emergence of the specialist shop to stock this documentation on vinyl and in print.

Some of the post-1950 events I do mention in my final chapter, but the entire story is deserving of a separate volume. So, although I have dealt only with part of the span of jazz history in Britain, I hope that many might, after reading this volume, seek out the records of the musicians discussed in it. I thus end this introduction with a note of missionary zeal, the zeal that fired the movement in the twenties and thirties and without which there would have been no jazz in Britain, nor this book to honour that phenomenon.

'"The Original Dixieland Jazz Band has arrived in London," says an evening paper. We are grateful for the warning.'

Punch, 16 April 1919

1

When I Hear That
Jazz Band Play

During the last fifty years or so, people in public life or the media have been able to consult a vast library or refer to a host of experts before making any comment about jazz, but it remains a musical form that many, even to this day, do not consider worth the effort of checking before pronouncing upon. Judges, in particular, are notorious for their facetious questions and observations concerning the music, and in 1976 the future Prime Minister, Margaret Thatcher, committed, via a spokesman, a gaffe which inspired many a coarse guffaw in the jazz community.

In August of that year the Fulham and Hammersmith Conservative Associations booked the bands of Chris Barber, Kenny Ball and Dave Morgan to appear at the Royal Albert Hall to raise funds. The *Daily Mail* ran a picture of Mrs Thatcher, ostensibly playing clarinet in the company of the three bandleaders, all with instruments to their lips. The accompanying report stated that Margaret Thatcher couldn't actually play the clarinet but that she liked 'New Orleans Jazz, especially Duke Ellington'.

If the fact that a political association, and right-wing at that, booked jazz bands to raise funds reflected the drawing power of bands playing music once despised and derided by the Establishment, it was also reflective of its 'cultural' acceptability that the leader writer in a 'serious' daily paper should remark upon Mrs Thatcher's alleged comment. That paper was the *Guardian*, which under the heading 'Educating Mrs Thatcher' pulled her up very sharply:

The other day, in the high cause of something or the other, the Conservative leader, Mrs Thatcher, was photographed with a group of jazz musicians. In what looked like a naked bid for the woodwind vote, she was nervously grasping a clarinet. Later, a party spokesman put the record straight. Mrs Thatcher, he admitted, didn't actually play the clarinet – but she is very fond of New Orleans Jazz, especially Duke Ellington.

Mrs Thatcher and her spokesman have a lot to learn. To number Duke Ellington among New Orleans musicians is like equating Shostakovich with Josquin des Prés or recalling the historic jam sessions in old Vienna when Wild Gus Mahler used to blow alongside Schubert and Johann Strauss. Much of the blame should rightly be placed on the niggardly attention paid to jazz by the BBC. In an age when the music of Beethoven and Bartók, Mozart and Messiaen, pours from our radios like water from a tap, jazz is kept on stand-pipe rations . . .

The representatives of the Jazz Centre Society, which this week told the Annan Committee on Broadcasting that we ought to have at least 25 hours of jazz a week on radio and much more, too, on television, would swing us too far in the opposite direction. But in asserting that jazz music gets a miserly deal at present they are fighting a justified fight, both for greater public enjoyment – and the further education of Mrs Thatcher.

This informed comment by a leader writer sympathetic to jazz was a far cry from the first press coverage of jazz or, in most cases, what the writers *thought* to be jazz.

These references can be traced as far back as 1917 and probably even earlier, long before anyone in Britain had ever heard a jazz band, on record or in the flesh. But, towards the end of the First World War, 'jazz' was all the rage and even the mighty *Times* gave it a mention. This voice of the Establishment did not, as might have been expected, 'thunder' in its denunciation of a music so patently non-conformist (although not, of course, the real thing) nor was the comment made in the leader column, in the space devoted to truly significant matters.

The acknowledgement that jazz existed came in *The Times* of 19 January 1919 and followed a list of forthcoming marriages, and condolences from their Majesties King George V and Queen Mary to Lady Wyndham on the death of her husband, theatre impresario Sir Charles.

Perhaps *The Times* thought there was a connection between Sir Charles' activities and the show then running at the Coliseum which gave it the opportunity to mention this new craze. The comment was headed:

THE ART OF THE JAZZ

DRUMMER AS CHIEF CONSPIRATOR

Not the least interesting feature of a capital programme this week at the Coliseum is the effort of the orchestra to convert itself into a jazz band, one of the many American peculiarities that threaten to make life a nightmare. The object of a jazz band, apparently, is to provide as much noise as possible; the method of doing so is immaterial and if music happens to be the result occasionally so much the better. The chief conspirator is the drummer, or the individual who held that position in normal days for the drummer merely becomes a side show.

Granted, around him there are as many things as he can possibly need, motor horns, bells, sheets of tin, anything from which noise can be extracted. The object of the drummer then seems to be to strike as many things as possible in the shortest possible space of time, and it may be said to the credit of the gentleman who officiated at the Coliseum that he certainly hit something every time; whether or not it was the object at which he was aiming it was hard for an outsider to say. At any rate he didn't tie himself into an inextricable knot – so presumably he won the game.

The Times failed to mention the name of the show or the band. It must be assumed that the athletic percussionist was the drummer in the pit orchestra.

Before *The Times'* historic mention of a music that was to sweep throughout the world, the word jazz, according to some historians, had been used in America at least from the beginning of the century. Spelt 'jass' or 'jas', it was a slang African-American term meaning to excite erotically; and with such connotations it soon became associated with a music springing from low-life origins.

The word became increasingly used as this new music developed, although not always in respect of the music itself or of the sex act. Once the U-boat menace had been overcome at the end of the First World War, American artists came to perform in Britain, some bringing with them songs that included the word. Many, American and British, used it to describe their act. One called 'The Little Fields' advertised their performance as 'Jazzing on a Wobbly Wire'. Because many of these acts included dance routines it was generally thought that jazz was a dance. A common question at dances and parties was, 'Do you jazz?', the enquirers almost certainly unaware of the word's original meaning. The US magazine *Etude*, September 1924, commented: 'If the truth were known about the origin of the word "jazz" it would never be mentioned in polite society.'

Murray Pilcer and his American Sherbo Sextette. In 1919 Pilcer made the first British recording by a group claiming to be a jazz band.

It was the percussion in these so-called jazz acts and bands that entranced the writers in the music and trade papers. Indeed drum-kits used to be known as 'jazz-sets'. In the 11 October 1917 issue of *Encore*, a paper devoted to the flourishing variety profession, there appeared a feature by Thomas Reece, headed 'Mr Jazz Arrives':

America is a country which apparently delights in the invention of weird bands. It is to America that we owe the trap drummer, usually a powerful negro, which has made the drum solo an instrument of force and power, if not attractiveness. The building up of a peculiar combination of instruments to go with the trap drummer has now been proceeding for some time and the latest fruit of this is the jazz band.

Examples of this reached this side some time ago and comprised of piano, banjo, violin, saxophone, trombone and trap drum. Exceptional noisiness is, of course, the result; but at the same time these bands may be held to justify their existence. They are certainly correctives against air-raids because no matter how loudly the anti-aircraft guns roar outside the trombone etc. can be guaranteed to drown all extraneous noises. Sometimes the performers are brave enough to dance to a jazz band and this has led to the jazz tango.

In August 1917, Francis, Day and Hunter published 'When I Hear That Jazz Band Play' and 'Stick Around for the New Jazz Band'. In the same year the Edison Bell Record Company issued a record by song duettists Collins and Harland called 'That Funny Jazz Band from Dixieland'. *Encore*, 1 February 1918, reported that, at the Grand, Hanley, Stoke-on-Trent, 'A new American invasion is heralded by the appearance "fresh from the United States" of the Jazzbo Band. This is a combination of instrumentalists, vocalists and dancers, the instruments consisting of pianos, double bass, saxophones, trombones, banjos, piccolos, mandolin and trap drums. From their Transatlantic reputation the Jazzbo Band are the last-minute rage and are expected to leave the old Tango craze standing.' *Encore*, 8 November 1918, carried a half-page advertisement which read:

Harry and Burton Lester
The 'Jazz Boys'
writers and composers of
My Jazz Band Down in Dixieland (Reilly and Bertrand)
That Piccaninny Child of Mine (Francis, Day and Hunter)
More in the making

The 'Jazz Boys' appealed to Thomas Reece. Reviewing their appearance at the Metropolitan Theatre, Edgware Road, he commented, 'John Lester's Frisco Five, featuring Harry and Burton Lester . . . with that ragtime singing and dancing and violin playing and eccentric Jazz band antics would be the life and soul of a musical or burlesque piece. They possess a real genius for entertainment, Harry the smartest and cleverest and most amusing Jazz drummer I have ever seen. The audience was convulsed with amusement.'

In January 1919 'All Bound 'Round with the Mason–Dixon Line' coupled with 'That Moaning Trombone' was recorded for the Edison Bell label by Murray Pilcer and his Jazz Band. It was the first-ever British-made record by a combination claiming to be a jazz band, but the music hadn't the remotest affinity with jazz.

In the *Performer*, 23 January 1919, there appeared an advertisement for 'Jazzin' the Jazz' with the Brazilian Trio led by Captain T. Jackells, of St

John's Wood House, Shoeburyness, whose latest composition for the act was a number entitled 'Jazzers, Jigs and Nigs, You All Look Alike'. The advertisement ended on a defiant note. 'Producers, managers and agents! See this act for yourself and don't listen to what the nincompoops have to say!'

In the 12 February 1919 issue of *Era* the song publishers Darewski, with offices in Denmark Street, Britain's 'Tin Pan Alley', advertised their 'jazz' titles separately from the rest of their list.

GREAT JAZZ HITS

Jazzin' Around One Step (one step)   Hawaiian Jazz (fox-trot)
Hong Kong Jazz (fox-trot)   At the Jazz Band Ball (one step)

Only one of these titles, 'At the Jazz Band Ball', had any staying power. It was a composition by the first genuine jazz band to visit Britain and subsequently became one of the most frequently recorded by jazz bands.

In *Era*, 19 February, a paragraph headed 'Joy Bells' was as unintentionally portentous as the title 'Stick Around for the New Jazz Band': 'Albert De Courville seems to have selected March the 12th for the Hippo's next revue, *Joy Bells*. In this you will see and hear the Original Dixieland Jazz Band, all the way from New Orleans where the crocodiles come from! There will also be displayed a marvellous Electroller all-a-beaming and gleaming – and George Robey doing ditto.'

While the Original Dixieland Jazz Band were still aboard the RMS *Adriatic* bound for Liverpool, the British public and press, quite unaware of what was about to assail their ears, continued listening to songs whose affinity with jazz went no further than items such as 'The Yiddisher Jazz' and 'The Corned Beef Jazz Band' to name but two songs with titles of that ilk.

In the same issue *Era* reported: 'The jazz band and the shimmy are all the rage just now and have been introduced into the Broadway Roof Garden Scene in *Bing Boys on Broadway* at the Alhambra. Miss Violet Loraine, Mr Gus McNaughton, Toots and Lorna Pounds participating therein with great gusto. The jazz carnival is one of the features of this successful piece.'

In the 15 May 1918 issue of *Performer*, there appeared a crude illustration of a black man with the following caption:

> First he brings us his slave ditties,
> Then he charms us with his Coon songs,
> Now he's sending us barmy with Jazz
> What's his next stunt?

Yet it wasn't the black man who first sent 'us barmy with Jazz' in Britain.

The Original Dixieland Jazz Band as it appeared at Reisenweber's restaurant in New York in 1917. *Left to right*: Eddie Edwards, trombone; Henry Ragas, piano; Larry Shields, clarinet; Nick La Rocca, cornet; Tony Sbarbaro, drums.

* * *

On 1 April 1919 the *Adriatic* berthed at Liverpool and the Original Dixieland Jazz Band travelled to London by train, reporting late that night to producer Albert De Courville at the London Hippodrome. *Era*, 4 April 1919, commented:

> The Original Dixieland Jazz Band which arrived in London last night and is now one of the attractions in *Joy Bells* gave a private performance at the theatre on Thursday last between the afternoon and evening shows. The bandsmen are white men from New Orleans and the instruments on which they operate with such enthusiasm are a piano, cornet, clarinet, trombone and trap drum, the last named having an especially busy time.
>
> A saucepan and a bowler hat were also used as adjuncts to the brass instruments in some of the selections, which include the 'Tiger Rag', the 'Barnyard Blues' and other exhilarating numbers. A clever and wonderfully agile dancer

is a member of the combination, the expert instrumentalists of which also prove their ability in 'straight stuff' and accompanying the Dixieland Band are due to be a big success.

On 10 April a contributor to the *Performer* revealed his perplexity:

> I had an experience the other evening. Whether I am to be envied or not depends on personal tastes . . . a semi-private exposition of real jazz by the Original Dixieland Jazz Band. At least I was told by Mr De Courville that this was the Original Dixieland Jazz Band, and from the noise 'kicked up' I may well believe him . . . I am assured that there are only two original jazz bands in America. Why two, I cannot say . . . I am told that the other of the two original bands is but an imitation; a fact that seems to clear the atmosphere somewhat. Then I'm told that the Dixieland lot are the original, so it seems that poor America has to be content for the nonce with a mere substitute . . .
>
> At any rate I've come to the conclusion that the best qualification for a jazzist is to have no knowledge of music and no musical ability beyond that of making noises either on piano, or clarinet, or cornet or trap drum which, I believe, are the proper constituents of a jazz orchestra. Of course, I may be mistaken, for I place myself amongst the musically uninitiated.

Press men were now hearing jazz proper for the first time, and played by a band that laid specific claim to being the originators. It was the journalists' opportunity to enquire of the visitors the origins and true meaning of the operative word.

The *London Daily News*, 4 April 1919, reported:

> . . . as to the word 'Jazz' the bandsmen rejected both the current explanations. They will not have it that the word is of Red Indian origin, or that 'jazz so' is a term of praise in the dialect of the negroes in the Southern States. The word was invented by someone in Chicago . . . It is possibly a purely onomatopoeic expression . . . In view of the unkind and disrespectful things which have been said about Red Indians and negroids and West African Savages, it should be stated that the players are all white – white as they possibly can be.

H. O. Brunn, in his *The Story of the Original Dixieland Jazz Band*, recalls how the band opened at the Hippodrome in *Joy Bells* on 7 April, appearing in a specially staged cafe scene. The ovation following the opening number was deafening, due in large part to the number of American doughboys in the audience:

The fever spread throughout the theatre until every last man and woman was on his feet, shouting and clapping in a manner that was peculiarly un-British. When the curtain came down, George Robey, the star comedian of the show, strode up to De Courville in a seething rage and served an ultimatum. Robey or the Jazz Band would have to go – De Courville could have his pick. De Courville gave in.

The ODJB as they appeared in Britain in 1919. *Left to right:* Billy Jones, piano; Larry Shields, clarinet; Nick La Rocca, cornet; Emile Christian, trombone; Tony Sbarbaro, drums.

Thus the first engagement in Britain of the Original Dixieland Jazz Band (or the ODJB, as it became known) lasted for just one night.

On 29 April *Era* reviewed the show, but omitted mention of both the ODJB's appearance and their dismissal. They made an oblique reference to the fracas:

A DISSERTATION ON JAZZ

The world these days seems to be dividing itself into two camps – the pro-jazzers and the anti-jazzers. To Jazz or not to Jazz – that is the question.

I must confess that I derive some entertainment from the unexpected twists and turns of a good jazz band. As I sit indolently in the halls the ethics of the question do not concern me. The music hall idealist may worry over jazz as his more solemn confrères worry over Richard Strauss, but to me it is . . . April 19th that counts and if I am cheered on this chilly eve in April 1919 by the orchestra's tiddley-poms, I think not of the years ahead when, according to the anti-jazzers, the house that Jack built will come toppling down.

There is, however, much to be said for the anti-jazzers, and it is imposs-ible to deny that jazz music is impertinent and hath no respect for persons. My recent experience at the Palladium and the Coliseum provided many illustrations of this. At the Palladium I turned round suddenly one moment to see the damage apparently caused by an attendant dropping her tray of ices and lemonade. Her tray was intact – the crash had come from the orchestra.

This appraisal is both appreciative and heavy-humoured, but it employed a splendid analogy in the arguments for and against this new experience by mentioning a 'classical' composer notorious for 'imperti-nence' and then unacceptable to the academic musical establishment.

On 12 April 1919 a paper called *Town Topics* speculated on the reason for the sudden withdrawal of the ODJB from *Joy Bells*:

> The Dixieland Jazz Band appeared in *Joy Bells* at the Hippodrome last Monday but since has been withdrawn, presumably on account of that ubiquitous complaint influenza. On the occasion of their performance they gave us a demonstration of undiluted jazz, and it must be admitted, despite all that has been thought and said to the contrary there was a certain charm in the mournful refrains, dramatically broken up by cheery jingles and a mis-cellany of noises such as one generally hears 'off'.
>
> At one moment the whole orchestra would down tools while one member tootled merrily or eerily on his own account, and the whole would resume again, always ready to give a fair hearing to any other individual player who had suddenly developed a stunt. The conductor was most urbane about it all, but everybody was perfectly happy, not excluding the audience who appreci-ated a novelty not unartistic.

One decidedly unhappy person was George Robey. He wasn't, as fore-cast in *Era* on 19 February, 'all-a-beaming and gleaming' and his perform-ance in the show received a poor notice in the 22 March issue of *Encore*.

Despite the Hippodrome setback – or maybe because of the contro-versy it aroused – the band opened at the London Palladium on 12 April. An evening paper, the *Star*, 19 April, commented: 'It is an interesting study to watch the faces of the dancers at the Palladium when the Original Dixieland Jazz Band, which is said to be the only one of its kind in the world, is doing its best to murder music. Most are bewildered by the weird discords but some, to judge by their cynical smiles, evidently think that it is a musical joke that is hardly worth while attempting. Perhaps they are right.'

From the programme for the ODJB appearances at the London Palladium, April 1919

****

8. The Great Original American

DIXIE-LAND JAZZ BAND

and JOHNNIE DALE, a Jazz Dancer,

Presented by Albert de Courville for the first time in England.
The creation of Jazz.   The sensation of America.

****

Encore didn't mention the ODJB's one-night stand at the Hippodrome, but carried a review, unsigned, of the band's appearance at the London Palladium. The tone of the piece was entirely different from Thomas Reece's mention of 'jazz' in the same paper on 11 October 1917, but the earlier appraisal wasn't of any particular band and was based only on Reece's notion of jazz. This particular writer was vitriolic about the genuine article:

De Courville presents the Dixieland Jazz Band, the sensation of America. I once heard of a man who jumped from a ten-storey building and dashed his brains out. He caused a sensation. President Wilson has departed. Jazz has arrived. I do not know which is having the worst effect. In this act there are seven. Piano, trap drummer, flageolot [sic], cornet and trombone and male and female dancers. After what seems to one like loud rolls of dreadful thunder, a girl arrived, dressed in a half green muff and some other stuff who tried to sing to a discordant row in a music shop. Her song was something about a 'Wonderful Smile'. It is wonderful what the world is coming to. The lady is indeed clever, for she danced without moving her feet – in fact when she danced with her partner she was more danced against than dancing. After her departure to moderate applause a man came in and wiggled himself about like a filleted eel about to enter the stewing pot. This is the most discordant and uninteresting entertainment I have ever seen at the Palladium.

The resident orchestra fast asleep could amuse me more. These jazz bandsmen played like a swarm of bees who had lost their hive and found a home at the Palladium. After seeing jazz musical studies are of no account, I can see clearly that if I can rattle on any old tin my future is made.

They got a cool reception despite a few Americans who travelled especially across the big spit to give them a lift up. I know some rattling good English acts walking around who can really entertain the public.

Clearly the writer was evaluating them as a variety hall act and his on-the-spot report of the audience reception differs from Brunn's retrospective account of the Hippodrome performance. *Encore* made an allusive reference to the incident at the Hippodrome in a regular feature headed 'What *Encore* would like to know', listing as many as twenty 'in' questions. One of these was: 'What does George Robey think about it?' – an obvious reference to his displeasure.

Era, 23 April, also gave a different impression of the Palladium performance:

> [The] Dixieland Jazz Band . . . appeared at the Palladium last week . . . and met with hearty approval – the band numbers five, in addition to a lady and gentleman, the lady singing a couple of numbers excellently. Johnny Dale is the male jazz dancer and his steps and gymnastics are little short of wonderful, especially in the 'Darktown Strutter's Ball'. 'Everybody Shimmies Now' in conjunction with the lady is a great duet with jazz chorus and the lady sings 'I'm Sorry I Made You Cry'. The band itself gave us 'Barnyard Blues Jazz' [*sic*], 'At the Jazz Band Ball', and 'Tiger Rag', in the latter a saucepan and bowler hat serving as accessories to the various instruments. The Dixieland band is retained for this week.

The personnel of the band that came to England was Nick La Rocca (cornet), Larry Shields (clarinet), Emile Christian (trombone), Tony Sbarbaro (drums) and J. Russell Robinson (piano). La Rocca, Shields and Sbarbaro were from New Orleans. Robinson came from Indianapolis and was replaced during the tour by a Londoner, Billy Jones.

The records they made here for Columbia and those made in America for the Victor label (released on English HMV) reveal their spirited, if jerky and inspirationally limited, collective improvisation on, mostly, their own tunes. They convey some of the impact such unorthodox and unfamiliar sounds must have had on British audiences accustomed to polite Edwardian ballads or so-called 'ragtime'.

They were a totally new experience. Despite their early, very mixed reception, and being dismissed after only one night at their first engagement, they stayed in the country for fifteen months, doing good business at the Palladium, Rector's Club in Tottenham Court Road and the Hammersmith Palais.

They were even received at Buckingham Palace, the twenty-year-old Marquis of Donegall arranging a performance before King George V.

Brunn quotes La Rocca as saying that they were all carefully scrutinized by a gathering of British nobility who peered at them through lorgnettes 'as though we had bugs on us'. According to Brunn the band, once allowed across the royal threshold, exploded into a

Hammersmith Palais – the ODJB played here in 1919

steaming version of their most famous tune – since played a million times over by bands throughout the world – 'Tiger Rag'. 'The audience appeared petrified at first, a few members of the court glancing uneasily at the nearest exit. At the conclusion of this number and after an embarrassing silence King George laughed his approval and began to applaud energetically, his example taken up by the loyal but frightened entourage. The encore, "Ostrich Walk", was received with somewhat less tension.' (The English magazine *Tempo*, undated, but published in 1947, contains an article by the Marquis of Donegall, which relates his meeting with La Rocca in the Silver Bar of the Roosevelt Hotel, New Orleans, in 1936. He quotes La Rocca as stating that the band broke up in 1925, that they started 'swing' [then in 1936 the currently fashionable word for jazz], and that the proudest moment in the band's life was playing at the Peace Ball at the Savoy Hotel in 1919 at which Earl Haig was one of the guests. No mention was made of the visit to the Palace, either by La Rocca or Donegal.l)

The ODJB returned to America in July 1920 to find that jazz had been prettified. Bands like Paul Whiteman's, Art Hickman's and Paul Specht's had introduced written arrangements of Tin Pan Alley songs, and largely eschewed improvisation, retaining only the four beats in a bar rhythm for the dancers. These bandleaders and their supporters genuinely believed they were 'improving' jazz by stripping it of improvisation.

The ODJB underwent several personnel changes, and added a saxophone to keep up with the fashion, before disbanding. They reassembled briefly in 1936. It was not until the mid-thirties that their significance was evaluated from a more informed perspective.

Many historians, all of them white, denied them a role other than that of imitating the black man's music. Much of this criticism was inverse (or 'Crow Jim') racism, but certainly the ODJB's claim to be the originators of jazz proved to be insupportable. In a highly perceptive analysis of their music in his *Best of Jazz – Basin Street to Harlem*, Humphrey Lyttelton writes, 'For all their shortcomings . . . they provided a sort of blue-print of how the line-up of trumpet-clarinet-trombone could be organized and from that blue-print a lot more creative jazz in what has come to be called the dixieland style has stemmed.'

The Original Lyrical Five, 1923. This British band emulated the ODJB and played at the Hammersmith Palais. Included are: Syd Roy, piano; Lew Davis (who became Britain's first recognized jazz trombonist in the 1920s), and future bandleader Harry Roy, clarinet.

The ODJB's direct musical influence in Britain was negligible, since most of the local bands were emulating the prettifying processes then prevalent in America and heard on records issued in Britain. Even so, the word jazz was now widely bandied about, thanks to their visit. In *Era*, 20 November 1920, Leonard Fisher and Sylvia Lees, a dance act, advertised 'Jazzs [*sic*!] and Whirls' and the *Era*, March 1921, carried an advertisement for Abbot's Jazz School, 215 High Street, Kensington.

If eighteen months of the Dixieland Band hadn't shown British musicians how to play jazz, an academy for such tuition in genteel Kensington was hardly likely to do any better. But now 'jazz' was all the rage, and no doubt there were individuals with the naïve belief that it could be instructed. As was later seen it was an art that could be absorbed but not 'taught', but while it was a novelty, dance halls capitalized on the fact. *Musical Mirror Pictorial*, February 1921, carried an advertisement placed by the Hammersmith Palais, which had been host to the ODJB:

CONCERNING JAZZ MUSIC
at the Palais de Danse

'What is the secret of the success of your jazz bands?' we are often asked. There are definite reasons to be given in explanation. All the musicians are specialists in syncopation – we scoured two continents to procure the best – and besides being musicians they are great fun provokers. Musicianly and mirthful they are at all times in perfect harmony with the dancers – they inspire one to ecstatic dancing happiness. They give 'life' and 'vim' and 'go' to the whole proceedings.

For the best dancing and perfect dance music go to the Palais de Danse, Hammersmith.

Two sessions daily:
3 to 6 p.m. 2/6d   8 to 12 p.m. 5/-

PALAIS DE DANSE
THE TALK OF LONDON HAMMERSMITH

But the palais didn't renew its advertisement in this paper, perhaps because of the sustained editorial hostility to what was thought to be jazz. Under the heading 'The Origins of Jazz' the paper reported that John Philip Sousa, the 'March King', had been:

> busying himself in research work with the object of discovering the origin of Jazz. He declares that the term originated with the darkie minstrels of the southern states. To these worthies, knockabout humour was a source of irresistible merriment and a good sound thwack on a musician's head, or a playful squirt of water in his face, reduced the audience almost to a state of hysteria. These adventitious aids to the charms of the music were known as 'hokum' or 'jazzbo' and it was, Mr Sousa thinks, the second of these that gave its name to the dance.

Among the numerous references to jazz was a report in the May 1921 issue of *Musical Mirror Pictorial* stating that a Russian pianist had been concerned with experiments to ascertain the effect of different kinds of music on the insane. 'Of course the thing should be done properly. It might be the reverse of judicious, however, to administer a violent dose of concentrated jazz three times daily though, on the other hand, such music might conceivably be effective in the case of a madman of the quiet morbid type, or any form of lunacy in the classic melancholy category.'

While the music and the stage act of the Dixieland Band were creating a minor furore in the press, a black band from America, Will Marion Cook's Southern Syncopators, were attracting relatively little attention,

Ernest Ansermet – 'first ever jazz critic'

probably because the music they played was more formal, more acceptable to Western ears. Its repertoire, played in semi-symphonic style, included popular ballads and novelty pieces including 'Jazzin' at the Harem', 'The Music Box', 'Tarantine' and a work by the black composer Samuel Coleridge-Taylor, 'Imaginary Ballet No. 4'. The vocal items were tunes like 'Roll, Jordan Roll', 'Jazzamine', 'The Sweetest Flower' and 'Why Adam Sinned'. Clearly, no jazz band; but they had in their personnel a twenty-year-old creole from New Orleans, Sidney Bechet.

Thirty-six-year-old Ernest Ansermet, founder-conductor of the Suisse Romande Orchestra, heard the Southern Syncopators at the Royal Philharmonic Hall, 35 Great Portland Street, and the then little-known conductor wrote about their orchestra and particularly about their clarinettist in the 19 October 1919 issue of the Swiss music magazine *Revue Romande* under the title 'On a Negro Orchestra'. Ansermet's warm appraisal of their performance stands in sharp contrast to the bluster of the English journalists who, in their assessments of the Original Dixieland Jazz Band, were being abusive, heavy-humoured and preoccupied with the loathed percussion. He wrote: 'The first thing that strikes one about the Southern Syncopated Orchestra is the astonishing perfection, the superb taste and the fervour of its playing . . . ' But it was Bechet's playing that impressed him most:

There is in the orchestra an extraordinary clarinet virtuoso who, it seems, is the first of his race to have composed perfectly formed blues on the clarinet . . . they are admirable for the richness of their intonation, their force of accent, their daring novelty and unexpected turns . . . their form was gripping, abrupt and harsh with a brusque and pitiless ending like that of Bach's Second Brandenburg Concerto. I wish to set down the name of this artist of genius, as for myself I shall never forget it: it is Sidney Bechet.

When one has tried so hard so often in the past to discover one of the figures to whom we owe the advent of an art . . . what a moving thing it is to meet this very black, fat boy with white teeth and that narrow forehead who is very glad one likes what he does, but who can say nothing of his art save that it follows his 'own way' and then one thinks his 'own way' is perhaps the highway the whole world will swing along tomorrow.

Benny Peyton's Jazz Kings, a contingent from the Southern Syncopated Orchestra, c.1920. Sidney Bechet is on the far right.

Ansermet's speculation on future musical fashions was, at least in part, accurate and his phraseology (i.e. 'swing along') uncannily pre-echoed vernacular which was to be so widely used by the jazz community in later generations.

The Southern Syncopated Orchestra didn't record either here or in America, although a contingent from the band, led by drummer Benny Peyton and including Bechet, recorded for the English Columbia label. The sides, however, were never released, and the masters were subsequently destroyed. A shame: it would have been instructive to hear exactly contemporary recordings of the playing that so impressed the 'classicist' Ansermet, although Bechet made records in 1923 with Clarence Williams' Blue Five, that demonstrate how he must have sounded four years earlier.

Like the ODJB, the Southern Syncopated Orchestra appeared before the royal family at Buckingham Palace. The curiosity value of these visitors appears to have exerted an unexpected fascination on the royals. They had listened to the first band that truly despatched the word 'jazz' round the world and here they gave audience to an orchestra that contained an instrumentalist who was later to become universally acclaimed. Allegedly Bechet found the Palace 'like Grand Central Station with lots of carpets and lots more doors'. They played in the Palace garden and Bechet claimed that King George liked his 'Characteristic Blues'. In 1937 Bechet recorded this title with a trio (and singer Billy Banks) from Noble Sissle's orchestra. If the sheer force of this was the same that King George heard he was indeed a swinging monarch!

The jazz cognoscenti who were shortly to emerge were, however, slow to echo this approbation from an eminent conductor and the King of England. The records Bechet made subsequently (none of them under his own name until 1938) were paid scant attention.

In 1920 Bechet was charged with attempted rape and appeared in Bow Street magistrates court. He was acquitted, but a deportation order was made against him which ended the first English sojourn of a brilliant musician who had earned both academic and royal approval but had to wait until the forties for wider critical recognition. Nearly thirty years after this brush with the law he was to become the central figure in a unique and dramatic event in the history of jazz in Britain.

* * *

The appearances in Britain of the first jazz band ever to make gramophone records and of a band that included a player of such great talent were simply the result of booking agents seeking new 'acts', rather than an expressed wish on the part of the public to embrace jazz. In their different ways the ODJB and Bechet with the Southern Syncopated Orchestra sowed the seeds of a situation when there would be a genuine desire to see and hear those playing the new and exciting music flowering in the United States.

2

The *Melody Maker*

January 1926 saw the first issue of a paper whose subsequent history was intertwined with the popularization of jazz in Britain. This was the *Melody Maker*, which in its early days was as confused and convoluted in its critical judgements about jazz as the variety journals and national newspapers. Slowly, however, criteria of a kind emerged from the confusion, misinformation and prejudice rampant in its pages.

It was launched by the popular music publisher Lawrence Wright, who also wrote songs under the pseudonym Horatio Nicholls. Typical of the period, many of these songs had titles in which sheikhs and deserts and other oriental associations were included, following the success of the twenties matinee idol Rudolph Valentino in silent film epics such as *The Sheik* (1921). The illustrations on the song covers were frequently of young, white maidens looking soulfully into the lustful eyes of a handsome sheikh, some of these reproduced in the publication that was to be Britain's first 'jazz' paper.

The *Melody Maker*'s first editor was Edgar Jackson, real name Edgar Cohen. He was born in Edgware in 1895 and died in London in 1967. His change of name is mentioned to illustrate the prevailing attitudes to race at a time when Jewish stage and variety performers often parodied themselves in a manner unthinkable today or, as in the case of Jackson, felt the need to anglicize themselves. Significant in all this was his own highly offensive attitude to, and descriptions of, black musicians.

The publication announced itself as 'A Monthly Magazine for All Directly or Indirectly Interested in the Production of Popular Music'. The editorial claimed that its aims were to co-ordinate the branches of popular entertainment and ended, 'We have decided to devote our frontispiece each month to some prominent member of the musical profession. In this, our first issue, we are indebted to the famous British composer, Mr Horatio Nicholls, for allowing us the privilege of publishing his photograph. Born in Leicester, Mr Nicholls rapidly came to the fore and is now admittedly one of the finest and most popular composers of lighter music, not only in England but throughout the world.'

The imprint merely stated 'Published at 19 Denmark Street (Charing Cross Road) WC2', and the first advertisement for the Lawrence Wright Music Co. on page three gave the firm's address as Denmark Street, Charing Cross Road, WC2 – omitting the number.

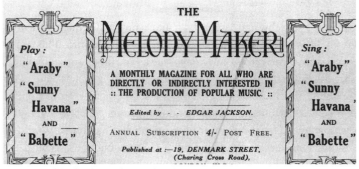

Masthead of the first issue of the *Melody Maker*, January 1926

It is obvious from this succession of omissions that, naïvely, they hoped the connection between the editorial and publishing activities at the same address under the same aegis wouldn't be noticed. This reluctance on the part of the publishers to declare their interest was maintained for subsequent advertisements, which appeared on almost every page until the last, where they gave their address for the second time.

The first issue carried news of variety acts, including the Houston Sisters, José Collins, Dick Henderson and Will Fyffe under the heading 'Over the Footlights', a military band section, manuscript arrangements of light music and an article by bandleader Jack Hylton blasting critics of 'jazz'.

The first mention of a 'jazz musician' concerned violinist Hugo Rignold . . . 'leading a band at Kettner's Hotel, Church Street [now Romilly Street], Soho, a famous landmark which achieved the height of its popularity in the days of King Edward VII who, rumour has it, was very partial to this secluded and select spot. Lunch and dinner are served, as in the old days, unaccompanied by aught else but the tinkle of plate and glass, and the subdued laughter of the elite of London Society.'

The first record review was of a tune called 'Araby' composed by Horatio Nicholls and played by the Savoy Orpheans, resident at the

Savoy Hotel, in the Strand. Not surprisingly, the notice was highly favourable and this was followed by:

> For those who want red-hot syncopated rhythm with a good deal of 'dirt' thrown in, 'Riverboat Shuffle' played by Hylton's Kit-Kat Band (No. B2167) and 'Stomp Off, Let's Go' by the Savoy Orpheans (No. B2174) should prove eminently satisfactory. Both these numbers are excellent compositions and contain an abundance of modern style, harmonic effects and rhythm. The former is conspicuous for an excellent hat-muted trumpet solo and some real 'dirt' on the fiddle by that super-jazz artist, Hugo Rignold.* The latter has a lilt all through that is irresistible and contains fine examples of the excellent rhythmic effect which is obtained by accentuating the fourth beat of the measure. 'Jazz' enthusiasts will find their appetites thoroughly appeased by these two red-hot numbers.

* Rignold, then twenty-one years of age, later played in Hylton's band, joined the RAF during the war and conducted the Palestine Symphony Orchestra when in uniform. On demobilization he conducted the orchestra of the Sadlers Wells Ballet Company (1947) and then the Liverpool Philharmonic Orchestra until 1957. He was musical director of the City of Birmingham Symphony Orchestra, 1960–68, and resident guest conductor of the Cape Town Symphony Orchestra in 1956, 1971 and 1973.

The reviews were unsigned, but almost certainly were by Edgar Jackson. The February issue continued much in the same vein, and included an article by saxophonist and bandleader Bert Ralton that contained unintentionally significant comment. It was headed: 'The Evolution of Jazz and a Saxophonist':

> Although there have been dance bands, or perhaps I should say some form of dance music, almost since the world began – certainly since music in any form originated – the 'Jazz' or syncopated dance band really originated in New Orleans, one of the southern of the United States of America, where small outfits, comprising usually three or four instruments manipulated more or less successfully by negroes, were becoming increasingly popular on account of the excellence of the rhythms they produced, even though other qualities were lacking. But rhythm alone, as we all know, is insufficient to satisfy the educated ear, and the advent of the white man into Jazz marked the commencement of the struggle to perpetuate the spirit of the negro rhythm and at the same time introduce and maintain the many other qualities which the great classical masters have shown us to be music.

In its quaint fashion the article bows to the musicality of the black pioneers of New Orleans (here elevated to the status of a state) while claiming the improvement of jazz by introducing 'classical' elements. Jazz was to suffer many such 'improvements'.

The *Melody Maker*, February 1927, reported that Ralton, on tour with his band in South Africa, had accidentally been shot while hunting on the veldt. The report ran: 'originally an American, he was a graduate to music from the ranks of newsboys . . .   Then came the tragedy of his accident which deprived the profession of one of its most respected stars. According to reports he died bravely playing the ukulele and singing to his attendants while on the stretcher taking him to hospital.'

In the March 1926 issue the thorny matter of reciprocity in the employment of British and American musicians in their respective countries was commented on. The concluding note put the matter in a nutshell:

> Let it be distinctly understood that these are the days when the employment of British musicians must be rigidly safeguarded. No foreign musician should be enabled to do a British musician out of a job. There is no argument about that.
>
> Yet if it can be shown that foreign bands are booked because they can deliver the goods which home talent cannot, then let us have the opportunity of further studying these experts before we permanently lock them

out. Let us be sure they are doing harm instead of good before we adopt any safeguarding measures in unnecessary panic.

Here the writer (Jackson, presumably), was making the same mistake as the Musicians' Union in later years of lumping American jazz and dance-band musicians together (although often these were one and the same) and yet, unknowingly, he hit on a truth that was subsequently to be disregarded by the Musicians' Union and by the Ministry of Labour, which meekly accepted the former's restrictive recommendations in the mid-thirties through to the early fifties.

The pertinent truth was: 'If it can be shown that foreign bands can deliver the goods which home talent cannot, then let us have the opportunity of further studying these experts before we permanently lock them out.'

* * *

The first reference in the *Melody Maker* to a genuine American jazzman was by an English dance-band trombonist, Richard MacDonald, in the April 1926 issue. Referring to 'Duck's Quack' by the Cotton Pickers (the Original Memphis Five) he notated and analysed a 'break' by the trombonist on the record, Miff Mole.

MacDonald commented, 'It is one of the finest breaks I have ever heard and a fine example of New Orleans style of trombone playing.' Mole, an extremely talented white musician who played on literally hundreds of records of varying quality, was not from New Orleans, but was one of the very few trombonists responsible for developing the instrument's role in jazz from the rudimentary and semi-comic grunts and groans of the early practitioners. This was the first-ever technical analysis of a jazzman's recorded solo to appear in print in this country, albeit with misplaced reference to 'New Orleans' style.

This issue marked the appearance of a radio critic with the pseudonym of 'Stayatome': surely the redoubtable, eventually multi-pseudonymous Jackson. In the same pages a new item announced a 'Novel Series of Tutors':

> We have had a novel series of tutors sent to us for review by Messrs A. J. Stasny Music Co. Ltd., of 62 Oxford Street, who publish them in this country. They are, however, the products of the famous American Winn School of Music, and are presented here in a very novel and concise manner. They

are all excellent and very useful, the series including the following: *How to Rag and Jazz on the Saxophone*; *How to Play Ragtime*; *How to Play Jazz and Blues*; *How to Play Breaks and Endings*; *How to Play Popular Music*; *How to Play Melody on the Uke*, and *A Chord and Jazz Book*.

In the December 1926 issue Jackson, under the pseudonym 'Needlepoint', reviewed the usual collection of dance record issues – the now forgotten ephemera of the time – with an appraisal of probably the first black band he ever heard, and this only on gramophone record. Made in 1926, the recording was one of the earliest made by trumpeter King Oliver after departing from the smaller instrumentation of his Creole Jazz Band.* The arrangement is ponderous and turgid and Oliver is in decline, but the playing has a hot timbre. Jackson wrote: 'And to finish with, the lowest of low-down, mean, blues renderings is portrayed by the Savannah Syncopators in "Jackass Blues" which is a curious mixture of 1926 and 1916.'

In the January 1927 issue Jackson committed his first really big gaffe. He praised Fred Waring's Pennsylvanians' rendering of 'Bolshevik' as 'a comedy dance record as good as anything I've heard. The orchestration is fine; it opens with four bars of the Russian National Anthem, leading cleverly into a paraphrase of Tchaikovsky's "1812" after which we are introduced directly into the verse of the number. The comedy vocal effects are excellent and this is a record to amuse both grown-ups and the kiddies.' He followed this enthusiastic appraisal of such trivia with the following critique:

> A band of which I have not heard hitherto, called Jelly Roll Morton's Red Hot Peppers, is introduced in 'The Chant' and 'Black Bottom Stomp', both 'hot' Charleston numbers. No one can say that the musicians are not wonderful performers. Nevertheless we are treated to an exhibition of the bluest jazz, not as it should be today, but as it was six years ago. The fact that this is about the best record I have come across for Charleston dancing owing to the 'hot' rhythm behind it certainly does not excuse the fact that it is crude in orchestration and poor amusement to listen to.

Both sides of this record have since been acknowledged as classics of jazz, but were not likely to appeal to someone who found 'Bolshevik' 'as good as anything' he'd heard.

* The Creole Jazz Band recordings made in 1923 were not issued in Britain until 1936 – see Chapter 8.

Like most of the British (and American and European) public, Jackson had long been over-conditioned by the easily grasped arrangements on typical dance-band records to block appreciation of the free-flowing lines springing from the quintessential New Orleans instrumentation of trumpet, clarinet, trombone, piano, guitar, bass and drums on Morton's recordings.

In the March 1927 issue Jackson reviewed a release on the Pathé Actuelle label which synthesized the 'European' approach to jazz. His praise, typically ecstatic, was quite out of proportion to the record's quality and contrasts strongly with his condemnation of the Morton record.

An example of what modern style in rendering dance music really means, 'Alabama Stomp'/ 'Brown Sugar' by the Red Heads are far and away the finest records I have ever heard. They are about two years in advance of anything ever issued in this country of which I know and it is absolutely certain that even to those who cannot appreciate the subtlety of the style and thus obtain enjoyment when simply listening to it, the wonderful rhythm is bound to be ideal for dancing, and its recognition and consequent

Edgar Jackson, former army officer, professional dancer, and first editor of the *Melody Maker*

introduction as the most perfect form of rendering evolved to date is only a question of how long it will still take to overcome the retarding influence of the lay public which, even after all these years, seems able to understand little more than melody and a slapped out four-in-a-bar.

Nearly sixty years later it is easy to mock this jangled and breathless eulogy of a typical white jazz record, made by this group under the combined leadership of trumpeter Red Nichols and trombonist Miff Mole. The phrasing is nervy, crimped and staccato, and this particular recording was not helped by the boxy 'acoustic' recording (before the general introduction of 'electrical' recording from which the HMV Morton records benefited).

Indeed, the comparison with the free-flowing lines, the strong tone and genuinely rhythmic beat of the Red Hot Peppers which Jackson found so old-fashioned is striking. Withal, in Jackson's appraisal of a 'hot' record there was a growing awareness that small-group improvising was superior to a melody 'slapped out four-in-a-bar'. The Red Heads had nudged him a shade further towards an appreciation of true jazz. Many others found Red Nichols and his associates a stepping stone to acceptance of more fundamental and rewarding truths. Later, Nichols and company, particularly Miff Mole, developed a maturity that stood in sharp contrast to their earlier recordings.

However, in the April 1927 issue, Jackson soon returned to fulsome praise of the commercial dance records preferred by the lay public until he reviewed another Red Heads' release, 'Black Bottom Stomp'/'Heebie Jeebies'. Always one for emphatically alleging artistic improvement with the passage of time, Jackson surprisingly failed to mention that this December 1926 recording of 'Black Bottom Stomp' was made four months later than the Jelly Roll Morton version which, it may be fair to assume, inspired the Red Heads' version. Jackson guessed, partially inaccurately, at the personnel, getting some of the names wrong, but there were no discographies in 1926 for him to consult, and in truth his endeavours to establish the personnels were highly commendable. It was the start of the jazz aficionado's concern – obsession, even – with person- nel identification. After speculating on the personnel, Jackson wrote: 'Now, I don't know how much this will mean to you, dear reader, but to those who know the names it will convey a canful.'

He reviewed Jelly Roll Morton's 'Sidewalk Blues' in the same issue:

> Following are the records by the American bands, and I'm disappointed in most of them. Oh yes, they are good, of course, but there's nothing much out of the ordinary rut in any one excepting 'Sidewalk Blues' by Jelly Roll Morton's Red Hot Peppers, the extraordinary point about which is that it was ever issued at all, as it is hopelessly old-fashioned in style, even if the musicians can play their instruments, and recalls the old Dixieland Jazz Band. Paul Whiteman's 'Why Do Ya Roll Those Eyes' is exceptionally good and has a wonderful 'stunt' trombone solo.

Red Nichols

Whiteman's 'Why Do Ya Roll Those Eyes' is properly relegated to total obscurity. The Red Heads occasionally appear on compendium LPs for their relative historical and musical significance but the Morton records have become accepted as jazz classics, their constant availability a measure of their enduring worth. In his spatial references to 'six years behind' and his praise of work two years ahead of its time Jackson again confused the passage, or anticipation, of time with artistic value.

In the same issue Jack Miranda, saxophonist and clarinettist with Bert Ambrose's band at the Mayfair Hotel, wrote about the role of the clarinet in the modern dance band:

> From the days when Jazz was in its primitive form when drummers had kits composed of tin cans, rattles, etc., and used to make queer noises, like an antiquated Ford chastising its young, when Jazz was a noise and nothing but a noise, to the present day dance music with its advanced state, with its beauty of tone and colour, artistic blendings, clever rhythms that compel even the most hardened of 'Crowhards'* to admit that dance music is an art, the clarinet had to take its place in the dance band.

In outlining the part the clarinet plays in the modern dance band he refers to 'that supreme artist of Jazzdom – Larry Shields, clarinet player in the first jazz band to visit us – the Original Dixieland Jazz Band'.

* Term of contempt for opponents of jazz derived from the name of a bitter critic of the music, Dr Henry Coward. See page 48.

His playing in that classic of Jazz 'Tiger Rag', if it does not go down to posterity, was nevertheless the work of genius. Some of the breaks are being used by the hottest and finest players in America. True, they are phrased and accented in the modern style, but fundamentally they are the same. What magnified Shields' great genius was the fact that he couldn't read a note of music; but his tone, technique and novel ideas left nothing to be desired.

Miranda, after this honest acknowledgement (however contradictory it may have appeared after his pronouncements on the primitive form of jazz), notated one of Shields' more renowned 'breaks'. Again there is an aspect of the duality of thought clogging the minds of both musicians and critics of the time. In acknowledging the 'genius' of Shields, Miranda unintentionally denies the philosophy of 'improvement' that was the substance of his article.

In the May 1927 issue, under the heading 'Who's Who in American Bands' by Fred and Manuel ('Liz') Elizalde, was the first mention in the *Melody Maker*'s pages of trumpeter Louis Armstrong and cornettist Bix Beiderbecke, misspelled 'Bidlebeck'. Another trumpet player mentioned was Ted Schilling. Bracketing him with Louis Armstrong, they wrote, 'We foresee a bright future for Schilling, especially. We expect him to be the best across the Atlantic before a couple of years have gone . . . he is the only performer on that instrument who has absolute originality of phrasing and style who hardly ever does the same things, or anything like them, twice in the same tune. In our opinion, he is already the "hottest trumpet in the States" . . . ' Of Schilling, as history tells, nothing has been heard since. A lot has been heard of Louis Armstrong and Bix Beiderbecke. Schilling was on Fred Elizalde's first records, made in Hollywood in 1926, probably accounting for the eulogistic tone of his description.

The article mentions saxophonist Frankie Trumbauer, Jimmy Dorsey and Fud Livingston, clarinettist Benny Goodman, Miff Mole and Red Nichols. Except in the case of Mole, this was the first occasion on which these players had been mentioned in the *Melody Maker* (although Jackson had already guessed Nichols' playing on the Red Heads' records as by Ted Schilling). They were to impress the emerging jazz cognoscenti in this country and those dance-band musicians with a yearning to fill the occasional solo spot allocated by a grudging bandleader. Shortly afterwards

Fred Elizalde went to Cambridge University and formed a student band, the Quinquaginta Ramblers.

The recordings of white dance/jazz musicians made up the bulk of the record companies' issues, but when records by black bands were released the editor of the *Melody Maker* in his role as record critic was persistently virulent in his denunciation of them.

In retrospect it would appear strange that the only paper in the twenties ostensibly propagating and defending jazz should have for an editor someone so antagonistic towards black jazz. But Edgar Jackson was a rare bird; educated at Claysmore and Cambridge, one-time officer in the Tank Corps, he led his own band, on drums, at a 'roadhouse' called the Spider's Web on the Watford by-pass and toured the music halls – in what capacity is not known – in a performing dogs act and, among other activities, conceived and organized the *Melody Maker* dance-band contests. Regarding his bias against black jazz it is no surprise that a certain picture hung at the Royal Academy in their spring 1926 collection outraged him. The oil painting in question was by a John B. Soutar, RA. It portrayed a naked white girl clapping her hands next to a black man dressed in formal evening wear of top hat, white shirt and bow tie with swallow-tail coat, and playing a saxophone. He was seated on a broken classical statue. The picture was entitled *Breakdown*. Under the heading, 'The Problems of an Immodest Masterpiece', Jackson thundered his denunciation:

> There are doubtless many who, while admiring the technique of this year's problem picture, by John B. Soutar, will affect to be able to interpret his pictorial metaphor as a further slap in the face for modern dancing and its particular type of music . . .
>
> The hanging committee of the Royal Academy, too, with its usual dispassionate disregard for subject, will have viewed it only for its artistic merit – that is to say, on its quality as a work of art alone. All the same, speaking as we do for dance musicians in this country, we object to this picture because of the inferences it is capable of bearing to the many others who may view it less as a work of art and more as a sermon.
>
> We jazz musicians are not thin-skinned, fortunately, for we are subjected, by those who know less than nothing about us, to the most bitter and illogical criticisms of this generation, but this picture bears such possible alternative interpretations as to be positively indecent. Those who bear us ill-will will undoubtedly interpret it in this wrongful manner.

It is not our intention to labour the point, and so to give this picture a publicity disproportionate to its value, but we state emphatically that we protest against, and repudiate the juxtaposition of an undraped white girl with a black man. Such a study is straining beyond breaking point the normal clean inferences of allegory. We demand also that the habit of associating our music with the primitive and barbarous negro derivation shall cease forthwith, in justice to the obvious fact that we have outgrown such comparison . . .

Breakdown is not only a picture entirely nude of the respect due to the chastity and morality of the greater part of the young generation but in the degradation it implies to modern white woman there is the perverse danger to the community and the best thing that could happen to it is to have it . . . burnt!

Stop Press: We are informed that, at the request of the Colonial Office, *Breakdown* was recently withdrawn from exhibition from the Royal Academy.[*]

The suggestion that the offending piece should be burnt reads like an unpleasant portent of evil days to come, when literature and paintings, mostly by Jewish artists, were thrust into bonfires in the streets and squares of Nazi Germany. And the editor of the *Melody Maker* was to prove, in his constant belittlement of 'negro jazz', as racially prejudiced as the creator of this grotesque and unintentionally funny painting. In retrospect, one wonders what the fuss was about. Who was more absurd – the painter or his critic?

Jackson's tirade, however, was merely consistent with his bias against black jazz, a prejudice repeatedly emphasized in examples which follow later. This is not to smirk at distant folly, nor to wish to show superior understanding in hindsight, but to demonstrate how extraordinary it was that the editor of a 'jazz' paper made such determined efforts to smother interest in the genre's genuine music and how, despite the fact that others shared his antagonisms, this music thrust itself forward to become internationally acclaimed – thereafter – with Jackson's enthusiastic help.

But then musicians generally do not read the writings of jazz critics and certainly American black jazzmen of the twenties did not read the *Melody Maker*. Had they done so they would surely have been highly bewildered. They entered the recording studios to earn a few dollars

[*] A photograph of Soutar's painting in the 1926 catalogue was seen by the author in the 1980s at the Royal Academy. At the bottom of the photo a pencilled note stated that it was withdrawn at the request of the Colonial Office.

The Problems of an Immodest Masterpiece

THERE are doubtless many who, while admiring the technique of this year's problem picture, by John B. Soutar, will affect to be able to interpret this pictorial metaphor as a further slap in the face for modern dancing and its particular type of music.

We will impugn no discreditable motive to the artist, but, on the other hand, will freely admit that he was surely animated with the highest artistic motives when he composed this work. The hanging committee of the Royal Academy, too, with its usual dispassionate disregard for subject, will have viewed it only for its artistic merit—that is to say, on its quality as a work of art alone. All the same, speaking as we do for dance musicians in this country, we object to this picture because of the inferences it is capable of bearing to the many others who may view it less as a work of art and more as a sermon.

We jazz musicians are not thin-skinned, fortunately, for we are subjected, by those who know less than nothing about us, to the most bitter and zoological criticisms of this genera-

tion, but this picture bears such possible alternative interpretations as to be positively indecent. Those who bear us ill-will will undoubtedly interpret it in this wrongful manner.

THE BREAKDOWN ... ... John B. Soutar.

(Copyright reserved for owner by Watter Judd, Ltd.)

It is not our intention to labour the point, and so to give this picture a publicity disproportionate to its value, but we state emphatically that we protest against, and repudiate the

juxtaposition of an undraped white girl with a black man. Such a study is straining beyond breaking point the normal clean inferences of allegory. We demand also that the habit of associating our music with the primitive and barbarous negro derivation shall cease forthwith, in justice to the obvious fact that we have outgrown such comparison.

Problem pictures are capable, we reiterate, of a thousand and one different and antipodal interpretations. The artist visualises one and every thinking spectator visualises another ; rarely can they be reconciled. In this case we will extract what comfort we can from this indelicate creation by interpreting for ourselves the only suggestion of a conventional and fair allegory which appears to us in the whole picture.

We see Minerva lying shattered and neglected in the background. It is said that, for the purpose of this picture, represented the "old order of things" which the iconoclasm of jazz has hewn down. Minerva, however (Continued on page 3, col. 3)

Melody Maker article with photograph of John Soutar's picture, *Breakdown*

and were now being critically analysed by white critics over three thousand miles distant.

The *Melody Maker* then ran a regular feature called 'Paras from the Press', a monthly round-up of comments about jazz, mostly critical, with the editor's answer at the end of each quote. A typical example was:

DR FARNELL FULMINATES ABOUT JAZZ

'Nigger music comes from the Devil,' said Dr Farnell, the Rector of Exeter College (as quoted in the *Daily Chronicle*) when welcoming members of a Summer School for Music Teachers which opened at Oxford last night.

Vulgar music might not be as criminal as murder, but it was far more degrading. Our civilization was threatened by our own inventions, by dreadful noises, our horrible motor traffic, Americanisms and jazz music.

'Don't take your music from America or from the niggers,' he said; 'take it from God, the source of all good music.'

There was nothing more degrading than vulgar music, which was worse than poisonous drink.

There was no editorial rejoinder – the usual practice in this feature – to this Christian pronouncement.

In the July 1927 issue Jackson reviewed a stage show and headed his piece:

BERT AMBROSE'S BAND AT THE PALLADIUM
The Tragedy of 'The Nigger'
How Failure Turned to Success
(from our Special Correspondent)

An augmented orchestra led by the Mayfair Hotel dance-band leader Bert Ambrose played a week at the London Palladium commencing on Monday June 6th.

In fact, it was solely the sheer excellence of the combination as a straight-forward dance band which turned what looked like being on the first day a ghastly failure into a complete success . . . and I make no apology for the unusually long space for me to tell for the first time the true facts.

The Palladium appearance first became mooted when that young genius, Fred Elizalde, burst in one morning to the managing director of British Brunswick Ltd. and explained to him that he had evolved a story which had inspired him with ideas to write a more ambitious symphonic suite for modern dance-band instrumentation.

The suite, said young Elizalde, in asking if they would record it, was to be called 'The Heart of a Nigger' and to comprise four movements depicting the life of the negro: (1) Water Melon Memories (2) Coloured Love (3) Dissipation (4) Nigger Heaven. These titles fully explain the story to be interpreted by the score.

The 'Special Correspondent' lamented in detail the reasons (mostly about costumes and settings) for the breakdown on the opening day, and related how Ambrose on subsequent days rallied, although having to withdraw the suite from the performance because of the inadequate prior arrangements. He concludes the review, 'I only hope we shall all be given another chance of hearing Elizalde's suite played by the same band again. It is a work the world cannot afford to lose.'

Although by-lined as by a 'Special Correspondent' it is also signed 'E. C.', the initials of Jackson's real name, Edgar Cohen. He used the same initials at the end of a footnote which read: 'I have referred to the suite under the title "The Heart of a Nigger". This is correct, as Mr Elizalde entitled it, but some authority evidently found objection to the word "nigger" and compromised by renaming the suite "The Heart of a Coon". This mawkish fastidiousness ruined the only possible title to convey the real sense of the idea.'

As late as 1932 Elizalde recorded the suite, under the original title, for the Decca label on two twelve-inch 78 rpm records. This is entered in the massive jazz record discography, *Jazz Records 1897–1942*, by Brian Rust, followed by details of solo records Elizalde made for the same label three days later, one of which – 'Yes, We Have No Bananas' – was a trivial comedy number. The 'suite' hardly bears one listening. It is a very insubstantial example of light music. It has never been performed since.

Bandleader Bert Ambrose

In the same issue, Jackson, under the pseudonym 'Needlepoint', was obviously still smarting about the substitution of a term only marginally less offensive than the one it replaced and wrote: 'You will find a full report of the appearance at the London Palladium of Bert Ambrose when he presented a new symphonic suite especially composed for the occasion by Fred Elizalde and actually entitled "The Heart of a Nigger", although somehow on the playbills the Nigger became Coon.'

Reviewing a vocal group called the Revellers he wrote: 'Not having looked at the label I nearly mistook the Revellers for a nigger quartet.' The 'mawkish fastidiousness' of some authority who compelled a composer to change a title wasn't going to have that subduing effect on the right of Edgar Cohen/Jackson/E. C./'Needlepoint'/'Stayatome' to say exactly what he thought.

The *Melody Maker* continued to quote anti-'jazz' comments from the lay press, but started publication too late to pick up an article in the *Sunday Chronicle*, 24 June 1924, which for its naïvety, misconceptions and racial bias verges on the bizarre and unwittingly contrives to be hilariously funny. The piece was entitled 'Jazzing to Jeopardy', with the subheading, 'Violet Quirk Goes to a Dance and Brings Back Disturbing Impressions'. In a contribution nearly two thousand words long Miss Quirk's impressions included the following:

The dance room was half-ballroom, half-restaurant, and as I entered it I heard jazz music for the very first time. I recognised it at once. To give its name to the syncopated tunes I had heard in the past was like putting cocoa in a wine-glass and calling it brandy. That music was awkward but civilised. This was savage, and unseemly.

The negro musicians knew well how to recapture the inflaming noises made by their far-back ancestors, and which are still enjoyed by cannibals during their most important ceremonies. They disdained the cultured violin and the highly-involved piano. Such instruments make too subtle a sound. They merely please and delight. They give sensations too delicate for the tastes of the animal devotees of jazz, who like to be maddened, not enchanted . . .

See how it whips them about! They obey it like slaves. That it stuns their intelligence is beyond question. Coquettishness is so deeply implanted in women that they do not make themselves ugly and ridiculous if they know what they are doing . . .

These women cannot know how revolting they appear, as they shuffle round the room with striding legs too far apart, rigid bodies, and fixed staring eyes. They are so closely clasped by the men that free movement is impossible. Yet only a few years ago girls, among themselves, unanimously condemned the partners who didn't keep their proper distance. They drew a sharp line between dancing and embracing. They didn't give to the casual stranger that which they reserved for a chosen man.

The band has begun again. The negroes clash their instruments together, their bodies excitedly jerking, and sometimes singing out aloud. This must be a new dance. For though the music is rushing the couples hardly move. At least their heads remain stationary. But what are they doing with their feet? Why! They are like paralysed invalids trying to walk, and not quite succeeding. They vibrate and stagger and shiver.

Before mothers give permission to their girls to go alone to jazz dances let them know first where they are going, or else go with them.

The self-appointed guardians of morality in the early twenties found plenty in 'jazz' to threaten the purity of Britain's young womanhood.

3

Stumbling

Towards Criteria

In the *Melody Maker*, May 1927, Edgar Jackson devoted a whole page to record classification and suggested that the record companies split their releases into three separate categories:

Hot Style Dance Record
Popular Dance Record
Rhythmic Concert Record

Jackson obviously didn't favour the word jazz and in the September issue that year, he wrote:

> One of the most significant happenings since the advent of modern dance music is the inclusion in the Columbia lists of decidedly 'hot' records. And not only are they hot but Columbia advertise them as being so, including them in their catalogues under the special heading 'Hot Jazz Records'.
>
> There is no question that this must be taken as a sign of the times. It is probably the most conclusive proof one could possibly have that a big demand for this style of performance is likely to arise in the future – that is, if it's not already arisen. A number of other companies have been issuing records of this kind catering for a more specialised public.

In the November issue Jackson, apparently forgetting his tacit acceptance of Columbia's innovation, attacked the company's designation in an article that echoed his three categories in which the odious word 'jazz' was eschewed.

> Well, they say a rose by any other name smells just as sweet and I suppose a dance record under this sort of description can be good. To me the above

description – under which Columbia are advertising their most up to date and stylish renderings – seems quite enough to put anyone off hearing them. I'm not quarrelling with the word 'Hot', hopelessly inadequate as a sensible description that it is. It is best understood by those in the know to mean something which can be musical, ingenious, well performed and modern in style.

For the want of a better word I use the word 'Hot' myself. I do so because I write only for musicians and those whose interest in modern dance music keeps them in close touch with the meanings of the colloquial term to describe it. I shouldn't write it if I were writing for the lay public.

But jazz! I wonder if the Columbia people wonder what this word conveys to musicians. If not, let me hasten to enlighten them by saying it signifies everything that is old-fashioned. It is a word of sarcasm. It is nearly as bad as ragtime. One can understand the uninitiated members of the lay press using it. But for an informed recording company to use it to advertise their wares to the man in the street . . . well!

Anyway, thank heavens the records are not what their descriptions would make one believe . . .

'Delerium' by the Charleston Chasers, under the direction of Red Nichols, is a wonderful performance perfectly recorded. It's composed by Arthur Schutt whose piano solo is a masterpiece of ingenuity in the modern dance style. It embodies solos of the 'hottest' order and having a marvellous dance rhythm running all through.

On the reverse face is 'Down in Our Alley Blues' played by Duke Ellington and his Washingtonians, a coloured unit in which the expected faults of the coon bands – a noticeable crudeness and a somewhat poor tone – are by no means as apparent as usual. The orchestration of the number is clever.

But when it comes to really good nigger style, I'm afraid that Massa Ellington will have to give pride of place to . . . Fletcher Henderson and his orchestra, who have excelled themselves for Columbia this month. Their orchestration of 'Whiteman Stomp' is a masterpiece. It contains stuff worthy of any symphony. The performance is unusually musicianly (some extraordinary technique displayed) and the rhythm and syncopation for which the coloured races are noted has not been lost in any way.

In his reviews Jackson posited a critical dichotomy between black and white jazz, coming down heavily in favour of the latter. In the 27 May issue he described the Red Nichols Five Pennies recording of 'That's No Bargain'/'Washboard Blues' as: 'The hottest thing that has happened. It's full of novel ideas.'

In the same issue he wrote of King Oliver's Savannah Syncopators,

'They display a strong nigger atmosphere in "Sugar Foot Stomp"/"Snag It". In the latter number the rhythm is undeniably clever but there is too much "wow" on the brass and lack of good phrases to conform to modern dance music standards.'

These were by no means Jackson's only references to 'niggers', and he

PARLOPHONE
NEW RECORDS OF MODERN DANCE MUSIC.
ALL 10-inch BLUE LABEL RECORDS, 3/- EACH

FRANKIE TRUMBAUER
King of all Saxophone Players and the greatest figure in Modern Music.

HAVE YOU HEARD
THE NEW WONDER RECORD BY
FRANKIE TRUMBAUER
AND HIS MARVELLOUS ORCHESTRA
FEATURING
THE RHYTHM BOYS.

R 3526 MISSISSIPPI MUD, Fox-Trot
THERE'LL COME A TIME, Fox-Trot

FRANKIE TRUMBAUER has made another wonderful record, this time he introduces the famous RHYTHM BOYS. "Mississippi Mud" a tune in a thousand, will be a great popular favourite with all followers of this outstanding Orchestra. In "There'll Come a Time" FRANKIE TRUMBAUER'S chorus is at his very best, never before have such marvellous breaks for saxophone and trumpet been heard as on this side. Listen to the double break by the trumpet in the trumpet chorus, and to the final sax break by Frankie Trumbauer just before the coda. Note here how the last two notes of this break are miraculously taken up by the trumpet from Trumbauer playing sax.

MIFF MOLE'S LITTLE MOLERS
— with MIFF MOLE Himself —
THE REAL HOT-TIME ORCHESTRA.

R 3530 ORIGINAL DIXIELAND, One-Step
MY GAL SAL, Fox-Trot

MIFF MOLE and his LITTLE MOLERS need no introduction. They are old favourites. MIFF MOLE is the greatest trombone player in the world, and the originator of more hot breaks and new phrases than any other dance artiste. He has certainly made a dance record all appreciators of hot records will enjoy. ADRIAN ROLLINI puts in some strong work on both sides of this record.

EXCLUSIVE ON PARLOPHONE

MIFF MOLE
The world's greatest Trombone Player and the most brilliant creator of modern music phrasing

Insist on hearing these wonderful Records at your nearest stores or dealers. In case of difficulty apply to
THE PARLOPHONE COMPANY, LTD., 85, CITY ROAD, LONDON, E.C.1

Advertisement from the *Melody Maker*, May 1928, promoting the launch by Parlophone of their 'Rhythm Style' recordings.

was beginning to have doubts about Red Nichols. In the September issue, apropos a selection of Charleston Chasers records following his report on Columbia's new policy, he commented:

> With all his hot style he is, as usual, a perfect little gentleman and never in one note does he overstep the bounds of artistry. His rhythmic style and phrases are absolutely original and for technique and tone there is probably no-one to compare with him. In fact he is so perfect I have come to look at him more as a machine than a human being. I must confess I would like him more if he could thrill my heart as he inspires my admiration.

*J*RAM

A TALL, gaunt figure, very old for his years, greatly changed from the youthful and debonair "Tram" of the old photographs ... has a world of experience behind him, from shovelling coal on a railway engine to playing saxophone in the U.S. Navy Band ... fired the jazz world's imagination with his historic records featuring a contingent from the Goldkette Band ... has spent many years with Whiteman, and nearly forgot hot jazz in his passion for aeroplanes; still has time, though, to slip away and record with a band of his own now and then ... whether in the cockpit or perched behind a C Melody, he can still send you sky-high ... that's "Tram," the Melody Man!

FRANKIE TRUMBAUER
Drawn by B. ten Hove

Frankie Trumbauer drawn by Boy ten Hove for a feature in *Rhythm* magazine

His doubts were confirmed when yet another company, Parlophone, launched specialist jazz issues. In the mid-twenties, they had sporadically issued jazz on their Red and Purple labels by the white bands of clarinettist Tony Parenti and trumpeter Johnny Bayersdorffer – recorded in New Orleans – and the black bands of Benny Moten, from Kansas City, and Clarence Williams with Louis Armstrong and Sidney Bechet.

In 1927 Parlophone's advertising in the *Melody Maker* was slanted towards the 'hot' enthusiast, prior to their launching the since renowned 'Rhythm Style' series in 1928. Their 1927 releases included records by Frankie Trumbauer's band with Bix Beiderbecke, Miff Mole's Molers, the violin and guitar duets of Joe Venuti and Eddie Lang, the Goofus Washboards featuring Adrian Rollini on bass saxophone – all white players. Later, their issue of black jazz recordings presented another face to jazz criteria, these releases including the celebrated Armstrong Hot Five and Seven recordings. All were drawn from the American OKeh label – a veritable treasure trove of jazz masterpieces – and it was a freak of fate that such were available to Parlophone. In the involved machinations of recording company tie-ups, the owners of OKeh, the General Phonograph Company of New York, passed the rights to CBS as far back as 1926, but English Parlophone, for a variety of reasons, retained the English rights.

One of their first releases in July 1927 was Frankie Trumbauer's 'Singing the Blues' with Bix Beiderbecke, about which Jackson remarked: 'The Elizalde Brothers have told you about Bidlebeck [*sic*]. Here is your chance to prove the statement that he is the king of trumpet players. What soul, too, is in his playing; what beautiful phrases he works out.'

The next Trumbauer/Bix release was 'Riverboat Shuffle'/'Ostrich Walk' two months later. Jackson perceived the superiority of Beiderbecke over Nichols:

> Neither of these is a new tune. 'Riverboat Shuffle' was published in this country about Christmas 1925 (and was a winner too) while 'Ostrich Walk' was one of the star turns of the famous Dixieland Band when it was over here. Personally, I am all in favour of reviving these old numbers. Not only are they excellent, but they give the public a chance to compare the old-fashioned styles of playing with the new . . .
>
> And I am convinced that anyone who compares the modern renderings of these two old numbers will be bound to acknowledge the great strides in what for the moment, may I call 'Novelty' rhythmic renderings? All that was

worth having was retained, while all the crudeness is being rapidly elimi-
nated by the musical artistry that is now being given its rightful importance.

These are two of the hottest but at the same time most artistic performances of really inspiring dance music as played by small combinations I have
ever heard. The Laurels . . . must go to Bix Beiderbecke, the trumpet
player, who loses nothing when compared with the famous Red Nichols. It
may be true that Bix slightly lacks the perfection of tone and technique,
which has given Red such world-wide fame, but Red always seems to have
something of the coldness, even though he includes the purity of crystal.
Whereas Bix has a heart as big as your head, which shines through his playing with the warmth of the sun's rays.

He sometimes seems more human than Red whose perfection always
makes me think of the majesty of the snow-clad mountains.

Anyway, even if this is rather far-fetched the fact remains that Bix has one
of the best rhythmic styles of the day, and with the wonderful phrases he
invents and the manner in which he performs them is bound to be a constant
source of delight.

Jackson was right that Beiderbecke's playing was to be a constant source
of delight, but he continued to berate black jazz, sometimes offensively.

In 1927, Levy's, a record and gramophone shop in Whitechapel, east
London, issued specialist releases on their Oriole and Levaphone labels
with material drawn from the American Vocalion label. Their releases
included records by blues singers Rosa Henderson and Viola McCoy, two
piano solos by Jelly Roll Morton, two sides by Duke Ellington's band,
two by Luis Russell's orchestra and two by Louis Armstrong's Hot Five,
'Drop that Sack'/'Georgia Bo-Bo' (issued as by 'Lil's Hot Shots').

Levy's were the first independent company issuing purely jazz records
and Edgar Jackson was rather cool towards them all. The Morton piano
solos were 'not wonderfully conspicuous in any direction and old-
fashioned' and of Lil's Hot Shots he said, 'It is not easy to bestow praise
on these discs. They reach the limit of blueness. The vocal chorus on
"Georgia Bo-Bo" is particularly blatant and unmusical.'

On the next page he reviews 'Yale Rhythm' by the original Washboard
Beaters. 'This is probably a coloured outfit, as I seem to recognise the
style of Louis Armstrong, the famous coon trumpet player, particularly in
the vocal chorus. Anyway, whatever conclusion you come to, it is certain
that you will have to agree the vocalist is a nigger and if you can judge
from his voice and style, a big bluff one at that.'

The vocalist was the band's leader, Clarence Williams, height five feet eight, weighing approximately nine stone ten. Louis Armstrong wasn't on the record. The reverse side, by the Goofus Washboards (the California Ramblers, a prolifically recording white group) received Jackson's praise and he appeared not to notice the absence of a washboard.

Throughout his reviews in 1928 he blundered through the problematic terrain of race relations like a rogue elephant recklessly inflicting the maximum damage. In the January issue he reviewed 'Slow River'/'Zulu Wail' by the Clarence Williams Bottomland Orchestra: 'Two numbers that yield well to hot treatment . . . Although slightly crude in places they are entertaining to listen to and certainly show that the coons are not afraid to "swing it". The rhythms are penetrating to a degree and the singing has a true nigger flavour. The trumpet – very nigger style – is strongly featured throughout.'

Early advertisement for Britain's first specialist jazz record shop

If for nothing else the review is notable for its use of the phrase 'swing it', widely used in the years to come, as 'swing' became the recognized generic term for jazz in the thirties, typified by Benny Goodman becoming the 'King of Swing'.

In the same issue Jackson reviews 'I Ain't Got Nobody' by the Coon–Sanders orchestra. He writes, 'The hot playing is far more restrained than we usually expect from a coloured combination.' Here he is confused by the name of the band, correctly given. He thought 'Coon' signified the pigmentation of the personnel. Coon was the surname of drummer Carleton Coon, co-leader with pianist Joe Sanders of the orchestra, whose leaders and personnel were all white.

Two pages later Jackson becomes further entangled by again taking as gospel the information he had read on the label. This read, 'Candy Lips'/'Nobody but My Baby' by 'Louis Armstrong's Original Washboard

Beaters'. 'This should be heard if only to learn how bad a coloured combination can be. They are both old fashioned "jazzy" renderings with an
overpowering washboard rhythm (and bad at that!). The hoped-for
redeeming feature of Louis Armstrong's amusing and original style on the
trumpet (he can play if he wants to) never materialises.'

Quite unintentionally this was fair comment. Armstrong's 'amusing and
original style' didn't materialize as he wasn't on the record, but it was virtually the same band, led by Clarence Williams, that Jackson thought
entertaining to listen to and 'not afraid to swing it' on page 59, six pages
earlier.

The turmoil of his own confusion was exaggerated by many other
instances of record companies mistitling their records, usually unintentionally, although some may have been guilty of deliberate misrepresen-
tation by using names on the labels they sensed were becoming significant and saleable.

Early researchers had to pick their way through labelling errors such as
these. Mislabelling was frequent; misleading pseudonyms were used and
often the same pseudonyms were used for several bands, and sometimes
different bands on the two sides of the same record, or the same band
with a different personnel.

In the March 1928 issue Jackson wrote:

> Louis Armstrong, the American negro trumpeter who is famous throughout
> his own country, is the leading light on 'Black and Tan Fantasy' by Louis
> Armstrong's Washboard Beaters and 'Wild Man Blues' by Louis Armstrong
> accompanied by his aforesaid Washboard Beaters.
>
> How this will appeal to you depends on how you look at them. Personally
> I don't think there's a great deal to be said about 'Wild Man Blues' except
> that it shows some pretty amazing technique both as regards Armstrong's
> solo passages and those taken by the clarinet – a technique which you may
> or may not think misapplied whether you are in sympathy with the negro
> temperament, which in this case shows somewhat crude and very exaggerat-
> ed sentimentality.
>
> 'Black and Tan Fantasy' is, however, quite a different proposition.
> Considering the composition itself – that is to say as it's interpreted – one
> must admit that Miley and Ellington, the composers (Duke Ellington I know
> is a composer of the coloured race – Miley I've not heard of before) have
> given us something which is far above the average in melody.
>
> Surely the highest of 'highbrows' will admit the beauty of it.

Then as to the interpretation, Armstrong pushes out some highly original effects, stunts, and styles which being so perfectly done must require outstanding technique, although they may not please the legitimate musician. Nevertheless I must admit they give me a thrill every time I hear them. On the other hand who could deny the legitimate artistry and beauty of tone with which the above theme is played by the solo saxophonist. The orchestration, too, cannot be passed over as unworthy of note.

The whole thing is, in every way, a great performance by a band, the records of which have hitherto been highly crude effects.

The mislabelling had led him further from properly identifying the artists concerned, nor did his ears help him to question the misinformation, or to recognize the vast difference in style or instrumentation between one side of the record and the other.

'Wild Man Blues' was by Louis Armstrong's Hot Five and contained no washboard in the instrumentation. 'Black and Tan Fantasy' was by Duke Ellington's band, and (apart from the absence of a washboard) the trumpet player who pushed out those 'highly original effects' and 'stunt' was Jabbo Smith. (To be fair, Jackson wasn't to know this – nor did anyone else!)

As for Jackson being surprised by this relatively sophisticated arrangement, and seeing it as an improvement on 'previous records', this is understandable as, in fact, these were by an entirely different band – the earthier Williams Washboard Band.

In June 1928 Jackson married off Louis Armstrong. He reviewed a record, labelled as by Butterbeans and Susie, accompanied by Louis Armstrong and his Washboard Beaters. The titles were 'That's When I'll Come Back to You'/'Why Do You Treat Me This Way'. Jackson wrote, 'Butterbeans is what Louis Armstrong's wife calls him. Both sing in the negro style which at least has rhythm. Ask any American dance-band musician to tell you the hottest trumpet players and he'll include Louis for a certainty. The rest of the band has the usual coloured crudeness.'

Both sides were by Armstrong's Hot Seven, and didn't include a washboard, Butterbeans or Susie. 'Armstrong and his Washboard Beaters' as a name to stick on the labels seemed to exert a peculiar fascination for one of the Parlophone executives, and it may have been a deliberate attempt to capitalize on Armstrong's name, which was fast becoming prestigious.

During 1928 the quality of African-American jazz became more apparent to Jackson as the number of releases increased and in August 1928, reviewing Duke Ellington's 'Take It Easy'/'Jubilee Stomp', he wrote:

> With perhaps the exception of Fletcher Henderson's 'Whiteman Stomp' and a couple of others by the same band on Columbia, the above are the best performances I have heard from a coloured band.
>   Both the compositions are by Duke Ellington himself. 'Take It Easy' is typical of him. There is something extraordinarily appealing about it. The misunderstood soul of the whole negro race cries out from it . . . This is a record which will, of course, evoke the usual abuse from the Crowhard fraternity. Personally, I must admit, I get a greater thrill every time I play it. I live with these coloured folk through every bar of it. I appreciate, particularly in 'Take It Easy', their fight for serious expression, as I do their childish humour. It is a record with which, in spite of the fact that its best friend could not call either side a great musical work, I shall never part.

Such pronouncements are now laughable but even allowing for the distance in time it is still amazing that such comments were ever committed to print. One still gasps at the twisted skeins in Jackson's critical confusion; still chokes at the effrontery in advising his readers to show a tolerance he never displayed himself; and boggles at his condescension towards black musicians. But withal it was obvious that some awareness of the black man's superiority in the special field of jazz creativity had impressed itself upon him, albeit inextricably mixed with horrifyingly racist ideas and attitudes.

He wasn't the only jazz buff of his time (and for a decade later) slow in grasping basic truths. Considering that contemporary ears had been conditioned to the purified jazz of the Red Heads and Five Pennies, the stark vitality of most black practitioners must have come as a shock.

In the 1929 issue there was an abrupt cessation (with one exception) of Jackson's references to 'coons', 'darkies' and 'niggers'. The exception was his review of 'Git wit It'/'Ideas' by Monk Hazel's Bienville Roof Orchestra, a New Orleans white band that played, according to Jackson, in 'nigger style'. 'Git wit It' was a vulgar spelling of a term enjoining a person to show more awareness, much used in the fifties and sixties.

In November 1929 Jackson visited New York and his place as a record reviewer was taken by someone who chose the rather unfortunate pseudonym of 'Pinhead'. Like 'Needlepoint' it was an allusive reference to the steel needles used to play the 78 rpm shellac records in those days.

In the next issue he sensibly changed this to 'Stylus' and announced the arrival of the Parlophone Rhythm Style series that included Louis Armstrong's 'West End Blues'. The reviewer thought the advertisements said quite enough about the records, and that further comment would be superfluous.

Reporting from New York in November, Jackson was shaken by the scanty clothing on the black dancers in Harlem's night spots, and on his return it was announced that he was leaving the paper to become Jack Hylton's manager. He was succeeded by Percy Mathison Brooks, a former manager of the Covent Garden Ballroom who joined the *Melody Maker* some time in 1927.

The convolutions of Jackson's logic as he stumbled towards a degree of awareness have been outlined to illustrate how ill-informed, prejudiced and confused was Britain's first jazz critic; to show the odd duality of his thinking; and to acknowledge his desire to propagate jazz (if not, at one stage, by that name) however contradictorily and inconsistently. He was the first to make vital research in record personnels, and it was his authority as an editor and his undoubted enthusiasm for jazz that resulted in the *Melody Maker*, a trade paper reliant upon advertising revenue from interests outside the jazz minority, becoming identified with that movement.

Later, there were several magazines dealing solely with the subject, but from 1926 to 1934 it was primarily the *Melody Maker* and *Rhythm* from which the growing jazz community could glean its knowledge.

In a mélange of widely spread coverage in the *Melody Maker* there were such quaint news items as the following quotation from the *Daily Express* in January 1926. Under the heading 'Order Against Saxophones Condition of Dancing Licence' it said: 'The dancing licence of the Liberal Hall, Wallasey, was renewed by the magistrates on the condition that saxophones are not used by visiting jazz bands. It is contended by residents that their music disturbs the quiet of the neighbourhood. Heavy curtains must also be drawn round the revelry within the hall.'

In the March 1927 issue an unnamed local paper was quoted as having reported a band that comprised 'two sets of bones, banjo and drums', and when the paper was informed that 'two sets of bones' should have read 'two saxophones' they replied that the difference was too hair-splitting to make a correction necessary. The *Melody Maker*'s only comment was to add an exclamation mark. And then, as now, there were the legal notables' witticisms about what was thought to be jazz, and saxophones, particularly, came in for many a learned judge's heavy humour.

'Paras from the Press' delighted in reporting the following:

> 'With remarkable persistence,' says the *Evening Standard*, 'lawsuits concerning musicians come before Mr Justice Eve, who of all his Majesty's judges is most renowned for being unmusical and not a little proud of the fact.
>
> '"What is a saxophone?" asked his Lordship in a chancery case the other day, with the traditional ignorance, which in this case was probably not assumed. Learned counsel replied that it is an instrument resembling a cornet (which is not true) and used in jazz bands (which is).
>
> At a subsequent hearing of the same case the *Daily Mail* quotes the following dialogue between Mr Justice Eve and Mr Peck, a barrister.
>
> 'Mr Justice Eve – "What is a saxophone?"
>
> 'Mr Peck – "A wind instrument."
>
> 'Mr Justice Eve – "What is the other instrument she [the litigant] plays?"
>
> 'Mr Peck – "I am told she plays a piccolo."
>
> 'Mr Justice Eve – "And what is that?"'

Such witty ripostes from gentlemen administering the law were common-place and served, apart from their dubious amusement value, only to bring jazz into further disrepute. Indeed 'jazz' had a hard time in the press and in the courts.

The Savoy Hotel in the 1920s from an LP sleeve

In the February 1928 issue of the *Melody Maker* under the heading 'Dance Band and Syncopated News' appeared a news item about the Glasgow Plaza Band, led by saxophonist Jock Scott. Jock was father of tenor saxophonist Ronnie, a pioneer of bebop jazz in Britain and founder of the internationally renowned London jazz club that bears his name.

In these gossip pages there were sundry references to 'vellum punchers' and 'gentlemen of the kitchen department' (drummers), 'iron tootlers' (saxophonists), and 'gobsticks' (clarinets). In one issue a whole page was devoted to how well the Savoy Hotel management looked after the resident bands, which included the pioneer 'hot' band in this country, Fred Elizalde and his Music.

Here is a typical menu provided for their exclusive delectation:

Menu -
Potage Cultivateur

Supreme de Plaice Bercy
Filet de Boeuf Pique
Macedoine des Legumes
Pommes Croquettes

Bananas – Gruyère

Gastronomically, this was a far cry from the stodge purveyed in the roadside transport cafes which touring jazz musicians in less gracious post-war days were forced to patronize; but how quaint that such an item was thought worthy of mention.

There were advertisements from record companies, gramophone and instrument and accessory manufacturers, arrangers, songwriters, publishers of tuition manuals and teachers, with sections for 'Light Music' and 'Music in the Cinema'. For this latter feature a certain William Oliphant Chuckerbutty, Mus. Bac., FRCO, one-time organist at Holy Trinity Church, Paddington and currently organist with the Café Royal Dance Band, wrote technical articles.

In addition there were news and gossip columns and record reviews covering all aspects of the paper's contents.

These were the heterogeneous ingredients of the early *Melody Maker*, but eventually it became concerned primarily with dance/jazz music. It enjoyed its role as the defender of 'Jazz', a Galahad persona consistent with the British attitude of protecting the underdog (although, in this instance, often giving the real underdog, the black jazz musician, many a vicious kick) and it took on all-comers in its 'Paras from the Press'.

The most famous opponent of 'Jazz' was Dr Henry Coward, born 1849, trainer of the Sheffield Festival Chorus and composer of anthems and cantatas now completely forgotten. Even in his day he was more famous for his attacks on jazz than for his own creative output. In July 1926 he addressed the London Rotary Club at the Hotel Cecil, in the Strand. He denounced jazz as 'atavistic, lowering, degrading and a racial question', adding that it was 'composed of jingly tunes, jerky rhythms, unquestionably grotesque forms, including untuned gramophones and noises from domestic utensils'.

What Coward heard was formal dance music; had he been subjected to the pristine exuberance of Armstrong's Hot Five or Seven and Morton's Red Hot Peppers, the jungle growls of Duke Ellington's brass or the Luis Russell band in full cry he would assuredly have expired in a fit of apoplectic convulsions. He became a figure of fun in the *Melody Maker*, his nickname 'Dr Crowhard' frequently used and applied to individuals sharing and pronouncing his objections.

Jackson was quite stern with the Crowhards. 'Yet abuse means nothing. Any person with a literary style and a little journalistic experience can string a number of colourful adjectives and other jargon into disparaging phrases which may sway the uninitiated by the mere preponderance of expression.' He could have been writing about himself . . .

The Crowhards condemned formal dance music that assaulted their ears, thinking it to be jazz. Generally Jackson condemned, in not dissimilar terms, the genuine jazz music that offended *his* ears.

In 1929 the *Melody Maker* changed hands. It was acquired by Odhams Press, publishers of *John Bull*, the *People* newspaper, *Sporting Life*, *Passing Show* and *Ideal Home*. In its notification of this there was a significant sentence: 'The passing of central control will not affect the *Melody Maker* in any way except that it will ensure complete editorial independence from vested interests.' This was an obvious side-swipe at editorial interference from the former publisher, Lawrence Wright. The brief announcement of Odhams' purchase, with the implication of previous editorial interference, only hinted at the developments leading up to the change of ownership. In its early days the *Melody Maker* was run on a shoestring in the basement of Lawrence Wright's office, with Jackson, his secretary Dorothy Newman, her assistant Gladys Birch and, later, Percy Mathison Brooks, who was brought in to seek the necessary advertising.

In three years it had grown in size and prestige. First distributed to the seven thousand subscribers to Wright's 'Orchestral Club', it was marked '3d a copy' to create the impression that it was being sold. Although it was soon known as Wright's house magazine, largely thanks to Jackson's salesmanship and latterly to P. M. Brooks' successful pursuit of advertising from other song publishers, it gained support from outside the Orchestral Club. Although publishers were forthcoming in support, it was the bandleaders who were found to be most sales-resistant, these worthies being somewhat cool towards a paper that openly supported hot jazz!

The third issue was published at 6d a copy while still being issued free to Wright's members. After a few months eight thousand copies a month were being sold.

Chris Hayes, who joined the paper in 1929 and stayed with it for fifty years, wrote:

> The magazine had become an authority on jazz respected by members of the profession and the lay public. It had become regarded as the voice of both professional musicians and jazz record collectors. This success, however, proved to be double-edged. Certain bandleaders were incensed by adverse reviews of their stage and record performances. As a revenge they refused to play Wright's numbers, a situation which, naturally enough, the paper's owner found intolerable. Here he was, with a house magazine edited by a jazz fanatic, upsetting the bandleaders upon whom he relied for his business. The bigger names (like Hylton), however, were not that put out. They were in receipt of considerable sums of money – from Wright and other publishers – to play their tunes, but the objections of the small fry – like Alfredo and Hal Swain – hardly names to conjure with – troubled Wright. Small fry to a publisher were just as important as the big names, and who was to know that the small names might not become big?
>
> He prevailed upon Jackson to tone down his adverse reviews but Jackson (and Brooks) had been made directors of the limited liability company that Wright had formed and spoke from a position of strength, turning down any suggestions that the paper should forsake its hard-earned reputation for honest and fearless commentary.

Good old Edgar! In his own inconsistent, befuddled and often offensive way he had fought the good fight. Wright sold the paper to Odhams for a mere £3,000, glad to be shot of those 'jazz fiends' who antagonized bandleaders.

During 1929 the paper carried a series of technical analyses. Notating the arrangement of 'Sweet Sue' by Paul Whiteman's Orchestra on a twelve-inch record, the analyst, Al Davison, bravely included the famous Bix Beiderbecke solo on this record, a thirty-two-bar chorus of considerable imagination, heat and swing that arose from the unsympathetic framework of an inflated arrangement.

Items like this indicated that the *Melody Maker* was moving slowly towards a positive jazz orientation. In July 1929 a readers' correspondence page was introduced. Later, the letters became filled with disputations about jazz-record personnels from knowledgeable collector-discographers. In the course of one of these, the *Melody Maker*'s new American correspondent Herbert S. Weill, erstwhile drummer with the massively recorded California Ramblers, felt moved to issue the following tribute: 'Incidentally, many musicians over here have remarked on the accuracy with which "Needlepoint", your Gramophone correspondent, recognises the various players on records. They point out that only on the rarest occasions is he at fault and that no-one over here would get anything like as near.'

This was probably true, as jazz scholarship in the country of the music's origin was almost unknown. It wasn't until the middle and late thirties that American aficionados emerged, lagging well behind the English and French in their investigations into the history of their one truly indigenous art.

Indeed, the *Melody Maker* was feeling its way as an authoritative jazz paper. In a feature called 'Backbeats' they upbraided the American magazine *Jacobs Orchestra Monthly* for (among other gaffes) misspelling Bix's surname as 'Binderbecke'. 'Surely they mean Beiderbecke' was the outraged cry from a paper that had consistently misspelt the name, but they were not too fussy about the spelling of trumpeter Sylvester Ahola, playing with Ambrose's orchestra. This was given as 'Ahoula'.

The allocation of space to jazz had grown considerably and the writers were better informed. At the end of the twenties the *Melody Maker* could – though not without a blush of embarrassment – look back on its highly significant contribution to jazz appreciation in Britain, and most of the credit was due to its editor and first record critic, the extraordinary, polymorphous and pseudonymous Edgar Jackson.

4

Early Definitions, Bands and Records

There were several definitions of jazz in the twenties' dictionaries and encyclopaedias. One of the very earliest appeared in *Brewer's Dictionary of Phrase and Fable*, undated but published circa 1920:

> A voluptuous dance of negro origin, accompanied by a wild, irregular kind of music, which has been spoken of as – 'that synchronising supersyncopation that, originating in New Orleans, has aggravated the feet and fingers of America into a shimmying, tickle-toeing, finger-snapping delirium and now (i.e. 1919) is upsetting the equilibrium of European dance music'. The dance and the music emerged from the negro shanties of New Orleans in 1915 and, in March 1916, Bert Kelly's Jazz Band (the first to be so-called) was engaged by the Booster's Club in Chicago and scored an immediate success and started the thing on its conquering career. The origin is uncertain. One account is that it is an adaptation of the name 'Razz' who was a band conductor in New Orleans about 1904; another one is that it has long been a common word to the negro and on the Barbary Coast and it means simply 'Mess 'em up and slap it on thick', and another that it was the spontaneous production of a brainwave on the part of the above Mr Kelly.

Another definition appeared in *Harmsworth's Encyclopaedia*, published in 1923:

> *Jazz*, name of dance and its accompanying music. A development of the modern one-step and two-step dances. The jazz, like ragtime dances and popular music generally, is of American origin. It was introduced into Britain during 1918. In the following year it became widely known and its popularity aroused some controversy.

Trumpeter Frank Guarante

The jazz band which provides the peculiarly noisy syncopated music is characterized by its percussion instruments and apparatus, drum, cymbals and sheets of tin.

Most of the bands, British and American, primarily white, were entertainment packages, the music purged of jazz crudities, the jazz tag having a publicly acceptable novelty value. They bore little relationship to the scholarly definitions. The year 1923 saw the appearance in Britain of two American bands that certainly didn't fit these. They were led by Paul Whiteman and Paul Specht, both classically trained violinists who, by refining jazz, had made it into a marketable commodity.

Whiteman was to become the self-styled 'King of Jazz' and Specht, entrepreneur more than bandleader, was one of the principal figures in the early disputes between the American Federation of Musicians and the British Musicians' Union which resulted in both countries operating a ban for over twenty years, with Britain the loser by being deprived of seeing and hearing genuine jazz musicians.

But Specht's band had a small contingent playing in the collective improvisational style of the ODJB. Called the Georgians, they comprised Frank Guarante (trumpet), Johnny O'Donnell, Harold Saliers (clarinet and saxophones), Ray Stilwell (trombone), Russell Deppe (banjo), Chauncey Morehouse (drums) and Arthur Schutt (piano). They occasionally split from the main orchestra, playing and recording in their own right. They appeared at Lyon's Corner House at the corner of Shaftesbury Avenue and Coventry Street and at the Royal Palace Hotel, Kensington.

After leaving Italy in 1910, Guarante played in New Orleans between 1914 and 1916. Here he met and swapped lessons with the black trumpeter Joe 'King' Oliver, since immortalized in jazz history. In a city notorious for its colour bar, social contact between the white and black races was rare, but in this instance it was of noticeable benefit to the young émigré trumpeter. If Guarante had been happy to exchange ideas with a black trumpeter the ODJB allegedly kept their distance from black musicians, except, it has been claimed, to listen and copy them. But Guarante and Nick La Rocca met and on the Georgians' records La Rocca's influence on the Italian is clearly demonstrated.

The American critic Rudi Blesh, in his book *Combo: USA*, asserts that the ODJB stole 'Livery Stable Blues', one of their most successful numbers, from the

Writer/promoter John Hammond at age sixteen

black trumpeter Freddie Keppard. Ironically, Keppard refused, in 1916, to record for the Victor label for fear that his rivals would steal his ideas from the records. Having failed to get Keppard, Victor approached La Rocca. Had Keppard accepted it might well have been that the first jazz band to visit Britain would have been black.

A young American boy of wealthy socialite parents who heard the Georgians in London was John Hammond, who claims they led him to jazz. It was Hammond who, in the mid-thirties, helped Benny Goodman towards international fame, and was instrumental in returning boogie-woogie pianist Meade Lux Lewis to a successful recording career after he had been discovered washing cars in a Chicago South Side garage. Hammond also brought the Count Basie band from Kansas City to New York and worldwide acclaim, was the first to record Billie Holiday and, after a long absence from the recording studios, 'the Empress of the Blues', Bessie Smith. These were the last recordings she was to make.

Hammond was also connected with the rise of genuine jazz appreciation in Britain through his passionate dispatches from America to the *Gramophone* and *Melody Maker* in the early thirties. In these he was mostly scornful about white jazz and, particularly, big white dance bands, but the man with such a distinguished history in supporting black jazz commenced his involvement when only a thirteen-year-old listening to a white group in a London restaurant in 1923.

As with the ODJB, the Georgians' influence on British musicians was negligible, and Guarante later joined a British dance band, the Savoy Orpheans, necessarily refining his style to suit their requirements. The Orpheans, and all other British dance bands, were much influenced by Whiteman's band which received its first British mention in *Era*, March 1923. 'Paul Whiteman is the only man who can make a Broadway audience stand up and yell,' it reported, quoting from the New York *American*. 'It has been specially engaged for Julian Wylie's show *Brighter London* to be produced at the London Hippodrome. Paul is due to arrive at Plymouth on Saturday.'

Era gave the names of the players, the first time the personnel of a 'jazz' band had been given in the entertainment press. 'His trumpet player is Henry Busse, famed as "Hot Lips". Pee Wee Byers on saxophone is a young man with a sunny smile. Harry McDonald is the drummer. Tom Galt and Sam Lewis the trombone players, Mike Pingatore the banjoist, Jack Busby the viol player and Ross Gorman and Donald Clarke the other saxophone players.'

In the 14 March issue of *Era* song publishers Francis, Day and Hunter placed an advertisement for a band arrangement of the tune 'Hot Lips' with an illustration of a pop-eyed black man apparently struggling to produce the notes on his cornet. This was misleading as Busse was white, but the supposed racial associations of the title were obviously thought more effective for advertising.

In *Era*, 21 March, *Brighter London* was reviewed: 'A capital episode is that of "Brighter Shakespeare" in which Mr Billy Merson gives us his idea of how Hamlet would be played in 1923. This scene concluded with the Shakespeare Jazz – Mr Charles Stone as the immortal Bard. It ends with a novel effect; not only do we see Shakespeare's characters jazzing, but the scenery jazzes also.'

This sketch received a bigger mention than the Whiteman contribution. And rightly so – judging by its striking originality as conveyed in the report. It continued: 'Mr Paul Whiteman and his Band are in the last scene – "Palais de Danse" – and play jazz music on instruments with much skill and effect and were loudly applauded.' The telling phrase 'on instruments' probably reflects the reviewer's pleasure at hearing 'jazz' on instruments other than percussive 'drums, cymbals and sheets of tin'.

Of his emasculating intentions Whiteman made no secret. In his book *Jazz* he wrote:

> We first met – Jazz and I – at a dance hall dive at the Barbary Coast. It screeched and bellowed at me from a trick platform in the middle of a smoke-hazed, beer-fumed room. And it hit me hard. Raucous? Yes. Crude – undoubtedly. Unmusical – as sure as you live. But rhythmic, catching as the small-pox, and spirit-lifting.
>
> I never stopped wanting to go into concert halls. If I have contributed anything to music, it is that I started the arranging business among the bands.

Programme for Specht's orchestra in New York. The band, including its jazz group, the Georgians, played in London in 1923.

His mission, he claimed, was to 'remove the stigma of barbaric strains and jungle cacophony from jazz'.

The English writer Iain Lang, in his *Background of the Blues*, made a sharp riposte to these woolly sentiments: 'In much the same way missionaries of another sort "contributed" reach-me-downs and Mother Hubbards to the barbaric nakedness of South Sea Islanders – and whole island populations incontinently died of the diseases of Western civilizations.'

Paul Whiteman's band, 1928

Whiteman received the accolade of a mention in a British encyclopaedia devoted to classical music. This, *Black's Dictionary of Music and Musicians*, edited by L. J. De Bekker and published in 1924, gave him twenty-two lines:

> WHITEMAN (Paul) conducted his own orchestra, specializing in JAZZ, and made successful European tour in 1923, and on his return gave a notable performance of this class of music at Aeolian Hall, New York. Son of supervisor of music in the Denver, Col., schools he studied with his father and mastered several instruments in early youth. His first important engagement was with the San Francisco Fair, in which city he first assembled his own organization. Returning to New York, he was soon established a popular favourite on Broadway and made numerous concert tours. B Denver, Colorado, *Add.* New York.

The same edition gave one of the first encyclopaedic definitions of 'jazz' in Britain, interspersed with Paul Whiteman's hardly erudite comments on the subject:

JAZZ, a development of RAGTIME, which began in about 1914 in the US, owed its deadly monotony to the exclusive use of dual time, and its interest chiefly to bizarre effects obtained through a new grouping of instruments in which saxophones, clarinets and trumpets and trombones, often muted, are often of primary importance and frequently played with portmanteau effects.

Its vogue was originally due to the ease with which certain dances could be learned and to instrumental antics which amused the crowds in dancing places and to thoroughly organized propaganda along commercial lines.

Almost without exception those concerned with its progress were young Jewish writers of popular songs, but, in 1924, Victor Herbert produced a 'Suite of Serenades': Spanish, Chinese, Cuban and Oriental, which demonstrated that the new form might be occasionally employed to advantage by real [sic] musicians. Paul Whiteman, 'King of Jazz', whose orchestra in 1923 introduced the higher type of this music to Europe, thus traces its genealogy:

'It really started with the Texas Tommy. Then came the Bunny Hug which brought into vogue the slow graceful hesitation waltz, which did not last long, and fell before the Frisco steps, the slow draggy blues and the Collegiate glide of to-day (1924) on which little attention is paid to the rhythm of the dancers.

'Syncopation has ceased to be an essential in Jazz, the Foxtrot being played in the 1 and 2 and 3 and 4 rhythm of the dactyle; but it continues to rule the Tango, which is slow, and the Cakewalk, which is fast and ragtime.'

The orchestra employed by Paul Whiteman on gala occasions includes eight violins, two double basses (interchangeable with tuba), banjo, piano, two trumpets (interchangeable with flugel horns) two trombones, two horns, flute and the complete group of saxophones, clarinets, oboes and one flute.

One performer may play several instruments alternately and the rhythm is fixed by drums, banjo, and bass strings, generally pizzicato and piano.

Dancing masters are of the opinion that the 'original jazz' is a combination of the backward glide and a flying dip, or a strongly accented Turkey Trot.

To quote Paul Whiteman again: 'You can stick on counter melodies like the barbershop quartets; you can call off imaginary figures, yell 'hot dog' in the midst of some perfectly decorous dance and make a donkey of yourself generally. That is Jazz. You can jazz 'Old Hundred' if you like, exactly as you can rag it. But the two are different. Anybody can jazz. It takes a musician to rag a tune.

It is difficult to understand exactly what Whiteman meant. Rarely can a pronouncement on any kind of music have been so puzzling.

The Harmsworth compilers were obviously impressed with the number of instruments used, some of these having 'classical' associations, and the multi-instrumental ability of the players, this being clearly superior in their view to the simple instrumentation of the original jazzmen and their crude improvisations.

Whiteman's comments are farcical although, in the early twenties, not surprising from a classically trained musician who, nevertheless, had

The Savoy Havana Band, one of the most popular British broadcasting orchestras of the 1920s. The Havana band and the Savoy Orpheans were the highest-paid dance bands contracted to EMI during the 1920s and made more than three hundred records between 1922 and 1927.

astutely realized the commercial potential of certain elements in jazz. Compare his comments with those quoted earlier from Ernest Ansermet, another formally trained musician, a European living far from the country of jazz's birth, but able to discern real creative ability in one listening and, incidentally, not himself mentioned in this encyclopaedia although he had been conducting the Suisse Romande Orchestra for five years when the volume was published.

Whiteman came to Britain again in 1926 with an enlarged orchestra, this time performing George Gershwin's much vaunted 'Rhapsody in Blue' at concert halls as well as playing pretty music for dances. Other visitors were the bands of Art Hickman, Johnny Hamp, Gus Arnheim, Fred Rich and Hal Kemp, their performances largely substantiating the Musicians' Union's disapproval of uncontrolled entry. Most of the British bands of similar calibre, although not as technically skilled and slick in their stage presentation, could have performed just as well.

In the Fred Rich Band a young New Orleans drummer, Ray Bauduc, drew the following praise from the magazine *Rhythm*: 'He puts over some flashy work and the public (including drummers) "eat him up". He is fifty per cent of the show. Go to see Ray's performance and have a thrill.' Bauduc was later a founder and long-standing member of the famous Bob Crosby band in the thirties. Certainly there were no British drummers of Bauduc's class in the twenties, or for many years later. While trumpet, saxophone, clarinet and, to a limited extent, trombone players grasped jazz essentials, rhythm sections, and drummers in particular, did not.

Ray Bauduc drawn by Boy ten Hove

* * *

The first definition of jazz in the *Concise Oxford English Dictionary*, in 1929, was the same as it gave as late as 1969.

> JAZZ, n.a., & v.i. & t.i. Music and dance of US negro origin with characteristic harmony and ragtime rhythm; noisy or grotesque proceedings.
> 2. adj. Discordant, loud in colour etc., rude, burlesque; – *band* (of such combinations as piano, trumpet, saxophone, banjo and drums).
> 3. vb. Play, dance, indulge in; – transform into, arrange as; (origin unkn.)

The combination of Whiteman's pronouncements which were echoed by British writers and musicians, the prestigious *Black's Dictionary* considering him worthy of twenty-two lines, and the various inadequate definitions: all of these contributed to misunderstanding about the true nature of jazz. Anyone looking to these sources for guidance would be wholly misled.

The Savoy Orpheans were but one of the English bands copying the Whiteman style. Another was that led by the Lancashire-born Jack

Hylton, at one time described as the 'English Paul Whiteman'. Whiteman's first record and the first issued in Britain was 'Wang Wang Blues'. It was a laboured, plodding performance by a band of seven pieces redeemed by the clarinet playing of Gus Mueller from New Orleans. Albeit badly recorded, Mueller plays a sinuous line in the classic New Orleans manner and although British record buyers were totally unconcerned with the fact, he was the first New Orleans clarinettist they had heard since Larry Shields with the ODJB.

Hylton recorded 'Wang Wang Blues' on the Zonophone label with Al Jenkins, a black musician, making an awful hash of his attempt to copy Mueller's ensemble playing. Just as the Georgians were the genuine jazz core of Specht's package (which included all manner of mechanical gadgetry like illuminated glockenspiels), Mueller was the one genuine jazzman in Whiteman's first band and, perhaps surprisingly, his comments to Whiteman on leaving the band are quoted in the latter's book:

> Gus Mueller was wonderful on the clarinet but he couldn't read a line of music.
>
> 'It's like this,' he confided one day. 'I knew a boy once down in N'Awleens that was a hot player, but he learned to read music and then he couldn't play jazz any more. I don't want to be like that.'
>
> A little later Gus came to say he was quitting. I was sorry and asked him what was the matter. He stalled around for a while and then burst out: 'Nuh, suh, I jes' can't play that "pretty music" that you all play. And you fellers never play blues worth a damn.'

The crux of the matter simply, graphically expressed – that 'pretty music' was soon to be the overriding fashion of white dance bands. As the Whiteman band increased in size (it was thirty-three strong at one stage) Hylton followed in his wake.

The few black orchestras to play in Britain during the twenties were not vastly dissimilar from the white 'show' bands. Will Marion Cook's Southern Syncopated Orchestra had only one jazzman in Sidney Bechet. Will Vodery's Plantation Orchestra, appearing in C. B. Cochran's presentation of the *Plantation Revue* in 1926, was of the same ilk, although it recorded two sides for the Columbia label that featured trumpet player Pike Davis.

A black band led by composer and singer Noble Sissle played in London in 1929 and 1930, recording for the HMV and Columbia labels.

Although it boasted such jazzmen as trumpeters Arthur Briggs,* Pike Davis and Tommy Ladnier and clarinettist Buster Bailey, little use was made in its shows or on record of their improvising abilities.

The 'English Paul Whiteman': Jack Hylton and members of his band

* * *

If jazz was being neutered by Tin Pan Alley to make it publicly acceptable it was another irony that the economic structure of the gramophone record business ensured the release of much genuine jazz, and some blues.

It has been estimated that there were two hundred British labels available to accommodate the widespread use of the gramophone after the First World War and many of these, having arrangements with American companies, were compelled to issue records they would perhaps have preferred to ignore. Most of these companies were independently owned, and those issuing jazz records from American masters were Aeolian, Ariel, Beltona, Cliftophone, Coliseum, Curry, Curwen, Duophone, Edison Bell, Grafton, Guardsman, Homochord, Imperial, Kildare, Pathe,

* Canadian-born Arthur Briggs (trumpet) was in the Southern Syncopated Orchestra but there is no reference to him taking solos.

Perfect, Scala and Winner. Often only limited numbers were pressed, the distribution being scattered and the attendant publicity minimal. The jazz on many of these was only fragmentary, but few picked up on the redeeming splashes of improvisation.

A player who was later to be regarded as the greatest of all jazz artists, trumpeter Louis Armstrong, can be heard on many records by Fletcher Henderson, issued by a variety of companies under a bewildering number of pseudonyms. The tunes were mostly current Tin Pan Alley pot-boilers, though some were to have lasting value. The arrangements were in the stiff and turgid period manner, Henderson at the time playing in the Roseland Ballroom, New York, a 'whites only' hall pandering to white tastes. He was billed as the 'Black Paul Whiteman' on some of his tours, but he engaged the brilliant young trumpeter from New Orleans in his band because, it is alleged, he thought Armstrong 'would be useful for our act'. It was quite accidental that these historic recordings were issued in Britain.

The joy of Armstrong's eight or sixteen bars of blazing improvisation is all the more keenly felt for emerging from the usual dreariness of the setting.* There were fifteen examples of him with Henderson issued in Britain in 1925/6 on various labels. One company, Imperial, actually credits Fletcher Henderson's band on the label and one title, 'Alabamy Bound' was the first record issued in Britain on which an Armstrong solo occurs. Later, Imperial released two versions of Henderson's 'Everybody Loves My Baby', one of them containing the first-ever examples of Armstrong's voice on record – a short 'scat' chorus at the end of the record, the words almost indiscernible on this muddy, acoustic recording. The voice that combined both earthy harshness and affecting tenderness was later to take Armstrong to the top of the Hit Parade many times with songs like 'Blueberry Hill', 'Mack the Knife' and 'Hello Dolly', but when 'Everybody Loves My Baby' was issued it went totally unnoticed.

Guardsman launched a special 'Race' series, 'Race' implying black artists. The pseudonyms they chose to emphasize this were the Old Southern Dance Orchestra, Southern States Orchestra, Pete Massey's

* Over fifty years later, the English trumpeter/critic Humphrey Lyttelton, in a broadcast featuring these records, remarked that it was almost as if the Louis solos had been spliced in, so different were they in concept and spirit from the arrangements, although, of course, no such process existed in the early twenties.

Sheet music cover, 1923. Composer Spencer Williams, long resident in Britain, wrote many standards including 'Basin Street Blues' and 'Careless Love'.

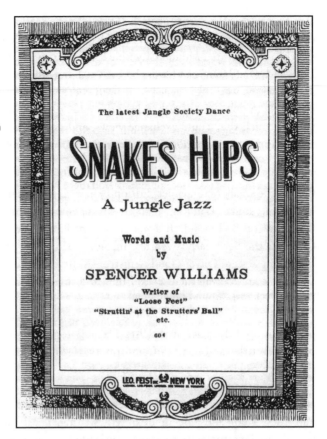

Black Band and the Original Black Band, the last featuring Fletcher Henderson again with Louis Armstrong. Actually many of these pseudonyms covered white bands, but Guardsman also issued records of blues singers Viola McCoy and Rosa Henderson as well as the Carolina Jug Band, all representative of jazz's true nature.

On the same label, under the pseudonym of the Californian Dance Band, one Henderson record, 'Dicty Blues', featured tenor saxophonist Coleman Hawkins playing a solo so clumsy and ugly that it is hard to believe listening to it now that he was shortly to burgeon into the world's supreme master of the instrument.

The willy-nilly release of Fletcher Henderson's records gave British listeners not only snatches of the greatest ever jazz trumpet player but also of a tenor saxophone player who was later to develop so dramatically. The contrast between these Henderson recordings and his work on, say, the reconstituted Mound City Blue Blowers 1929 recordings of 'Hello Lola' and 'One Hour' can hardly be believed, but when both Armstrong and Hawkins were first heard in Britain there were no knowledgeable jazz buffs to take note of either. Had there been, there was no organization in which they could exchange views, and no journal in which they could express their opinions, or seek further information.

* * *

One of the smaller companies, Edison Bell, with its studio and factory at Peckham, south London, had an arrangement with the Gennett Company of Richmond, Indiana, which had recorded many pioneer bands in the very early twenties, including King Oliver's Creole Jazz Band. These were Oliver's (and Armstrong's) first recordings, but Edison Bell chose not to avail themselves from this catalogue which represented the very best of pioneer jazz.

In those early days the executives of British companies must have peered in total disbelief at the lists available to them, wondered at the outlandish titles and names of performers of some of the blues records they were offered and pondered on the lyrics – had they been able to understand the unfamiliar diction – related to sexual needs, with many allusive references to the anatomy. Certainly they weren't in the usual Tin Pan Alley 'Moon and June' mode of lyric writing. These executives often complicated matters with their own misleading and unnecessary pseudonyms. Many of the masters were available to various companies and issued under different pseudonyms on miscellaneous labels at varying prices, a tangle discographers of a later decade had to unravel.

The two major combines then were the Gramophone Company, putting out HMV and Zonophone, and the Graphophone Company, issuing Columbia and Regal. Columbia pipped HMV by recording the ODJB on sixteen twelve-inch records at their studios in Clerkenwell Road, London EC1, even though HMV had had access to their recordings from the Victor label since 1917.

The doyen of British discographers, Brian Rust, states that 'Livery Stable Blues' was scheduled for release in mid-1917, but a high official of HMV blocked the release of a record with strange 'barnyard' effects he probably thought unacceptable to British record buyers. The nearest the company got to issuing jazz was in 1918 with 'Darktown Strutters Ball' (subtitled 'A Jazz Medley') by the Savoy Quartet, comprising two banjos, piano and drums. This was the sort of record the public associated with jazz before the Dixieland Band shattered this misconception.

Columbia's sister label, Regal, sporadically issued jazz records, including the Georgians' best record 'Snakes Hips', Fletcher Henderson with Louis Armstrong, Doc Cook's Band with many New Orleanians, and the Original Memphis Five, the ODJB's premier rival. The pseudonyms Regal Novelty Orchestra and Corona Dance Orchestra were used in preference to actual names.

After their enterprise in recording the dixieland band, Columbia were not to have any major additions to their jazz catalogue until 1927, upsetting Edgar Jackson when they did.

Most of the records mentioned here have since appeared in various formats, but the original 78 rpm discs are now collectors' items eagerly sought. Henderson's 'Everybody Loves My Baby', with the Armstrong vocal, commands considerable sums. That such prices were to be placed on records sold for two or three shillings on release would never have been envisaged in 1925 when they hardly warranted any mention, much less any reference to their enduring and later highly applauded 'hot' content. In fact, up to then the only truly perceptive observation on jazz (and this only in respect of one performer) was Ernest Ansermet's. True jazz quality, and genius in Armstrong particularly, went unnoticed, and by the time criteria began to emerge in the thirties these companies had become defunct and many of their masters had been destroyed when their factories were pulled down or used for other purposes. It was in the thirties when 'junk shopping' for these 78s became a feature of jazz research, with collectors foraging among bric-a-brac to find gems which, once found, heard and evaluated, helped to put the entire history of the music into some perspective.

Those early records, haphazardly issued by companies not the least interested in the 'art' of jazz, represented facets of the genuine article at a time when British bandleaders, following the Americans, were dressing it up. The true voice of the music could still be heard – albeit sporadically and fragmentarily, and although it seemed a tiny voice in the welter of prettified jazz.

The *Performer*, *Stage* and *Era* occasionally printed band news, and the *Gramophone*, from its inception in 1923, featured notices on dance music and jazz, although it was primarily concerned with classical music and technical appraisal of gramophone models.

In the *Gramophone*, January 1923, a piece, unsigned, read:

> It was I believe, the late Shah of Persia who, when taken to the opera, expressed preference for the tuning up of the orchestra and requested that it might be repeated. He would have revelled in modern dance-band records. They are indeed a source of wonder and joy.
>
> Ingenuity is taxed to the utmost to provide effects – beats, whirls, wails and quaint rhythms, whilst e'er so well marshalled that the result is quite masterly in its precision and completeness. Trombones laugh, saxophones sob and imaginary kittens flit across the keys of the piano. It is a mistaken conception that dance orchestras play by ear. The outstanding merit of modern dance records is the superb technique of the players enabling them to execute innumerable effects. Some are ex-symphony men.

The writer was a lot more generous in his assessment of jazz/dance than most of his 'classical' colleagues, but the few letters and articles about jazz published in the *Gramophone* were mostly in praise of Whitemanesque refinements. Henry Melville wrote: 'Paul Whiteman introduces to us brass instruments of vast size and barbaric splendour susceptible of infinite modulation. Will Vodery's orchestra, from the *Plantation Show*, appearing at a private party proved once more that black faces, like Oriental china, blend admirably with eighteenth century decoration.'

'Jazz' wasn't without its critics in their columns. Reader Stanley Smith described it as 'immature, mercenary and mechanically made. Fit only for the minute musical mentality of those poor devils, the masses.' He complained that 'Hylton is being encouraged by certain critics to vaunt in the glory of his aesthetic barbarism.'

A subscriber in Banbury wrote: 'It is up to the record companies to turn out their products in proper condition, particularly as the price for the best is high – for jazz records coarse surfaces are of little consequence – with a nice symphony it is another matter.'

Poor, maligned, misrepresented and maltreated jazz – not, some averred, even worth the benefit of good recording!

5

Odd Bedfellows

Immediately following Edgar Jackson's stringent criticism of Louis Armstrong's 'Georgia Bo-Bo' he warmly praised 'Brown Sugar' by Bert Firman's dance orchestra, resident at the Devonshire Restaurant, Devonshire Street, London. 'Brown Sugar' was an 'instrumental' with a few bars of mildly 'hot' trumpet and one of many that Firman recorded from 1926 with improvised solos. From 1927 to 1932 he organized 260 recordings for the Zonophone label issued under the name of the Rhythmic Eight. These were mostly of ordinary Tin Pan Alley tunes with some so-called comedy numbers, but many contained a surprising degree of improvisation. The personnel, constantly fluctuating and often in excess of eight, were British and American musicians, all clearly influenced by the Nichols Five Pennies and the Charleston Chasers. The collective personnel was Frank Guarante, Max Goldberg, Jack Jackson, Chelsea Quealey, Sylvester Ahola (trumpets), Perley Breed, Danny Polo, Sid Phillips, Arthur Lally (reeds), Max Bacon (drums), Joe Brannelly (guitar), John Firman (piano) and Billy Bell (brass bass). These Rhythmic Eight sessions were the first continuous series of recordings in Britain with any jazz content, however fragmentary, but much of this was provided by resident Americans. Significantly, when they departed the country the quality noticeably declined.

In the same year that the Rhythmic Eight appeared in the Zonophone lists the *Melody Maker*, April 1927, announced the receipt of a curious telegram, which they headed:

A NEW GENIUS IN THE DANCE BAND WORLD

Success of an Amateur Outfit
Cambridge, February 25th

The telegram read:

THE QUINQUAGINTA RAMBLERS, A DANCE BAND CONSISTING ENTIRELY OF UNDERGRADUATES AT THE VARSITY, WILL PLAY FOR THE FOOTLIGHTS CLUB BALL TO BE HELD AT THE MASONIC HALL HERE TONIGHT.

THE BALL, IT IS STATED, IS LIKELY TO BE THE MOST BRILLIANT FUNCTION HELD IN THE DISTRICT FOR THE SEASON, AS AT LEAST ALL CAMBRIDGE KNOWS THAT THE QUINQUAGINTA RAMBLERS IS THE BEST DANCE BAND NOW PLAY-ING IN THE COUNTRY.

Edgar Jackson promptly responded to the telegram:

The astounding claim made in the above telegram caused me to make a rapid decision to investigate there and then its accuracy . . . up at Cambridge the brothers Elizalde . . . ages 20 and 21 . . . are both musical genius-es. It wasn't long before they decided to start an undergraduate band. Told with some emphasis that others had tried it before and met with no success, Fred merely laughed and set himself, and his brother, who is an accomplished saxophonist, as a nucleus for the combination.

He found a bunch of youngsters whose enthusiasm was apparent despite their musical abilities. They commenced weeks of unending hard work . . . The result has been nothing short of uncanny.

In a short time Elizalde has produced a combination that is capable of holding its own with many bands considered good today but as a modern dance band it is, in style, in advance, I honestly believe, of any other now playing in this country.

From a purely commercial point of view it may be found that the public will find Elizalde's arrangements very advanced, being based on the modern harmony after the school of Debussy, Stravinsky and such like . . . they illustrate the coming vogue. As such, says Elizalde, they will eventually be recognised.

The foregoing may seem unduly enthusiastic. My excuse is that it is true. It also conveys a warning to which the highest of us must give heed. If a mere youth can take a bunch of greenhorns and turn them into a really first class modern dance band, what ought not the standard of professional combina-tions to be?

Elizalde's works force the idea that it is time that arrangers are awakened from the fantasy of self-satisfaction and they put out scores which are something more than the stereotyped and boringly orthodox ideas, which they excuse on the grounds that they are commercial, but with which we are all becoming thoroughly fed-up.

In the October 1927 issue Jackson reviewed Elizalde's HMV recordings, 'Clarinet Marmalade'/'Stomp Your Feet':

> If I didn't know otherwise my first thought would be that this is not an amateur band. I would wink my eye and wonder how many pros were wangled in at the last minute. But I know otherwise. Not only have I met every member of the band, but heard them play at Cambridge and can assure you the record is a faithful reproduction of their actual performance. Manuel Elizalde is the first sax; G. C. Monkhouse plays banjo; C. J. R. I. D'Arcy Hildyard, first trumpet; and R. A. F. Williams, sousaphone. I mention them as they are the outstanding instrumentalists on the record. Maurice Allom, the famous cricket Blue, is also in the combination as tenor sax.
>
> Of course, much of the excellence is due to Fred's arrangements of the scores – he is a genius at orchestration but they would be nullified if not well interpreted.

On the evidence of these recordings the suspicion remains that Elizalde's band obtained entry into a major company's studio because of their novelty in being university-based, rather than their musicality or jazz ability. Any semi-professional dance band entering the *Melody Maker* contests must have been at least equal and probably superior to the

Records were reviewed under this heading in the *Melody Maker*.

Quinquagintians in style and execution, and it is certain that Allom, a fast bowler, was considerably more proficient as a cricketer, achieving the hat-trick against New Zealand at Auckland on his Test debut in 1930, than as a tenor saxophonist.

In 1928 Elizalde made further recordings with musicians from other dance bands until he took a band into the Savoy Hotel with a nucleus of American musicians whose playing was now relatively familiar to the jazz record collector: Chelsea Quealey (trumpet), Bobby Davis, Max Farley, Arthur Rollini, Fud Livingston (saxophones) and the most notable of all – a multi-instrumentalist most famous for his prowess on the bass saxophone – Adrian Rollini.

Rollini, one of the most puzzling figures in jazz, was a child prodigy, performing Chopin on the piano in public at the age of twelve, and of the hundreds of records he made with a variety of bands only relatively few display his considerable talents to the full. The most impressive are the records he made with Bix Beiderbecke and his Gang, recorded a few months before he came to Britain.*

Most of the Americans had recorded with the California Ramblers on hundreds of largely mediocre recordings redeemed only by Rollini's dexterous manipulation of his bulky bass saxophone and Quealey's trumpet. Their variable talents were also largely wasted in the Savoy band, at least on the evidence of their recordings.

The largely 'commercial' nature of Elizalde's Anglo-American band was consistent with its primary role in playing dance music at the insistence of the Savoy management. The management naturally feared that their patrons' digestions would be impaired by hot jazz but, apparently, Elizalde wasn't over-concerned with the dancing requirements of the well-heeled patrons. He often used arrangements that suddenly changed tempo, halting the bewildered socialite clientele in their steps and leaving them standing awkwardly on the floor waiting for the band to resume the original tempo.

Not surprisingly the jazz tinge in Elizalde's performances led him into dispute with the management and the engagement terminated in 1929. He was involved in various (mostly disastrous) activities, including an

---

* Curiously, during the 'revival' of the forties and fifties which brought many musicians from retirement or obscurity on hundreds of recordings, Rollini did not figure on these at all.

unsuccessful tour of the provinces, being actually shouted off the stage at Edinburgh. He was in a revue which lasted a single night, and was restored later to continue only for a further week. A moral can perhaps be drawn from one feature of his last big concert played in Britain, at the Shepherds Bush Empire and sponsored by the *Melody Maker*. His concert suite 'Bataclaan' was much less enthusiastically received than the performance of his 'hot' contingent, which included a seventeen-year-old British trumpeter, Norman Payne, who was to solo on many British jazz recordings in the thirties.

Fred Elizalde and his Anglo-American band resident at the Savoy Hotel. *Left to right*: Dick Maxwell, vocals; Len Fillis, guitar; Elizalde, piano; Adrian Rollini, bass sax; Ronnie Gubertini, drums; Rex Owen, tenor sax; Norman Payne and Chelsea Quealey, trumpets; Harry Hayes, alto sax; Bobby Davis, clarinet and alto sax.

One of Elizalde's recordings, 'Nobody's Sweetheart', made in April 1929 for the Parlophone label with a contingent from the larger band, strongly demonstrates the superiority of small-group improvising to those pretentious 'suites' like 'Heart of a Nigger' or 'Bataclaan'. A considerable momentum is developed by the band, this reduced by the leader's jangled piano solo and dramatically restored by a magnificent solo by Rollini, one of his greatest ever. The ensemble joyously rides out the final chorus.

Elizalde's bold attempt to present jazz in the unlikely and unsympathetic milieu of a smart hotel was doomed to failure, and his 'concert' works are totally forgotten. Despite Jackson's panegyric he was limited in his talents as composer, arranger and pianist. He returned to Spain, studied under Manuel De Falla and became a conductor, using the more dignified first name of Frederico. He was an officer in Franco's army during the Spanish Civil War – a strange role for the former leader of a jazz band.

Fred Elizalde (left)
and
Adrian Rollini

The Firman and Elizalde endeavours, with the latter receiving considerable publicity in the *Melody Maker* and appearing 'live', owed much to the resident Americans, as did another series of recordings issued on the Decca label. In 1929, Decca's Light Musical Director, Philip Lewis, recorded 130 sides under his name and others using the pseudonym 'Rhythm Maniacs'. Some were heavily jazz-oriented, with Ahola and Polo in the personnel. These sessions were the chrysalis of another series, organized by a young Anglo-Irishman Patrick 'Spike' Hughes, bass player, composer and arranger, and the son of Herbert Hughes, music critic of the *Daily Telegraph* and *Saturday Review* and collector of Irish folk songs.

As a boy Spike Hughes travelled widely in Europe listening mostly to classical music in the great capitals, but he heard his first jazz in the Weinburg Bar, Weibburggasse, Vienna, played by a black band led by trumpeter Arthur Briggs.

Later, at Cambridge University, he attended hot record circles and was very impressed by Red Nichols' 'Washboard Blues'. On leaving university he became a professional musician and at the age of twenty-two, in February 1930, recorded the first of his hundred sides for Decca made over a period of two years. He called his band the Decca-Dents, a jocular title consistent with the prevalent conception of decadent jazz, but after twelve titles the management elected for the more formal title of 'Spike Hughes and his Dance Band' on their labels and adverts. The advertisements bore the quatrain:

> There was a young man named Spike Hughes
> Who holds the most original views;
> You must hear him on Decca,
> In Hot Choruses, fox-trots and blues.

As with Firman, Elizalde and Lewis, Hughes' early records include a sprinkling of American musicians – Ahola and Polo yet again – but from June 1930 to November 1932 all the musicians were home-born. These sessions were the first series of British recordings of an almost wholly jazz nature. The collective personnel was: Danny Polo, Max Farley, Bobby Davis, Rex Owen, Harry Hines, Billy Amstell, Harry Hayes, Dave Shand, Philip Buchel and Buddy Featherstonhaugh (saxophones), Max Goldberg, Jack Jackson, Jimmy Macaffer, Norman Payne, Sylvester Ahola, Bruts Gonella (trumpets), Lew Davis, Don Macaffer (trombones), Eddie Carroll, Gerry Moore, Claude Ivy (piano), Len Fillis, Alan Ferguson (guitar) and Bill Harty (drums).

The Decca-Dents' repertoire, a mixture of jazz standards, popular tunes and Hughes' own compositions, suffered from poor recording, but as

Spike Hughes by Spinky Alston

Max Goldberg

evidence of the dance-band musician coming to grips with the jazz idiom over two years they have extra-musical interest. The brass, and Lew Davis particularly, display more solo ability (and section strength) than the saxophones, although Amstell and Featherstonhaugh were clearly developing into assured players. The rhythm section was patently unrhythmic.

That such a young man as Hughes should land a prime recording contract with a major record company had some 'members of the profession' and their spokesmen sniffing with disapproval, especially those who regarded jazz with distaste, and more especially those who believed that the sweet arrangements they played were superior to hot improvisation.

In the spring of 1930 two American bands, Hal Kemp's and Ted Lewis', were playing in London. With Kemp were trumpeters Bunny Berigan and Mickey Bloom and Lewis' band included alto saxophonist/clarinettist Jimmy Dorsey and trumpeter Muggsy Spanier. Hughes invited Berigan, Bloom and Dorsey to record with the Decca-Dents. The conditions of their work permits prevented Berigan and Bloom from accepting, but Dorsey agreed and on 23 May brought Spanier to the Chenil Galleries, King's Road, Chelsea, where the Decca-Dents recorded (Hughes not having thought to invite him). In *Swing Music*, April 1935, Spike Hughes wrote:

> In the summer of 1930 there was a stir in West End jazz circles when Jimmy Dorsey, American clarinet and saxophone player and worshipped the length and breadth of England, came to London with Ted Lewis' band. I prevailed upon Jimmy, almost before he had got off the boat, to come to Chelsea and record. He came down one hot afternoon bringing with him the second trumpet player from Lewis' band, called 'Muggsie' [*sic*] – nobody ever discovered his other name.
>
> It was an exciting session, but the records we made were never issued, which was probably the saddest thing that ever happened to me in the two

years I recorded at Chelsea. Things went wrong from the first. Muggsie was not used to playing lead trumpet and we could not make satisfactory records of the numbers I had arranged. We improvised on well-known themes, but these were rejected on technical grounds.

Hughes did not elaborate on Spanier's alleged inability to play a satisfactory 'lead' and there are many Ted Lewis records where his exceptional capacity in this role is clearly exhibited. Only four weeks previously (24 April) Spanier recorded 'Sobbin' Blues' with Lewis (Jimmy Dorsey also on the session) and one of the record's strong features is his lead trumpet.

Years later, in the *Melody Maker*, Hughes referred to this abortive session and revealed that the tunes recorded were 'I Like to Do Things for You', 'Dinah', 'Avalon' and 'Kalua' but did not refer to Spanier's failure as a lead trumpeter.

On 15 July Dorsey recorded four titles with the Hughes rhythm section that were released and are now available in compendium albums.

* * *

In 1933 Hughes visited America, using John Hammond's flat as a base for his exploration of the New York scene.

Hammond and Hughes were indeed kindred spirits: of about the same age group, both precociously successful, both from comfortable backgrounds, both knowledgeable about 'classical' as well as jazz music, both enjoying sufficient affluence and the confidence of their class to indulge their activities and proselytize (to good effect), with a certain arrogance and presumption.

Spike Hughes, in his *Second Movement*, wrote:

> It was John's innate and sincere sense of justice that first endeared him to me. His championship of the negro cause was not the sentimental, patronizing doting on all things negro which characterized the negromania of some sections of British society during the late twenties. Indeed he heartily detested some of the coloured people because they let their race down in his estimation. He formed genuine friendships with negro artists, writers and musicians and is respected in Harlem as few white people ever were. He was never what is known colloquially as a 'jig-chaser'.

Through Hammond he met bandleader and multi-instrumentalist Benny Carter in March that year. Carter had already recorded one of

Hughes' compositions, 'Six Bells Stampede', in honour of the Six Bells pub (a few yards from the Chenil Galleries) where the Decca-Dents took refreshment before and after sessions – and the title was self-evidently descriptive!

Carter assembled the band that made sixteen sides under the name of Spike Hughes and his Negro Orchestra,* mostly of Hughes' compositions and arrangements and one of which, 'Donegal Cradle Song', is a classic with Coleman Hawkins at his most rhapsodically sublime.

In *Swing Music*, 1935, Hughes wrote: 'Without wishing to appear ungrateful for the British musicians who worked so hard for me at the Chenil Galleries, the New York band was technically of a higher standard than anything I had known before.' He also wrote of his problems at the New York sessions (experiencing what he called 'coloured people's time'), with musicians arriving late, and some not at all. He wrote of trombonist George Washington as the band's 'tame comic', round-headed and irrepressible, arriving at a rehearsal carrying 'his own very small, very brown baby under his arm and his trombone over his shoulder'. 'Trombonist Dicky Wells was a complete contrast. A quiet, sad individual whose playing had the same sad quality, but I rather thought this was helped by regular swigs from a bottle of gin,' a fondness for which was noticeable during Wells' tour of this country in 1967. Hughes found trumpeter Henry 'Red' Allen 'very charming', a sentiment warmly endorsed by aficionados when Allen made several visits to this country in the sixties.

In a later report, Hughes hadn't familiarized himself with the names of the personnel, and some he got only vaguely right:

> The trumpet soloist on 'Air in D Flat' was known to me as Scotty [Red Allen]. The lead trumpet, who was always wearing a cloth cap, I knew only as 'Davis' [Leonard Davis]. At the first session there was a mysterious gentleman called Snad, or Chad [Shad Collins]. He too played in a cloth cap. The soloist on 'Pastoral' and 'Bugle Call Rag' I remember as Bill Dillard, but only found that out when the *Melody Maker* published his solo on the latter and I had to cable to America for his name.

In January 1934 an unnamed reviewer in *Rhythm* sourly remarked about 'Donegal Cradle Song':

> Spike Highes and his orchestra again appear in the Decca list . . . It is a pity that he had to go all the way to America to record this dreadful row with

---

* Now listed as Spike Hughes and his All-American Orchestra.

a negro orchestra . . .   I candidly admit that with twenty years' practical experience I don't know what on earth 'Firebird' [one of the titles] means as a title or musical composition. There's nothing Irish about 'Donegal Cradle Song'. It might as well be called 'Guinness Blues'.

The critic revealed that he – probably Julian Vedey – was a facetious Philistine but it was typical of the convoluted attitude of the time that such a review should appear.

In the *Swing Music* article, Hughes summarized his jazz career:

In 1933 my ambitions in jazz came to a logical end. I am proud that some of the music I helped to create is still played in Europe and America, although my pride is mingled with a little sadness knowing that Benny Carter and his players are still making music somewhere in Harlem, that gay friendly world where time and the Depression mean nothing. I shall always remember that in four albums I have a few ten inch circular pieces of shellac with gold-lettered blue labels that will for my life-time remind me of the happiness and the experience of those three years in jazz. Sometimes the memories are tinged with melancholy. The parting is indeed sweet sorrow.

Hughes had ceased playing or leading bands, but continued to write music and contribute to the *Melody Maker*, *Rhythm* and *Daily Herald*. In the *Melody Maker*, under the pseudonym of 'Mike', he reviewed his own 'negro' records. The 'Mike'/Spike Hughes pretence was maintained for years, 'Mike' even referring to correspondence with Hughes.

As he became less and less interested in jazz his articles became increasingly repetitive and discursive. On a post-war BBC 'Brains Trust' programme he couldn't answer questions about Jelly Roll Morton. 'It's after my time,' he said. Chronologically, Morton was well before his time, but the Morton reissues and the 1941 recordings available in this country were totally unknown to him, but then Hughes was never historically or discographically minded. His achievements were on a truly creative level, as a genuine trailblazer in the thirties. His list of achievements was remarkable for one so young.

It was a racially and socially mixed quartet that made such positive efforts to present jazz, live and recorded, to the British public in the late twenties and early thirties: a British-Jewish dance-band leader in the London-born Bert Firman, a wealthy Cambridge University undergraduate from Manila in Elizalde, an orchestral violinist from Wales in Philip

Lewis, and an Anglo-Irish, Chelsea-born Cambridge undergraduate in Spike Hughes. The then emerging British jazzmen, stuck in the dance halls and hotels to earn their living, had every reason to be grateful for the opportunities these odd bedfellows gave them to develop the craft they'd heard on records from America. Their efforts hardly stand comparison with the American records that first inspired them, but history should give a kindly nod to these pioneers who played their part in spreading the gospel of jazz.

Decca advertisement, *Melody Maker*, February 1932

6

Leading up to Louis

The visits of big stage bands from the USA, playing highly organized arrangements, were interspersed with those of smaller bands that had some claim to the title of 'jazz band', even if the improvisational nature of the music was subservient to 'entertainment' considerations. They paved the way for a truly major artist to make a shattering impact in 1932.

The successors to the Original Dixieland Jazz Band at the Hammersmith Palais were a group of white students from Carolina University calling themselves the Southern Rag-A-Jazz Band. In 1921, they recorded seven sides on the Edison Bell Winner label, including 'Tiger Rag', the first recording of the tune in Britain after the ODJB version.

Another American band, the Original Capitol Orchestra, also playing earthier music, appeared at the Grafton Galleries in Regent Street in 1923 following a spell on the Mississippi riverboats. They recorded twenty-five titles for the Zonophone label. They had much of the Original Dixieland Band's character, and their clarinettist, Tracy Momma, played in the style of Larry Shields.

Another group, appearing in Britain in late 1924 and early 1925, was the Mound City Blue Blowers. The Blue Blowers were primarily a novelty band with the instrumentation of comb and paper (played by leader Red McKenzie), kazoo (Dick Slevin), banjo and guitar (Jack Bland and Eddie Lang respectively). The one accredited jazzman was Lang, who played on literally hundreds of records and was to enjoy international fame in jazz circles before he died in 1933.

In the US magazine *Jazz Record* Jack Bland recalled their trip to England:

> We had to get birth certificates to get to England and Langie [real name Salvatore Massaro] didn't know whether he was born in Philadelphia, Atlantic City or Italy. First thing that happened when we got off the boat Lang wanted to go back immediately. The English fog hit him, his hands turned blue and he got scared.
>
> Before we opened at the Piccadilly an agent put us on at Haggerty's Empire [probably Hackney Empire] at Limehouse. We played the first number – 'Tiger Rag' – real fast. Nobody understood or clapped or anything and the orchestra leader in the pit looked at McKenzie, McKenzie spat at the leader and said: 'Which way do we go out boys?' – and out we went!
>
> We finally got through the first show, didn't play the second and wanted to cancel the whole thing, but the agent said: 'All you have to do is play "Red Hot Mama" and they'll learn it and sing it with you and everything will be OK.' So we played 'Red Hot Mama' for the rest of the week.
>
> Langie was a swell guy – a nice disposition – you couldn't make him mad. He was about five feet eight inches, had curly dark hair and was one of the best card players in the country. He stayed with us for four years. I'd say he was about twenty-six when he joined us. He used to unpack and play on a street corner, or a bathroom, or anywhere if a friend wanted to hear us. He had the best ear of any musician I know.
>
> In London Langie took his guitar to the London Sporting Club and played and they made him and me charter members. This really meant something because the Sporting Club was composed of sportsmen who could bet up to a million without cutting up the money.
>
> He died from an operation on his tonsils. He bled to death. He had one of the biggest funerals ever held in Philadelphia. Joe Venuti was mad because Bing Crosby got to ride in the first car and he had to go in the second. Of all the records made I like best the ones he made with Bessie Smith.

* * *

Ted Lewis, christened Theodore Leopold Friedman, born 6 June 1892, Circleville, Ohio, was a showman in the American burlesque theatre tradition in which so many Jewish performers like Eddie Cantor, Al Jolson, Sophie Tucker and George Burns excelled. Lewis postured in the extrovert burlesque manner and sang in a pseudo-dramatic recitative fashion; his clarinet playing was sheer hokum. His stage apparel consisted of a dress suit, patent leather shoes, white shirt and black bow tie, with a carnation in his lapel and a row of peaked handkerchiefs in his breast pocket. He wore a battered top hat and flourished a silver-topped walking cane. He was dubbed the 'High-Hatted Tragedian of Jazz', and spent fifty continuous years as a bandleader, death finally retiring him from the business in 1964 at the age of seventy-two.

He selected tunes that had a 'message for the folks'. On one of his records, 'When the Curtain Comes Down', he emotively milks the quasi-philosophical lyrics, acknowledging that death comes to rich and poor alike. The other side of his dramatic persona was seen in his singing of snappy 'cheer-up' songs written as antidotes to the gloom of the Depression. 'Look for a Silver Lining', 'There's a Choo-Choo Headin' for Better Times', 'Sunny Side of the Street' and 'The World is Waiting for the Sunrise' are a few examples he recorded. His catchphrase was the rhetorical question, 'Is Everybody Happy?' Any listeners left unmoved would be further assured that he was their 'Medicine Man for the Blues', one of his best-selling records.

From 1921 to 1927 the band played quasi-dixieland, its corny style set by the atrocious clarinet playing of the leader. When it came to Britain in 1925 to play the Kit Kat Restaurant in London's Haymarket, a genuine jazzman, trombonist George Brunies, had been added and on a repeat visit in 1930 to the Kit Kat the jazz strength had been increased by the addition of Muggsy Spanier and Jimmy Dorsey, the presence of these accredited jazzmen considerably raising the standard of performance. But inevitably, their talents on the 1930 trip were subjugated to the vocalizing and posturings of the ebullient Ted.

The June 1933 issue of *Rhythm* reported: 'On Sunday May 4th – a day more like mid-summer than early spring – Ted Lewis and his Band opened at the delightful riverside Hotel de Paris at Bray-on-Thames. Booked at short notice there was little advertising but the place was packed.' In such an essentially English setting, in a milieu redolent of middle-class prosperity, the High-Hatted Tragedian of Jazz made an unexpected and incongruous appearance on this balmy evening with three players who were later to achieve recognition from jazz enthusiasts throughout the world, particularly Muggsy Spanier with his 1939 Ragtime Band recordings with George Brunies on trombone.

Rhythm continued:

> It's Ted's showmanship that counts. With his old top hat set either side at a rakish angle on his mop of black hair or being waved about to point any one

of his characteristic gestures he magnetized the audience from the moment he appeared before them. The band is the curate's egg. 'Corn-fed' wa-wa's mingle unnecessarily with the perfection of style, musicianship and originality which are the features of every note played by Jimmy Dorsey and the excellent 'hot' man 'Muggsy', neat and alluring work from Dave Klein and amazing rhythm and execution from Harry Barth on string bass and tuba.

George Brunies also gave the impression that he needs only the slightest encouragement to produce the right stuff, but Ted apparently believes that the work of the trombone begins and ends with 'wa-wa', so friend George doesn't get much to do.

The *Rhythm* writer wasn't to know that Brunies had been a member of the New Orleans Rhythm Kings; nor did anyone else as their records had not been issued in Britain, nor had anything been written about them.

The employment by Lewis of another star clarinettist (Jimmy Dorsey) was an act untypical of a clarinet-playing bandleader. He also hired and made records with Benny Goodman, Tony Parenti, Frank Teschemacher and Don Murray, all acknowledged jazz clarinettists. The best of these recordings, with Spanier and Brunies, appeared on the Columbia 'Hot Jazz' series, some of the most notable being recorded just prior to his 1930 visit, and the presence of the jazz players bringing out the best in their non-jazz colleagues.

Lewis, theatrical ham and dreadful clarinettist though he was, probably made more genuine jazz records (with the exception of Ben Pollack) than any of the big-time contemporaries, and he will be remembered for a trenchant remark he made on hearing Stravinsky's 'Ragtime'. 'That guy don't know nuttin' about it,' he asserted. Which was true, but then neither did Lewis. Evaluation of true ragtime was to become a seventies phenomenon when the compositions of Scott Joplin and others were to enjoy academic scrutiny and unprecedented public acclaim.

The violinist Eddie South, a black musician described as 'The Dark Angel of the Violin', led a four-piece band at the Café Anglais in June 1930. The *Melody Maker* reported:

> Eddie South plays a very stylish fiddle, sometimes shooting out phrases of an absolute white-hot variety and scarcely ever failing to maintain a standard both interesting and artistic, even if it is occasionally 'corn-fed'. Several of his choruses follow the real Venuti tradition and his executive ability is at times quite astonishing. Legitimately trained, he studied at Chicago Musical College and with Professor Deason in Budapest.

No bands of any significance visited Britain in 1931, but there were continuing and ominous rumblings from 'members of the profession' about the entry of foreign musicians, this issue frequently being debated in the columns of the *Melody Maker*. These objections led to an almost total twenty-year ban, but before this was enforced jazz enthusiasts revelled in two stupendous happenings – the separate visits of Louis Armstrong and Duke Ellington and his Famous Orchestra.

Eddie South (*centre*) with his band

In July 1932 the *Melody Maker* announced that Armstrong's visit was certain, but professed concern about his supporting band and the limited time for rehearsal before opening at the Palladium on 18 July.

Armstrong's reputation had been steadily building since his records were first released and here, for the first time since Bechet's almost unnoticed appearance, was a colossus of jazz shortly to be seen actually performing on an English stage. It is nothing short of extraordinary that a man of such stature should have arrived without a band, or a musical director, not even a pianist, just a handful of arrangements, himself, his wife, and manager Johnny Collins, a Chicago hoodlum. The *Melody Maker*'s apprehensions about the sort of band that would accompany him proved to be justified.

In the *Melody Maker*'s August issue (the publication was then still a monthly), Dan S. Ingman, former theatre pit drummer and then technical editor of the paper, wrote a long, welcoming article. It commenced: 'He's here! and by the time this report appears he will have been here for two weeks.' Recounting his meeting with Louis and his party at Waterloo Station, Ingman expressed his surprise at finding a youthful, short black man. (He had imagined – from the sound of Armstrong's voice and the power of his trumpet playing – someone older and bigger.) He recalled the hassles over permits and hotel accommodation, due to the colour of Louis' and his wife's skin, and went on to report the opening night, Monday 18 July, at the Palladium where Armstrong was one of a bill of average variety acts:

Ballad singer Robert Chisholm introduced Louis who played 'Them There Eyes', 'When You're Smiling', 'Chinatown', 'You Rascal, You' and 'Tiger Rag'. Of the latter Louis said, 'This tiger moves very fast, very very fast so I expect I'll have to play five choruses to catch up with him.'

He played eight, all different!

His technique, tone and mastery of his instrument (which he called 'Satchmo', a contraction, I believe, of 'Satchel Mouth') is uncanny. Top Fs bubble all over the place and never does he miss one. He is enormously fond of the lip-trill which he accomplished by shaking the instrument wildly with the right hand. He works with a microphone and loud speakers – except for his trumpet playing, which varies from a veritable whisper to roof-raising strength, mostly the latter.

The amazing thing is his personality. He positively sparkles with showmanship and good humour. When he is singing he carries a handkerchief and mops his face – the perspiration drops off him. He puts enough energy into half an hour's performance to last the average man several years. He is, in short, a unique phenomenon, an electric personality – easily the greatest America has sent us.

The band – well, to tell the truth, beyond that it is painfully unrehearsed and had very little quality – I didn't notice it. He should have had – could have had – much better support.

Brought over at two days' notice, this band comprised Paris-based club and restaurant musicians of less than average technical prowess, with only clarinettist Pete Du Conge, a New Orleanian, displaying any real jazz ability. It wasn't the most auspicious way for Louis Armstrong, jazz genius, to make his debut in a strange country, and it was the first time he had ever been abroad.

In the same issue, the *Melody Maker*'s new American correspondent, the forthright John Hammond, wrote expressing the hope that there'd 'be no attempt at commercialization in the presentation of Louis and cheapen someone who has more than a touch of genius. Even so, I have a lurking suspicion that Armstrong will be more appreciated by the English than our own tripe-fed fans.' In the same issue 'Mike' (Spike Hughes) wrote: 'The secret of Armstrong's greatness lies in himself. With the barest of backgrounds and a minimum, or indeed, a

Louis Armstrong around the time of his visit to Britain, 1932–33

complete absence of arrangements with, in many cases, the lousiest of bands playing numbers by immigrant Caucasian Broadwayites he can create a welter of sound that, whatever one's personal tendencies, cannot be ignored as a tremendous force in modern dance music.'

The *Melody Maker*'s enthusiasm for the visit and concern for the presentation contrasted with the observations of columnist Hannen Swaffer in the *Daily Herald*. In the course of a long article he wrote:

> If you want to test your intelligence and the courage of your own mind, go and see Louis Armstrong, the negro trumpeter brought over here at great expense from the Cotton Club, Los Angeles, who is now at the Palladium arousing furious arguments as to whether he is or not. [*sic*!]
>
> Excited young men of the pseudo-intellectual kind are bleating and blahing in ecstasy. Men about ten years older come to me and demand that I shall tell the truth.

When he did his show hundreds cheered him as if it were Kreisler, but others went to the bar. One woman I know put her hands over her ears. A newspaper friend of mine, demanding that I solve his problem, said: 'Tell me if I am right or wrong. I think he's dreadful. When he blows his neck swells out as though he's swallowed a melon. I never heard such a noise in my life! Why do they like it?'

'That man, why he did everything with the trumpet but play it!' said a London editor intimately acquainted with the music hall for the past thirty years.

One critic in the front row left after five minutes saying: 'Do you mind if I go to the back of the house?', but a theatre manager next to him sat grimly determined to see it through. 'I wanted to know what he was going to do next,' he said. 'I have never seen such a thing. I thought he might even play the trumpet before he was through. Besides, I couldn't understand one word he said. It sounded to me like . . . No I cannot say it, I cannot spell it.'

Yet they say he is a genius – perfect technique. None of these Transatlantic turns please everybody.

On 25 July Swaffer returned to the fray in the same paper:

Louis Armstrong, the negro trumpeter, is the most amazing performer the stage has seen for months. When I saw his turn on Saturday night, five out of six people seated in a row in front of me walked out while he was on; so did two people to my right – and several others at the back. Yet pale aesthetes were lily-like when he appeared and the young Jewish element at the back were enthusiastic.

There have been more arguments over Armstrong than any turn at the Palladium since Gibbon built it. People have called it 'an insult'; others have gone every night.

Armstrong is the ugliest man I have ever seen on the music hall stage. He looks and behaves like an untrained gorilla. He might have come straight from some African jungle and then, after being taken to the slop tailors for a ready made dress suit, been put straight on the stage and told to 'sing'.

His singing is dreadful, babyish, uncouth. Yet, while he makes animal noises into the microphone which sends the sound to the loud-speaker at the side, he makes love to the instrument as though it were a dusky belle.

Now and again he charges his all-black orchestra like a drunken bull, yet he caresses his trumpet like a lover – and then making it do things I've never heard a trumpet do before, emits from it a rapid succession of notes which have nothing to do with the melody.

I was reminded of the first London performance of *Elektra* for which Strauss invented new instruments to imitate the bleating of lambs.

Armstrong's head, while he plays, is as unique as his music. Gradually it is covered by a thousand beads of perspiration. Occasionally they fall off him in a shower. He tries in vain to keep dry with a handkerchief. He is a living shower bath. And his neck swells out like a gorged python.

In a later issue of the *Daily Herald* he wrote:

Armstrong is by no means angry with my reference to his looks. After all he has seen himself in the glass several times and got used to it. Nor was it the 'African jungle' he minded, but the part about 'slop tailors'. He feels this is an unkind reflection on his tailoring as he says he owns one hundred and thirty-nine suits, travels with forty-eight trunks and has not worn the same suit twice on the Palladium stage. The reason for this is that he perspires so during his rainbath act, that his clothes are always wringing wet.

Well, Louis Armstrong's band in America is paid £1,400 a week at par. Prince George, when he went to hear him the other day, thought he was 'marvellous'. So do thousands of young people who have been back several times. In spite of this you can hear from the back every now and again the sounds of ridicule. In case I am misunderstood I consider Louis Armstrong a brilliant trumpeter and repeat that I regard his syncopated methods as revolutionary, as were the operatic orchestrations of Richard Strauss as quarter of a century ago. A thing does not frighten me because it is new.

The last sentiments indicate a typical Swaffer volte face.

The *Melody Maker* boasted:

When Louis Armstrong made his electric appearance at the Palladium he vindicated everything the *Melody Maker* has said about the aggrandisement of popular music.

Melody Maker readers packed the Palladium for every one of his twenty-eight appearances. About this there can be no argument. Before the *Melody Maker* came into existence seven years ago the name of Louis had never appeared in print in this country. Not a record had been issued,* not a word had ever been heard on the subject of the coloured trumpet wizard, even in

---

* As stated previously, solos by Armstrong could be heard on records by Fletcher Henderson's band issued in this country since 1925 and the writer was forgetting, or wasn't even aware, that Edgar Jackson had derided early Armstrong releases as 'crude and exaggerated sentimentality'. After Jackson's departure they didn't even review Louis' great 'West End Blues', relying instead on the Parlophone blurb, accurate though it was. Note, again, the reference to 'popular music'. There was still a reluctance to embrace the word jazz but, withal, their claim to have popularized Louis was largely true.

America he was considered one of a few eccentrics considered musically crazy and of no consequence.

The *Melody Maker* discovered some of his records issued here and immediately predicted that here was an artiste far in advance of his time who would surely leave his mark on modern music as it struggled out of the welter of 'jazz' rubbish which was all the go then.

The writer then complained about the blank weeks in his itinerary, berated hall managers for not seizing opportunities to present the great man, and outlined the problem of providing Louis with a suitable accompanying band when the scratch group of black musicians returned to Paris after the Palladium engagement.

Rudolph Dunbar, black clarinettist and teacher, classically trained and then playing formal dance music, attempted to recruit black musicians resident in this country, but without success. Jack Hylton's band was otherwise engaged. Spike Hughes was approached to form a band but was committed to writing music for a C. B. Cochran show in the West End. Eventually a British band was assembled by pianist Billy Mason. Max Jones and John Chilton, in their illuminating book *Louis*, rightly point out that these instrumentalists deserve a special place in the chronicles as Armstrong's first-ever white band.

The rest of the line-up was Freddy Mann and Bruts Gonella (trumpets), Harry Hayes and Sid Owen (alto saxophones), Buddy Featherstonhaugh (tenor saxophone), Bill White (bass), Len Bermon (drums) and Alan Ferguson (guitar). Armstrong made no records in this country with this or any other band, and this 'formidable outfit' was replaced during the tour by what the *Melody Maker* called 'a much cheaper collection', constantly subjected to cuts as the tour progressed.

Harry Hayes recalls:

> It was a breathtaking experience. What a *superb* player! I felt privileged to be one of his only British band. We all found him very friendly and charming, although we had little contact with him outside of the bandstand. Once the show was over he was whisked away by his manager, a very *offensive* fellow. I remember some of us had to go to his hotel in Tottenham Court Road to get our money. Yes, Louis brought arrangements with him. We were good readers and had no trouble with them at rehearsals, but I admit we were so engrossed with his playing our ears were more for him than our eyes were for the parts! I seem to remember some mix-ups in the travelling arrangements

that broke up the band. It was a great compliment to me that over twenty years later I walked into his dressing-room at Earls Court and he immediately recognized me, calling me by my Christian name. Louis was that sort of person – and he hadn't seen or heard from me in all that time since. One of my deep regrets is that we never recorded with him.

One of Hayes' recollections was of *Melody Maker* editor P. M. Brooks, upset that Hayes and Lew Davis had left the band, declaring that neither of them would be mentioned in the *Melody Maker* again! Neither Brooks nor the *Melody Maker* was directly connected with the Armstrong tour but Brooks became very friendly with Armstrong – so much so that the myth that Brooks coined the term 'Satchmo' gained currency. As Armstrong had used the original term 'Satchelmouth' in his 1930 recording of 'You're Driving Me Crazy' with Les Hite's band this was not the case, even though Louis himself often stated that it was.

Where responsibility lay for the bad organization of this tour is now a purely academic point but, at the very least, it was an off-hand way to treat a genius. It is not as though his superb artistry wasn't known, or that responsible parties were ignorant of the imperative need for at least efficient musicianship and fitting arrangements for 'the greatest that America has sent us'.

Louis, however, took to Britain. He had been fêted as never before; there was less overt racial intolerance; he wasn't bothered by gangsters as at home, although manager Collins lived up to his past when he demanded 'the dough' at the beginning of a dance at a Midland palais before allowing Louis to play. The money was put before him in notes and silver taken from the box office. Dan Ingman, present at the scene, recalls thinking at the time: 'He wouldn't know how to count it.'

During the early Palladium shows several members of the lay public left in disgust during the performance. Max Jones and John Chilton quote Nat Gonella and his brother Bruts, both fervent Armstrong disciples, claiming that as a gesture of solidarity with their idol, they tripped up the disgruntled as they strode angrily up the aisle to the exit.

The exodus was understandable. Jazz was the underground music of the era. Armstrong's 'flaring brilliance' (Jones' and Chilton's phrase) must have come as an acute shock to ears conditioned to polite dance music. Some were so incredulous that they suspected a trick trumpet, and asked to examine it. When a sceptic in an American audience threw the accusation at Armstrong that he employed such an instrument Louis smashed his horn against the nearest solid object, challenging anyone in the house to bring him another, from anywhere. He would show them if he relied on freak instruments!

According to Jones and Chilton:

> Louis set himself such high personal standards that it's possible to argue that he was in peak form for a span of ten to fifteen years, but in 1932 all the physical facets of his technique were in miraculous working order. He was the possessor of lung power and throat, jaw and lip formation which seemed ideally suited to the production of a trumpet tone. With these natural attributes went a control of the instrument giving him ease of performance in every department of the art. His mastery was matched by superior stamina and an artistic adaptability which was to be thoroughly tested on the British tour. As a jazz player he had it all; all, that is, except widespread recognition as a creative musician. This was something he was to pick up in Europe and not overnight.

He had done good business at the Palladium, and this had been a highly speculative booking. Many promoters had been wary of someone who, in the words of the critic 'Mike', must be enjoyed as a phenomenon, as 'something that will not be believed in years to come when you tell your grandchildren of the good old days at the Palladium in 1932'.

Louis left the country having made very little money and leaving behind him mixed impressions. But the British experience probably made him realize that he was playing a major role in the evolution of jazz.

After his initial appearances at the Palladium various musicians were asked their views on Louis Armstrong. In the following selection of opinions, taken directly from the *Melody Maker*, the sentiments expressed must be related to the profession of the interviewees. They were, almost without exception, dance-band musicians, although obviously some had strong jazz leanings and in a few cases, jazz ability:

Billy Mason (pianist and leader of the accompanying group for part of the tour):

> A child of nature. I doubt even if he could explain his secrets. Too much fuss is made of his high register acrobatics. The value of the Armstrong style is its extremely musical phrasing.

Bandleader Ray Noble:

Armstrong, the supreme artist, sacrificed a good deal of his creativeness for the sake of his stage show. He exercises no restraint upon the stage, which is bound to prejudice certain uninitiated people against him.

Clarinettist Phil Cardew:

Every note is a joy, every phrase superbly original. I am happy to have had the opportunity of hearing, in the flesh, the master of rhythmic music.

Clarinettist Joe Crossman:

His actual presence gave me in a sense, a shock, and I much regret to have to admit finding something barbaric in his violent stage mannerisms.

Reginald King (society bandleader):

I think the Louis Armstrong show offends against all reasonable definitions of good taste and I regard it as an insult to any musician.

Bandleader, later impresario, Maurice Winnick:

A great and inspiring artist and genius of the first water, but out of place on a London stage or, in fact, anywhere but in Harlem.

Drummer Maurice Burman:

A truly staggering performance but definitely too strong for the ordinary public and I didn't think some of the musicians who profess such enthusiasm for his work really understood it.

Stage bandleader Percy Bush:

A disgusting and abortive exhibition, likely to nauseate all decent men.

Drummer Bill Harty:

Marvellous, but certainly not for the public.

Tango bandleader Geraldo:

The greatest freak musician undoubtedly, but what an illogical position he occupies! Out of his numerous band of admirers I am convinced that many do not understand his work fully, if at all. The number of utterly ignorant people who use the parrot cry of 'Vive Armstrong' is incredible.

Tenor saxophonist Buddy Featherstonhaugh:

It was the swinging of his trumpet that stirred me profoundly. He was my idea of the perfect first trumpet and my enthusiasm made me play better, I am sure, than I've done before or since. There must be something very essential missing from the make-up of any dance-band musician who would not be similarly affected in such circumstances.

Trumpeter, later bandleader, Nat Gonella:

> Fancy asking me! Inspiration, guiding star, what more can I say? Ask someone who knows more complimentary adjectives than I do and leave me alone!

Pianist Eddie Carroll:

> A revelation! Definitely the artist of the century to me.

A mixed reaction! Many of these dance-band musicians had received a formal training that would have blocked any emotional response to such pristine force and the suggestion that Louis shouldn't play outside of Harlem was nonsense. It was also false to believe that he worked only in that district of New York. The dissenting bandleaders, perhaps unconsciously, were afraid that if Armstrong's music became more widely accepted they and their batons would be made redundant. In musical terms most of them already were, but while the public expected to see the smiling and bowing figurehead 'conducting' they were safe in their redundancy for a few more years.

Melody Maker front page, 3 June 1933, announces Louis Armstrong's visit.

Armstrong toured Europe but returned to play the Holborn Empire on 31 July 1933. Earlier, the *Melody Maker* ran the headline, 'Satch'mo Armstrong Again – Back from the Grave to the Holborn', a reference to a false report in the *Daily Express* that Louis had died. The 8 July issue demanded 'Justice for Armstrong' and 'a real band for a real artiste':

Already feelers have been put out for the provision of a British accompaniment band to support Armstrong in the £9 a head [weekly salary] class. We say boldly and authoritatively that an adequate support for Armstrong cannot be supplied at anything like this money. What Armstrong needs behind him is rhythm. He cannot get it from scratch bands and underpaid dance musicians, and he certainly cannot get it from pit orchestras.

One suggestion worthy of consideration in the absence of a really adequate band, is that a five piece rhythm section, including two pianos, would be a solution. Another, fanciful perhaps, but having the merit of imagination, is that a joint show be staged between Armstrong and Bert Ambrose's Orchestra which, since it will have left the Mayfair Hotel by then, will be available. This, of course, raises the question of whether the Holborn could afford to pay them both. Certainly, the association of such a band with a star like Armstrong would prove a draw at any time of the year in any theatre in Great Britain.

The latter idea was more feasible than the notion of a rhythm section with two pianos. Ambrose's band was the most polished and jazz-worthy band in the country and had, in Sid Phillips, a skilled and sympathetic arranger who could have provided the scores from which Armstrong's improvisational flights could have taken off.

As for the economics, there was no necessity for other 'acts' on the bill. Ambrose had two capable singers in Sam Browne and Elsie Carlisle, and many star instrumentalists, including clarinettist Danny Polo and a portly drummer, Max Bacon, who was later to tour 'the halls' as a 'Jewish' comic.

Had this association taken place and recordings been made assuredly they would have made worthy mementos of a historic event but it is doubtful, economics apart, that Ambrose would have entertained the suggestion that he should share a bill with an artist of Armstrong's class. While the orchestra would have played an integral role his baton-waving would have been totally gratuitous, with all attention being focused on the trumpeter and not on himself.

Yet another hastily assembled band was recruited from the Continent at the last minute and just how inadequate they were is illustrated on the records – from acetates by radio engineers – he made with them in Copenhagen and Stockholm and studio recordings in Paris, although an admirable pianist, Herman Chittison, had been added for this tour.

When Armstrong played the Holborn Empire on 31 July, the *Melody Maker* did not disguise its disappointment with the music:

Melody Maker headline, 5 August 1933

AMAZING RECEPTION FOR ARMSTRONG
FRENZIED APPLAUSE FOR MEANINGLESS
PERFORMANCE
LOUIS DELIBERATELY ALL COMMERCIAL

The report went on:

> Amazing! That's about the only word which adequately describes the reception accorded to Louis Armstrong at the first house, Monday night, at the Holborn Empire.
>
> The incredible trumpet player, whose falsely reported death a few months ago sent thousands of dance musicians all over the world into mourning, was due for a thrilling reception from his loyal adherents on the occasion of his London 'resurrection'.
>
> He got it – in an extraordinary scene after the show, which concluded as hundreds of elderly people were pouring out of the house in apparent disfavour. The younger element cheered wildly, unreasoningly, unjustifiably – out of sheer loyalty. Only the ringing down of the curtain and the playing of 'The King' by the pit orchestra stifled the fervid applause. But Louis must have caused many of his more enlightened followers to sorrow for him. His act was fifty per cent showmanship, fifty per cent instrumental cleverness, but nought per cent music. He seems to have come to the conclusion that a variety artiste's only mission in life is to be sensational, to pander to baser emotions, to sacrifice all art to crude showmanship; this from the most admired and individual musician in the world!

A different opinion was expressed in the 10 August issue: 'Armstrong Admits His Error' was the headline over a photograph of a long queue outside the Holborn Empire. The writer continued:

An amazing change has taken place in the calibre of Louis Armstrong's performance. We last reviewed his performance more in sorrow than in anger. We felt it a dreadful pity to see such brilliant musicianship wasted in clowning, and not too pleasant clowning at that. There was far too much striding about the stage, too many cheap laughs got by stressing his excessive perspiration, too many glisses, too many meaningless top notes.

It was sad because the Armstrong who came to the Palladium last year was a superb trumpeter with an exquisite tone, control and technique, a supreme player of extemporisation in dance rhythm. But Louis listened to the well meant criticisms. He realised these were from his best friends and from Tuesday onwards he began to play properly. By the end of the week he was almost his old supreme self.

Some of the superb phrasing began to return. Every now and again he tossed out a few bars which were flawless perfection. Louis is a great showman with a terrific personality. He had no need to descend to low comedy to get over, not with the following he has in this country. The world's greatest trumpet player mustn't be allowed to deteriorate even if we have to club him over the head to stop it! So take warning, friend Louis!

Having told the world's greatest trumpeter to be a good boy, the *Melody Maker*, in the editorial of that issue, berated the public schools which had banned jazz from their precincts:

Prohibition is just about the most dangerous device that any institution can employ to check the conduct of a community. Therefore when certain of our British public schools issue fiats to their pupils barring hot jazz, refusing to allow it to be played in school precincts, it can lead to those dangers of insubordination exemplified in illegal whiffing of Woodbines behind the woodshed. Do the MA's of our public schools really believe that there is anything pernicious about it? Do they honestly think that Duke Ellington, a humble disciple of Delius, is a black ogre conspiring to demoralise the youth of Great Britain?

This nauseating and entirely unjustified Victorian prudery, this incredible intellectual snobbery, this ranting ignorance can only result in turning out from our schools large numbers of junior intellectual snobs and repressed ignoramuses.

In the *Daily Express*, 1 August 1933, William Hickey (Tom Driberg, later Member of Parliament for Maldon, Essex, and subsequently Lord Maldon) wrote:

Louis (Trumpeter-what-are-you-sounding-now?) Armstrong re-appeared last
night at a London music hall. The event co-incides with the Wilberforce
centenary celebrations. Armstrong's father was a slave. He himself wears a
gold chain on his wrist, a memento of the old days of slavery.

Louis Armstrong is a negro artist of a different type from Duke Ellington.
Ellington is primarily a composer and the director of the world's most
famous dance band combination. Armstrong is an individual virtuoso, and
rarely keeps one band for long. Ellington is a sophisticated, highly civilised,
light-skinned Washingtonian. Armstrong is coal black, has a close-cropped
bullet-head, and was born in New Orleans. Both have charm, humour and
modesty.

Louis wears a swelegant [sic] light green suit. Smokes many cigarettes of
his own special brand. Drinks very little. One glass of brown ale suffices. It
harmonises decoratively with his skin. Says the best trumpeter in England is
Nat Gonella. He says: 'Some folks think all 'merican bands hot, but some
'merican bands makes yo' pull yo' hair.'

This quaint reportage was typical of the period. Driberg, lifelong
socialist, churchman and mildly conversant with jazz, revealed a host of
prevailing attitudes to the black race among privileged members of a
white society. Note the implied difference between the two men (correct
in essence) and the terminology used to make the point. Louis is 'black',
his hair 'close-cropped'. Duke is lighter-skinned, and there is no mention
of his hair, which was straightened, a common practice among northern
black Americans, many of whom dissociated themselves from their
'rougher' southern counterparts. Note, too, the phonetic spelling of
Louis' pronunciation. This was probably not inaccurate, but few journalists in these days of legislated race tolerance would dare use this device
to make a point.

It's highly unlikely that Louis ever drank brown ale. There is no coun-
terpart to this drink in America, but it had pigmentation and class associations to this well-meaning denizen of the middle class. Louis' father
wasn't a slave,* but Driberg was undoubtedly right in asserting
that Armstrong smoked his 'own special brand of cigarettes'. These were
likely to have contained marijuana, later frivolously described in Britain
by irreverent jazz musicians as 'naughty type African Woodbines'.
Armstrong was later convicted of growing cannabis in his back garden.
It may have been that Driberg was aware that his special brand of

---

*It was his grandfather who was a slave.

cigarettes contained a substance that it was illegal to possess, but this seems unlikely.

Apart from the recurring problem of a supporting band Louis had managerial and matrimonial problems and trouble with a much-scarred lip. Having to bear almost the entire burden of his show had physical repercussions. At the Holborn Empire one night in August he was barely able to play and resorted to clowning and singing for the best part of his 'turn'. He made a triumphant return to that theatre on 12 September and the *Melody Maker* enthused: 'Gone was the showmanship. In its place the sincere, musical Louis revered the world over. The band is bad; balance of the reeds is poor; and the rhythm section uncontrolled, but Louis' trumpet overshadowed everything. This is trumpet playing that can never be surpassed.'

In the 4 October issue a picture page at the back of the paper has a photo of Louis in diamond check plus-fours and a flat cap, reading the *Melody Maker*. Under this comical photo was the caption: 'The trumpet king reads that all is forgiven on his return to form.'

He visited Denmark, Norway, Sweden and Holland before returning to Britain. His British trail ended at Derby. On one of his trips to London he visited Clapham Baths with Jack Hylton, on the occasion of the *Melody Maker*'s first Annual South Western Dance Band Competition, and a paper in Harrogate carried the item that 'Louis Armstrong will be remembered, of course, for his fine performance with Duke Ellington who visited Harrogate a few weeks ago.'

Armstrong in Britain, reading *Melody Maker*, October 1933

He was not, of course, remembered for any such appearance, but vividly recalled for years afterwards as a genius who transcended a succession of problems, some of his own making, that had the critics and public weeping for him, as one would weep for any beloved person in trouble. For Louis, in all his professional life, was a much-loved man. His playing and personality reflected the individual whose childhood was spent partly in a New Orleans orphanage.

He finally left Europe for America in the spring of 1935, buoyed up with the knowledge that for the first time he was accepted as a celebrity and a player of rare ability. This awareness owed much to the *Melody Maker*, to the English enthusiasts who flocked to support and cheer him, to the record companies which released his records when he was an unknown quantity, and some journalists on the national press (though not Hannen Swaffer). Little thanks are due to the BBC who, in all the time he was here, accorded him only one twenty-minute broadcast, on 28 July 1932, relayed from the Palladium on the Regional Programme.

But if the establishmentarian BBC were too haughty to notice Louis Armstrong the public were not. They had seen as well as heard a supreme man of jazz and taken him to their hearts.

7

Duke and
Lesser Mortals

The jazz trumpeter supreme was a sensation, allowing that to many he was no more than a curiosity. His playing, singing, histrionics and his physical appearance had a tremendous impact, however varied the reactions, and it was essentially a solo *tour de force*. Generally, the accompanying orchestras' contributions were minimal and remembered only in that the star triumphed over their inadequacy. But the visit of Duke Ellington's Famous Orchestra in 1933 was a different matter altogether. Here was a regular ensemble of amazing talent at which the public and pundits, even those familiar with their records, gaped, wondered, and were utterly enthralled. Indeed they were overwhelmed by the spectacle of thirteen men performing, before their very eyes, magical flights of improvisation interwoven in a rich tapestry of orchestral colours on tunes ranging from the plaintively melancholy to the lustily exultant. It was a supremely imaginative and superbly executed distillation of African-American culture. No wonder it was a revelation! An exquisite assault on the ears!

The definition of jazz in *Black's Dictionary of Music and Musicians* could well have applied to the mechanics of this orchestra's performance: 'The interest of jazz is chiefly due to bizarre effects through new groupings of instruments in which saxophones, clarinets and trumpets and trombones, often muted, are frequently played with portmanteau effects.'

The first intimation of this visit was given in the *Melody Maker* in November 1932: 'A whisper has been heard that Duke Ellington and his orchestra are to visit this country next year.' By June 1933 that whisper had become a babble of excitement, and the now-weekly *Melody Maker*, 3 June, proclaimed: 'Musicians are getting thrill after thrill. 1933 is indeed a red-letter year for fans. Louis Armstrong is to return and Duke Ellington's visit is on everybody's tongue. The peak of that particular excitement is still to come.'

On 10 June they reported: 'Ready for Ellington on Monday. Today, June 9th, an unofficial reception committee awaits the arrival of the *Olympic* to welcome Duke Ellington's party to England.'

In its editorial the *Melody Maker* took issue with an article in *Era* – written by *Era*'s dance-band critic, Stanley Nelson. Nelson had quibbled about the advisability of Duke Ellington following the Crazy Gang's annual show at the Palladium and queried why the BBC should pay more than £30 for the broadcast that had been arranged. He wrote: 'I cannot see for the life of me that the Ellington band, good as it undoubtedly is, represents such a catch for the BBC. Its appeal is undoubtedly limited. They're lucky to get a broadcast at all.' But he did acknowledge that Ellington had a thousand or so fans and a 'few hundred curious attendant acolytes on these occasions'.

The *Olympic* docked at Southampton at 12.30 pm on Friday 9 June and from it disembarked the greatest jazz orchestra the world has ever known, then at the first of its many peaks. It was a truly memorable day in the history of jazz in Britain.

The *Melody Maker*, 17 June, splashed the headline 'The Duke at the Palladium' and showed Duke waving from the top of the ship's gangway. A 'Special Correspondent' wrote, 'As 6.30 approached on Monday I must confess that excitement rose to fever heat. Although Ellington's band was not on until nearly eight o'clock I felt I shouldn't miss a bit of the whole bill at the Palladium. As a matter of fact I could have done so without serious loss for, with the exception of Max Miller, the supporting acts were very poor. One supposed that the terrific cost of the band somewhat tied the hands of the bookers.'

It is surely one of the most striking of ironies in the history of jazz in Britain that the suave and sophisticated Edward Kennedy 'Duke' Ellington should, for his British debut, 12 June 1933, have been on the same variety bill as the irrepressible and irreverent 'Cheeky Chappie' Max Miller, the cockney comedian whose 'blue' humour frequently had him in bad odour with the BBC in the thirties.

Duke Ellington and his orchestra newly arrived at Southampton, 1933

The Special Correspondent continued: 'It is unnecessary to say that the house was full of familiar faces, everybody seemed to know everybody else. The preceding acts went all too slowly. Ellington was the last turn on the bill – No. 13. It seemed to me bad placing and the fact that the Duke's final curtain was cut short by people getting up and going out to avoid the rush appeared to justify my conclusions. In my opinion he should have either closed the first half, or been the last turn but one.'

Again, an event of great musical import, here involving an ensemble unique in the history of all music, was described as a 'turn', but in music-hall terminology that is what they were, and No. 13 on the bill at that. 'As number thirteen went up on the board,' continued the Special Correspondent:

> the applause grew into a roar, the pit orchestra faded out and we heard – for the first time in England – the magic sound of 'Duke Ellington and his Famous Orchestra'. The curtain went up and there they were! Even the six brass were inaudible – in the thunder of applause . . .   The band was

dressed in pearl grey dress suits, with Duke himself in the centre of the band down stage at the piano. On Duke's left there were the three trumpets; behind the trumpets on a higher rostrum were the three trombones; behind the saxes were the bass and banjo and high up at the back was Sonny Greer. There they were, the names we have met so often in the *Melody Maker* Gramophone Review: Barney Bigard, Johnny Hodges, Harry Carney, Otto Hardwicke (mis-spelt on the programme 'Ottox') (saxes); Artie Whetsol, Charlie Williams, Fred Jenkins (trumpets); Lawrence Brown, Juan Tizol, Joe Nanton (trombones); Wellman Braud (bass); Fred Guy (banjo) and Sonny Greer (drums).

When the applause subsided a little I discovered that the band was playing 'Ring Dem Bells', mostly as on the record.

They finished with a sudden and unexpected coda. Duke jumped up from his seat and walked to the footlights. It was minutes before he could make himself heard. He and the boys seemed overwhelmed by the reception.

The Special Correspondent listed the tunes played and bemoaned the interpolations from vocalist Ivie Anderson and the dancers Bessie Dudley, 'The Original Snake Hips Girl', and Bailey and Derby, who had travelled with the band as part of the package. He expressed the opinion that although the band was perfect the programme could have been better chosen, but concluded the eulogy with: 'Perhaps on second thoughts it is just as well that the programme was thus arranged, for it will throw into sharp contrast the *Melody Maker* concert.'

There is no reason to doubt that the band were overwhelmed by the reaction. It would have been far in excess of anything they had known in their own country, where the public could frequently hear and see them. For sure, there were more jazz enthusiasts per capita in Britain than in the country of its birth, the homeland of Duke Ellington and his Famous Orchestra. These British jazz enthusiasts worshipped this almost unbelievable constellation of stars and marvelled at the instrumental settings in which they glittered.

The correspondent's objections to the 'acts' Duke brought with him were justified. To have waited so long for an orchestra of this calibre and then have precious time frittered away on tap dancing and hip wriggling must have been particularly galling, but these extraneous performances were part of the American vaudeville tradition, and were perpetuated in Britain in the fifties when Louis Armstrong's first post-war show included a one-legged dancer called Peg-Leg Bates. When

Melody Maker, 17 June 1933, announces the arrival of Duke Ellington on board the *Olympic*.

Duke Ellington appeared here in 1958 he featured some particularly unappealing singers.

That issue of the *Melody Maker* was packed with manufacturers' advertisements for instruments carrying Ellingtonian endorsement, Ellington record reviews and news of the band's heavy schedule, necessarily rearranged as the tour was going to be extended by another week.

Duke Ellington and his Famous Orchestra had truly arrived.

The Times had not covered Louis Armstrong at the Palladium, but the paper sent an anonymous correspondent to report on Ellington's opening at this theatre:

> Mr Duke Ellington, whose performance is the chief item in this week's programme at the Palladium, is exceptional and remarkably efficient in his own line.
>
> He does at once and with a considerable show of ingenuity what a jazz band commonly does with difficulty and often fails to do [*sic*!]. And the excitement and exacerbation of the nerves which was caused by the orchestra was the more disquieting by reason of his complete control and precision. It is not an orgy but a scientific application of measured and dangerous stimuli.

Whether Ellington is so good that his performances differ not only in degree but in kind from the ordinary run of things it is difficult to say. The expert who could disregard their emotional effect might conceivably derive aesthetic enjoyment from his rhythms, but the ordinary listener probably does not, and is probably not intended to do so. It is enough the effect be immediate and violent. Certainly the audience does not fail to show its excitement, though it is curious that the most popular numbers seemed to be 'very old favourites' and actually advertised for their age, which may be presumably counted in years.

The performance of the orchestra is diversified by the excellent singing of Miss Ivie Anderson, the dancing of Bailey and Derby, more ingenious than interesting, and of Miss Bessie Dudley, 'the original snake hips girl' which is quite as interesting as it is ingenious.

It is doubtful if this was the same correspondent who wrote 'The Art of the Jazz' in 1919, but he was certainly cast in the same mould and characteristically unfamiliar with the subject he was reviewing. 'A scientific application of measured and dangerous stimuli' indeed! In the fever heat of enthusiasm for Ellington at the time such comments could have aroused a quite unmeasured but positively dangerous stimulus among the cognoscenti, with the Special Correspondent in mortal danger therefrom.

A report in the *Daily Express*, Saturday 10 June 1933, announced:

The High Priest of Jazz arrives – but what really is this Hot Music? The Duke of Jazz – Mr Duke Ellington – arrived at Waterloo Station last evening and met some Napoleons of English music.

He's good-looking, tall and the high priest of the new syncopation. Four thousand, five hundred enthusiasts have paid to hear his band give a semi-professional recital at London's biggest cinema tomorrow.* A party was held in his honour last night. Mr Ellington was late. There had been some difficulty in finding a hotel willing – because he is slightly black – to accommodate him and when he eventually found a home in Park Lane some of the guests went to the reception desk and protested.

Meanwhile the assembled musicians waiting to meet Duke Ellington discussed what 'hot music' really meant.

Mr Basil Cameron, whose name is familiar to all lovers of classical music as a distinguished conductor, had this to say: 'It's sort of spicy music . . . '

---

* A reference to the *Melody Maker* concert at the Trocadero, Elephant and Castle – not the following day.

Mr Henry Hall, the BBC jazz conductor, observed that 'hot music' was 'the natural result of the days when jazz conductors gave a few bars to various members of the orchestra and told them to go to it and improvise'.

This is what Mr Duke Ellington had to say: 'There is no such thing as "hot music". All I do is write and play negro folk music and if the public who hear it feel "pepped up" – well, that is "hot music".'

On Tuesday the thirteenth, the *Daily Herald* carried a lengthy article by Spike Hughes about Ellington on the leader page:

> A prophet without honour in his own country. It has remained for us to discover, if not at first hand, at least through the medium of the gramophone, that Duke is something more than a bandleader specializing in what are vaguely called 'voodoo harmonies' and 'jungle rhythms'. He is in fact the first genuine jazz composer. This may come as a shock to people who associate jazz with the 'Rhapsody in Blue' or who consider jazz to be any noise made by a dance band in the background to conversation or an excuse for those ungraceful, hiking movements which pass for modern 'dancing'.
>
> Jazz is not a matter of trite, unguarded melodies wedded to semi-illiterate lyrics, nor is it the brainchild of Tin Pan Alley. It is the music of the Harlem gin mills, the Georgia backyards and New Orleans street corners – the music of a race that plays, sings and dances because music is its most direct medium of expression and escape.

These words, much abridged but the essence of the article, were truly surprising in a daily paper in 1933, for the general level of reportage on jazz was uninformed and sensationalist.

In the *Daily Herald*, Saturday 17 June, Hannen Swaffer boasted: 'When I heard his shrillest trumpeter play the other night I gave Duke Ellington a name for his show – "Gabriel over the Black House". Ellington is now composing a tune called that. Next Tuesday he will record it.' If Duke wrote a tune with such a title, which is doubtful, he didn't record it as one of the four titles he made for the Decca label on 13 July. One title, 'Every Tub', he retitled 'Hyde Park' as a gesture to the country that had received him so enthusiastically.

In *Era*, 14 June, Stanley Nelson, completely won over by the band, expressed somewhat flowery sentiments that were in complete contrast to the derogatory tenor of his writing a month earlier:

> Duke Ellington and his orchestra. How to describe in so many words the most vital, emotional experience the vaudeville in England has ever known?

An orgy of masochism; an exercise in sensuality; the performance of the Ellington Orchestra was both these but it mined deep into the fundamentals of every human being in that multitudinous audience at the Palladium on Monday night.

I am not ashamed to say that I cried during the playing of 'Mood Indigo'. Here was music far removed from the abracadabra of symphony; here in the tenuous melodic line is distilled from the emotions all the heritage of human sorrow which lies deep in every one of us.

For one brief fleeting moment I looked around the auditorium. More than half of that usually phlegmatic sea of faces was bathed in ecstatic adoration of that tall, distinguished, grey-suited figure at the piano and the triangle of musicians building up to the back of the stage. The rest had bewilderment plainly stamped on their faces. 'Is this music?' said my neighbour. The band was playing 'Tiger Rag' with a *pianissimo* never achieved before. These half a dozen brass played so softly one could hear the golden whisper of those twisting rhythmic figures.

'What is music?' I might have answered. What, I thought, would Wagner have made of it all? Would he have condemned or exalted? I'm confident that he would have hailed this music as one of the most significant forms of modern musical art.

I want to close this panegyric of heady emotionalism by calling on the musical profession to thank Jack Hylton, the greatest personality in the world of popular music today, who almost alone made possible this visit of Ellington and his wonderful ensemble.

In *Era*, 5 July, Nelson wrote a lengthy eulogy of Ellington. This and his review of the Palladium concert were tacit acknowledgements that he had dramatically changed his mind about their appeal being limited and, supposedly, that they were lucky to obtain that broadcast for £30! The doubting Thomas had become a fervent convert!

Nelson interviewed Ellington and reported: 'How shy the musicians are with white people.' This was undoubtedly true as they had previously known little contact with Caucasians in the United States, outside of agents, hall managers, recording executives and white faces in the venues that operated the colour bar, including the socialites doing the 'uptown thing' at the Cotton Club.

In the *Melody Maker*, 24 June, the headline ran 'ELLINGTON FEVER HEAT' and the article read:

Duke Ellington and his orchestra just failed, on the week commencing June 12th, to set up a new record for takings at the Palladium. The dance that took place at the Streatham Locarno last Friday (June 16th) was a literal riot. Enormous crowds besieged the door and some forced in without paying. The attendance was in the neighbourhood of four thousand and hardly anyone attempted to dance. They just crowded around the stand and cheered themselves hoarse.

On Monday last another midnight dance was played at the Astoria Ballroom, Charing Cross Road, for which every table was booked in advance. With admission at five shillings a very smart audience of Ellington supporters was present.

It is still doubtful, however, if the band has yet done itself full justice. That consummation is expected to happen on Sunday afternoon next, June 25th, at the concert for musicians at the Trocadero Cinema, commencing at 2 pm and for which all seats were sold out weeks ago.

Room has been found for some additional standing tickets which will be on sale at the box office at five shillings each, including tax. The doors will open at 1 pm and the early arrivals will be entertained by a gramophone recital of hot records, given by Levy's of Regent Street, and organ solos from Quentin MacLean, England's leading cinema organist who is resident at the Trocadero.

We are confident that the model organization that has been set up to pass four thousand people into the theatre will work as intended if we have the orderly support of our visitors. May we also suggest that everybody keeps his enthusiasm within bounds and refrains from applauding individual solos so that subsequent sequences may not be drowned.

Beyond everything, it is expected that there will be no attempt to besiege the band after the concert, when, following a quick tea, it has to leave to fulfil an engagement at the Regal Luxury Cinema, Hastings, which commences at 8 pm the same night.

The concert will give an opportunity to the Duke to feature some of those quieter and more individual compositions of his which have not hitherto been played in London. We have promised him a quiet and attentive audience which will know what to expect and how to listen. The applause should come at the end of each number and not in the middle in the distressing and irritating way which has marred the work of the band elsewhere.

Let us show that ours is the real public, and then we shall hear something which we shall remember for many a long day.

This article was unsigned, but was probably by Spike Hughes. The schoolmasterly tone and phraseology reflect not only the mores of the time, but the intense desire of the organizers for the audience to conduct themselves properly on this special occasion when Duke Ellington had not to concern himself with the limited sensibilities of a 'vaudeville' audience. The *Melody Maker*'s request not to applaud after solos was eminently sound, but the information that organist Quentin MacLean would entertain a packed audience of jazz 'fanatics' bordered on the surreal. The usual organ repertoire of Strauss waltzes, a sepulchral 'Londonderry Air' and selections from the *Merry Widow* would seem rather out of spirit with the main proceedings, even if played by England's leading exponent of the instrument, but the doughty *Melody Maker* was determined to plug every angle to make a success of this endeavour, and history must thank them for their attempts to give the public a hearty push towards jazz appreciation, and this from a paper staffed by individuals not really knowledgeable about jazz and running it primarily for 'the profession'. Their editorial in this issue was understandably triumphant:

HOT MUSIC PAYS

And what have all the Dismal Jimmies got to say about it now! Hot music they have decried ever since they first heard it. Principally because they had only the vaguest conception of what it was all about. So far as they were concerned it only meant distorting the melody out of all recognition. Syncopated variations is how they would have defined it, and they have disliked it for several reasons. If they were musicians it's because they couldn't do it (although they might have persuaded themselves that they could). If they were music publishers it was because they thought that their precious melodies were not getting a chance to be hammered into the subconscious mind of that ephemeral creature, the man in the street.

The great cry that went up from these people was that 'it is not commercial – the public don't want it'.

What right have they to say that it doesn't? Has any one of them compiled an exhaustive consensus?

Well, the lie direct has been given to them all by Ellington's visit. The Palladium has done record business, the dances at the Locarno and Astoria were both jammed as these places have never been jammed before. The *Melody Maker* concert has been sold out for weeks. The sale of Ellington records, always high, has leaped higher still. Why? Because the Duke is a novelty? Because he's been ballyhooed by the Press?

Because he appeals to musicians? But musicians are not the only people who swarmed (and are swarming) to see Duke. The public, the man in the street and the anti-hotites are flocking, too.

Again, why?

Because Ellington is giving them something they've never had before, and they like it, and open their purses for it!

On 14 June at 8.30 pm Duke Ellington's orchestra broadcast on the BBC Regional Programme (the 'National' wavelength was strictly for 'serious' music). He was preceded by a talk on 'Industrial Relations', by Professor John Hilton, and followed by Phyllis Clare and her Boys, a polite song and instrumental act.

In the *Melody Maker*, 24 June, 'Detector' reviewed this broadcast in which the band played fourteen items, including the 'Blackbirds of 1930' selection. This sole broadcast was niggardly acknowledgement of genius from an organization that repeatedly avowed its obligations to present music of minority appeal, and the decision was no doubt reached after strong opposition from the 'anti-hotites'. And it cost them all of £30!

In the 1 July issue the *Melody Maker* covered the show at the Trocadero on 25 June in these terms: 'And what an electric affair was last Sunday's! The organization held out and ticket holders patiently and in an orderly fashion went to their seats and even applauded the hot record recital given by Messrs Levy's,* which relieved Quentin MacLean at the organ while the house was filling.'

'Mike' (Spike Hughes), less enamoured, asked:

Is Duke Ellington losing faith in his own music and turning commercial through lack of appreciation, or does he honestly underestimate the English musical public to such an extent that a concert for musicians does not include 'The Mooche', 'Mood Indigo', 'Lazy Rhapsody', 'Blue Ramble', 'Rockin' in Rhythm', 'Creole Love Call', 'Old Man Blues', 'Baby When You Ain't There' or 'Black Beauty'?

Is he afraid to play quiet music which will make an audience listen so that there is a moment's silence at the end, or would he rather play loud and fast so that it is greeted with instantaneous but less discriminate applause?

During the past two weeks I have had several talks with Duke and was glad to notice that his trip to London has had a most stimulating effect. The interest taken in his music by so many different kinds of people has given him something to think about, hasn't it? He had realised, I think, that in Europe there is a public which does not demand that the whole effect of

---

* Levy's recorded Duke Ellington talking, with his own piano illustrations, in an interview with Percy Mathison Brooks. The record, single-sided, was given away free to any customer at their Aldgate shop who purchased six Ellington records.

'The Mooche' be spoiled by the addition of three irrelevant and inartistic major chords – the result of the American convention that to be commercial you must finish fortissimo, regardless of the nature of the piece just played. I know he appreciated the visit of the sculptor Epstein in his dressing room and the discussion with Constant Lambert upon the restatement of the theme of 'Swampy River'.

But last Sunday it seemed as if all the courage he had acquired in London, all the determination to go his own way in music deserted him at the most inappropriate occasion.

There is a saying about 'giving the public what it wants' which had always struck me as being the greatest illusion from which any artist can suffer. In Ellington's case, as in any other, the public does not know what it wants and has never known.

Hughes' assertion was, at best, a questionable half-truth, to which it could be added that any artist hoping to please public *and* critics was labouring under an even greater illusion. In this particular instance Ellington's dilemma must have been insuperable. No one in jazz, then or since, had written *hundreds* of his own compositions from which to choose for a mere two-hour programme.

Hughes cited the tenor John McCormack and the violinist Fritz Kreisler as two major artists who had sacrificed their art pandering to an undiscerning majority. He recommended conductor Toscanini's take-it-or-leave-it philosophy as an example for Ellington to follow, seemingly unaware from his ivory tower that for a bandleader, and black at that, living and working in the United States, such an attitude would quickly have seen the end of Duke Ellington and his orchestra.

Ellington maintained a splendid integrity, yet achieving an amazing measure of success in a social, artistic and economic background unfavourable to the black citizen and performer. For nearly fifty years he led a large band. This, considering the attendant financial difficulties – especially in the inflationary fifties and sixties when most big bands, white and black, folded – was a staggering achievement. During this period he maintained a constantly high standard of bands, nearly always finding suitable replacements when key musicians left, keeping up a flow of memorable compositions, always exploring new tonal possibilities, surviving the hardships of continuous touring, the temperamental upsets inevitable in a big band and the indignities of racism in certain American states.

It is a quite extraordinary history and one which had nearly forty years to run after he first came to Britain. In retrospect it would seem that Hughes had an almighty cheek in telling him what to play. But it has always been a characteristic of jazz buffs to instruct their heroes, and in the particular mood of those days Hughes' advice was well intentioned and he was certainly correct in advising Duke Ellington that in England he had an infinitely more informed and well disposed audience than, say, his white patrons at the Cotton Club in Harlem.

Earlier that year Hughes had visited this club during the time he was recording his Negro Orchestra. In an article for *Rhythm* he damned the fact that Duke played a largely support-ing role to a succession of 'acts', berated the management for operating a colour bar and pointed to the ignominy suf-fered by two black artists, Paul Robeson and Ethel Waters, who were grudgingly allowed entry provided that they sat away from the white clientele.

Duke by Spinky Alston

Indeed, the audience at the Palladium, and perhaps more so at the Trocadero, were so admiring of his music in all its aspects that he had no need to play 'commercial' material.

What were Ellington's thoughts about his first English experience and particularly about this insistence on his playing 'quieter' tunes? Here, for the first time ever, he had an audience that, for the most part, had col-lected his records and studied and argued about their meaning and their differing personnels; people who intellectualized his music as well as reacting emotionally to its incredible fecundity. Off-stage he was being pursued by an awestruck press with an intensity that he had never expe-rienced in America. He was being courted by a stream of intellectuals, artists and musicians. He even had an audience with Edward, Prince of Wales, who would, by the Grace of God, become King, Defender of the

Faith, of the United Kingdom of Great Britain and Ireland, Emperor of India, and of the British dominions beyond the seas.

To what extent did he ponder on the ecstatic response to his opening night at the Palladium? Did he compare this audience with the café society patrons of the Cotton Club? Did he measure both against the responses he got in 'coloured' halls, where the reaction would be to dance to his music in the controlled abandon of jiving movements owing nothing to formal ballroom dancing, and where the dancers had no thoughts about his band's 'art' content? In a situation that starkly illustrated the difference between his professional and artistic standing in America and Britain did this – as in Louis Armstrong's case – give him a new perspective on jazz and make him realize his highly significant role in its evolution? Did he dwell on why jazz appreciation should have been an unexpected penchant of the white race and particularly a European (notably British and French) phenomenon?

Some of his recollections of this first London visit were set down in his book *Music is My Mistress*, published in Britain in 1974. Ellington was adroitly bland and uncontroversial in the relatively few comments he committed to print and in his personal interviews with the press. Throughout *Music is My Mistress* there is nothing but praise, often fulsome, of all the names he mentions, including Irving Mills, the manager with whom he parted company, and some of the most unstable characters he had in his various bands, but he allows himself a gentle side-swipe at Spike Hughes:*

> Irving's next coup was an engagement at the London Palladium, which he arranged in association with the British bandleader, Jack Hylton. The Palladium was then regarded as the number one variety theatre in the world. We sailed from New York on 2 June 1933, on the *Olympic*. Crossing the Atlantic for the first time was an exciting experience for all of us. There were many delegates from all over the British Commonwealth, and they were going to a big conference in London. We played a concert and made some valuable friends amongst them.
>
> We had a terrific reception at the Palladium. Ivie Anderson broke it up every time with 'Stormy Weather'; Bessie Dudley danced and shook to

---

* No ghost-writer is credited in this book, although in his acknowledgements he pays tribute to Stanley Dance for deciphering his handwriting. Dance, chronicler-in-residence of the Ellington entourage, may have had more than just a hand in this work, and it's been known for a 'ghost' to use his subject to fire his own bullets!

'Rockin' in Rhythm'; and we played 'Ring Dem Bells' and 'Three Little Words' to tie up with the Amos 'n' Andy movie. We always got a good response to 'Mood Indigo', too. But the 'jazz critics' [Duke's quotation marks] were not satisfied, and we had to give a special concert one Sunday at the largest cinema in Europe, the Trocadero at the Elephant and Castle.* It was organized by the *Melody Maker* and the audience was composed entirely of musicians, who came from all over the country. We were to avoid 'commercial' numbers [again Duke's quotes!] and apparently on this occasion we lived up to expectations because Spike Hughes, the foremost critic at that time, didn't criticize us at all. Instead, he criticized the audience for applauding at the end of solos and in the middle of numbers! That's how serious it was.

We were absolutely amazed at how well informed people were in Britain about us and our records. They had magazines and reviews far ahead of what we had here and everywhere we went we were confronted with facts we had forgotten and questions we couldn't always answer. Nevertheless, the esteem our music was held in was very gratifying. A broadcast we did for the BBC provoked a lot of comment, most of it favourable. Constant Lambert, the most distinguished British composer of that period, had written an appreciation of some of our early records years before.

Lord Beaverbrook, who owned one of the most important London newspapers, threw a big party to which the Prince of Wales and the Duke of Kent were invited. We were invited, too, and Jack Hylton's Empress Club band played until we got through at the Palladium. It was all very colourful and splendid. Members of the nobility, Members of Parliament and delegates to the imperial conferences, all in informal dress, mingled happily. There was a generous buffet and the champagne flowed freely.

Prince George, the Duke of Kent, requested 'Swampy River', a piano solo I had a hard time in remembering, but I was flattered, especially to have him leaning over the piano as I played it.

Later, the Prince of Wales had some kind words to say about us. When he suggested we had a drink together I was surprised to find he was drinking gin. I had always thought gin as rather a low kind of drink, but from that time on I decided it was rather grand. He liked to play drums, so he paid Sonny Greer a lot of attention, too. This is how Sonny remembers the evening:

'As soon as we got the band set up, the Prince of Wales came over and sat down beside me Indian fashion. He said he knew how to play drums, so I

---

* Not exactly fair comment. The Trocadero concert was obviously arranged well beforehand, but his use of quote and exclamation marks indicates puzzlement at Hughes' strictures.

said "Go ahead!" He played a simple Charleston beat, and he stayed right by me and the drums throughout most of the evening. People kept coming up and calling him "Your Highness" but he wouldn't move. We both began to get high on whatever it was we were drinking. He was calling me "Sonny" and I was calling him "The Wale".'

I think the Prince of Wales really did like us, because he came to hear us again at Liverpool, when he was up in that area for the races at Aintree. He was loved by the day people and the night people, rich and poor, the celebrities and the nonentities. He was truly the Billy Strayhorn of the crown princes.

So, strangely, jazz music was the common factor between the son of a Washington butler nicknamed Duke in his boyhood and the subsequently controversial royal who was not to take up his inheritance but, instead, to become a mere Duke. It must have been a heady experience for a second-class citizen in his own country being so royally fêted – and perhaps, just as heady an experience for a Royal who, as events proved, was patently a non-conformist.

* * *

The second Trocadero concert was more to Hughes' liking, as only three non-Duke tunes were played. He made pertinent observations about audience interruption and the use of mutes.

If a couple of thousands of people have learned within three weeks that Tricky and Cootie are really expressing something personal and moving indeed there is some hope that these same people will realize by the time Duke does another concert that applause during a piece is not done in the best circles.

During the first seven numbers the audience reserved its applause for the end, but in 'Echoes of the Jungle' the newly appreciated importance of Cootie proved too much and this player's solo was greeted by much tiresome handclapping. The result of this misplaced enthusiasm was that one of the loveliest bridge passages in all Duke's music was completely inaudible and we did not hear anything until Barney Bigard started that sinister clarinet solo.

This practice is grossly unfair to the next soloist.

Tricky Sam was clapped even before he'd played a note.

Jazz audiences the world over have persisted in the stupid habit of applauding at the beginning and the end of solos but it was obvious that the British public in 1933 were intrigued and excited by the nuances of

Melody Maker staff artist Leon Goodman's impression of Duke Ellington's Trocadero concert

expression and blend of tone achieved by skilful manipulation of mutes; and although these were often humorous they were not primarily used for laughs. Tricky Sam Nanton could eerily simulate the human voice on his instrument; he got it to cry and wail and snarl, almost to speak syllables. On one of Duke's records (and *not* one of his own compositions) 'In the Shade of the Old Apple Tree', Nanton's primeval cries are quite chilling.

Hughes' objections to Duke playing the compositions of 'Broadway Caucasian immigrants' were hardly fair. Even the jazz-conscious public like to hear popular themes and courtesy of his arranging skills and a fine understanding of his soloists' capabilities Ellington alchemized the most banal of Tin Pan Alley pot-boilers. The Special Correspondent of *The Times* had at least one good point in observing how well the pop tunes at the Palladium show were received.

In his day Spike Hughes was truly the demanding purist,* although his objections to superfluous applause were fully justified.

Ellington's tour was far more than a personal and artistic triumph. It was a revelation to the larger British public as well as the jazz buffs and 'members of the profession', demonstrating powerfully that jazz could be on a high inspirational level, combining emotion and technical skill yet remaining functional dance music. His visit gave the lie to the Pygmalion-like efforts of the symphonists who tried to make a decent woman out of this harlot jazz by dressing her up in extraneous fripperies. Ellington was a skilled, inspired orchestrator but, in the thirties at least, his mastery of instrumental textures never debilitated the music's essential beat. On the contrary, it substantially enhanced it.

The four 'London' sides (two of them non-Duke titles) were recorded at Chenil Galleries, where Spike Hughes recorded with his Decca-Dents, one of his titles being Duke's 'Mooche' (labelled 'Mouchi') and another, his 'Harlem Symphony', dedicated to Ellington.

On the Ellington sides all the characteristic Ducal devices were employed: brass solos, muted and open, with gurgitating saxophone figures in the background; saxophone solos against swelling and

---

* Like other musicians who were also journalists Hughes obviously didn't think those strictures applied to his own activities. Was he forgetting that he turned down the chance to lead Armstrong's accompanying orchestra because he, a Caucasian Anglo-Irishman, was writing tunes for a West End show, and did he forget that his own band, the Decca-Dents, played the popular tunes of the day?

diminishing 'organ' chords; Bigard's albatross-like clarinet soaring above the ensemble; Ellington's sprinkling chords ornamenting the section and solo parts.

*   *   *

During those two weeks at the Palladium it was the non-believers as well as the enthusiasts whose ears were pinned back, who gaped and gasped at the sheer brilliance of the performances, and in their heart of hearts the dance-band leaders and their musicians must have realized that however profitable and publicly acceptable their commodity had proved to be it was insignificant and ephemeral compared with the inspired creativeness of this colossus who was listed No. 13 on the Palladium bill.

In a post-tour article on the technical proficiency of Ellington's band Spike Hughes wrote of the moment when, at a rehearsal, he was watching bandleader Jack Hylton's expression of utter astonishment at the brass section's attack on 'Ring Dem Bells'. In thirteen years of bandleading Hylton had never heard a *sound* like that achieved by the homogeneous blending and execution, allied to jazz feeling, from Messrs Williams, Whetsol, Jenkins, Nanton, Tizol and Brown.

The *Melody Maker* on 29 July reported the departure of Ellington for fresh triumphs on the Continent and quoted his words before leaving: 'I'll be right back. Hope it will be soon!'

He wasn't to return for sixteen years, when he again appeared at the Palladium with only one other instrumentalist, trumpeter-violinist Ray Nance, and singer Kay Davis, and it was not until twenty-four years later that he returned with a full orchestra. His visit in 1933 with what many collectors believed to be his greatest-ever orchestra was made just in time.

By the early thirties Duke had become an international figure. He returned to the US to find letters from all over the world including one from Samarang in Java, reported in the *Melody Maker*:

> Dear Sir, How are you Duke Ellington? I hope quite well with you. I have hear, Mr Duke, that you played music in New York. When I money I will also go to American. Do you know who Louis Armstrong is? When you know him, helped to say he must be writing me. I am Mr Klink. Will you give me a photograph of yourself with your orchestra. I played the ukelelee at home but this is not much fun. When I have money I will learn the schiff

trombone. I am quite same with you writing Mr Duke Ellington. Goodbye. Your friend, P. Klink.

In the same year the *Melody Maker* ran an article by the American writer Warren Scholl headed, 'What's Happened to Paul Whiteman?' Whiteman was still leading an orchestra, still performing 'symphonic' trivialities and making a lot of money, but in the changed climate of opinion the question raised in the article's heading was more than apposite.

The 'King of Jazz' had lost the crown he had never been entitled to wear.

* * *

The *Melody Maker*'s editorial on 22 July ran: 'Ellington has been here and thrilled thousands of us. So has Louis Armstrong. We are told that Cab Calloway and the Mills Blue Rhythm Band are on their way. Our education, woefully neglected, is being attended to. We now have everything to learn. Let us, therefore, seize all the opportunities to hear these visiting artistes and learn what we can. It is madness and musical suicide not to do so.'

Two years later the British Musicians' Union saw to it that musical suicide *was* committed, by persuading the Ministry of Labour to impose a notorious and quite untenable ban which, but for a few exceptions, denied the entry of American jazz musicians for the next twenty years or so when most of those affected were at their creative and technical peak.

In March 1934, Cab Calloway played at the Palladium. Calloway, a 'personality singer', led an orchestra with many accredited jazzmen, but in his stage show they were almost totally subordinated to his exhibitionistic antics and brash vocalizing. He made famous the phrase 'Hi-De-Ho', punctuating most of his songs with this and inviting audience repetition. The *Melody Maker* reported:

> The show was much as we expected, and much as we feared it. The most impressive thing about this combination is its sartorial elegance, not only on the stage, but in everyday life, for this is a band of coloured Beau Brummells.
>
> The applause broke out in a frenzy as Cab strode out to the stage waving a large baton. We left it until the second show to review the performance seriously, but although a slicker show than in the first house it did not altogether remove the impression of dissatisfaction on the purely musical aspects.

The band of much talent is not allowed to show its paces; at least in the matter of orchestrations there was nothing worthwhile and Cab sings too much. Judged by what this phlegmatic critic heard there are British bands who play better stuff and are just as proficient musically. Comparison between Calloway and Ellington is impossible.

It is likely that the appraisal would have been more kindly had Duke not recently stormed the scene. This experience, seared into memory, was the yardstick by which lesser mortals like Cab Calloway were to be judged.

The *Melody Maker*, 24 March 1934, announced that saxophonist Coleman Hawkins was arriving to partner Louis Armstrong at a concert at the London Hippodrome on 7 April.

The tenor saxophonist supreme, first heard in Britain on Fletcher Henderson records in the mid-twenties when he was a very clumsy player (quite unlike Armstrong on the same 78s who was already displaying his 'flaring brilliance'), was to be reunited with his former colleague, and Hawkins was now much better equipped to deal with a challenging situation. But unfortunately, that reunion never took place. Armstrong, for reasons never clearly established, withdrew from the concert and it was cancelled.

Hawkins stayed to play with Jack Hylton's and Mrs Jack Hylton's bands, playing two numbers on the BBC's 'In Town Tonight' radio programme on London Regional. He recorded four sides for the Parlophone label with a British rhythm section. Of the two on which he is accompanied only by pianist Stanley Black he is alleged to have claimed that he was so hamstrung by Black's phrasing that he would have preferred to have played on his own and, in the view of some critics, the records bear witness to the justice of his complaint.

He toured and became resident in Continental Europe, where many black players found the social atmosphere more congenial than at home, and where they were not subject to bureaucratic interference by unions that were far less doctrinaire in approach than their British brothers. He recorded with many Continental bands, undoubtedly to their financial gain, musical delight and benefit. The same benefits, monetary and progenitive, could have been experienced by many British musicians but for a stupidly obdurate Musicians' Union.

In August 1934 the pioneer jazz violinist Joe Venuti, with Frank Victor on guitar, appeared at the Palladium. The *Melody Maker* was highly enthusiastic:

> On his opening night Joe Venuti 'registered' in no uncertain manner. It has been usual during the London appearances of celebrated 'hot' stars for the fans to cheer themselves hoarse, but for the majority of the audience to register boredom, if not sheer dislike.
>
> Not so with Venuti. He is a superb player, judged by any standards, and the Palladium habitués were not slow to appreciate it. There can be no argument against Joe's virtuosity. As a fiddle player he has an unusually brilliant technique – as a stylist he is so original as to be undating; the solos he originated years ago are still up to the minute.

The *Melody Maker* published a photograph of Venuti's hands, showing the shortness of his fingers, contrasted with the breadth of palm. There were difficulties over contracts and the kind of presentation which Venuti, not the most genial of persons, expected. He and Victor returned to the States in circumstances – as the *Melody Maker* put it – 'depressing and which give us cause to blush for shame for the way they have been overlooked in this country'. Venuti recorded four sides on the Regal-Zonophone label with the South African Don Barrigo (tenor saxophone), Britishers Arthur Young (piano) and Doug Lees (bass), and Frank Victor before he departed.

In 1934 the *Melody Maker* announced that Duke Ellington was to sail for London, but in the following week it noted that there had been a hitch in the matter of permits. In the 11 August issue it reported that permission had been categorically refused, and that the Ministry of Labour were 'becoming worried about the non-reciprocity' from the American side. The consultations between the Ministry and the Musicians' Union were the beginnings of a misbegotten alliance to block the entry of foreign musicians.

In 1935 the Ministry of Labour announced they would no longer grant permits for Ellington's Orchestra or any other band to play in Britain until satisfactory reciprocal arrangements had been made with the American Federation of Musicians, but before this cultural iron curtain finally fell a few more foreign bands appeared in Britain.

Teddy Hill and his orchestra played at the Palladium in the *Cotton Club Show* but only in an accompanying capacity. It was firmly stipulated in their permit that they were not to 'move', except in the mechanics of playing their instruments! The band had many notable soloists including trombonist Dicky Wells, clarinettist Russell Procope and trumpeter Bill Dillard. Another trumpeter was John Birks 'Dizzy' Gillespie, later one of the founding fathers of the revolutionary bebop movement that would give jazz another dimension from the mid-forties, and have a profound influence on so many British musicians. Denied any solo opportunity in the Palladium show he 'sat in' at the Nest Club in Kingly Street, near Regent Street, with local musicians who could have had no idea that this was the man, with alto saxophonist Charlie Parker, who was later to split the jazz world wide open. Not that Gillespie himself could have foreseen this in 1937.

Of Teddy Hill's orchestra the *Melody Maker* reported:

> The dizzy speed of the dancing, the garish colours of the settings and cos-
> tumes, the restless music and whirling movement of the whole production
> appeared to leave the public in a daze as they walked out. Teddy Hill's
> orchestra, compelled by the terms of its labour permit to play on the stage
> behind the show, is obviously handicapped in this position, but nevertheless
> it is a mixture of impressiveness and disappointment. When it goes to
> town it is something like a real Harlem band, but in the accompaniments
> demanding more repose the weakness of the saxophone section – thin,
> ragged and out of tune – is unfavourably revealed.

It was pure coincidence that the unnamed reviewer (probably Dan S. Ingman) should use the adjective 'dizzy'. A future high priest of bebop received not a single mention in the press.

* * *

Pianist of distinction, composer of brilliance and rumbustious enter-tainer Fats Waller opened a tour of Britain in Glasgow in August 1938. He appeared on a BBC television programme and recorded several sides on piano, organ and celeste with British musicians, the most notable of whom were George Chisholm (trombone), Dave Wilkins (trumpet) and Edmundo Ros (drums) who was later to become famous for his Latin American band, a favourite of the socialites at his Coconut Grove Club in Piccadilly. Waller also made a solo appearance at the London Palladium in August accompanied by the pit orchestra conducted by Clifford Greenwood. The *Melody Maker* reported that they were hardly adequate for the occasion.

* * *

The jazz pianist acknowledged to possess the most staggering technique, Art Tatum, visited Britain in March 1938 to play at the Paradise Club, Soho, but the visit of this brilliant musician went virtually unnoticed. There was no mention whatsoever in the *Melody Maker* and *Rhythm* confined itself to a small photo of Tatum being interviewed by clarinettist Rudolph Dunbar, the caption, however, referring to him as the 'keyboard wonder'.

* * *

In 1938 the Quintette of the Hot Club of France starring the Belgian-born gypsy guitarist Django Reinhardt and French violinist Stéphane Grappelli (then spelt Grappelly) toured the variety halls. Many British musicians complained that they had not received full critical recognition on account of their nationality and pigmentation and while most of these laments were unjustified there is no doubt that had Reinhardt been a black American his impact would have been considerably greater, for he was the Continent's outstanding contribution to jazz.

For the next seventeen years live jazz was heard only from British musicians, with occasional exceptions when American musicians managed to slip in as 'variety' artists or when off-duty members of the US forces visiting or stationed in Britain played in jam sessions during the war. It was a false premise that inspired the ban. How many British musicians had been rendered unemployed by Louis Armstrong or Duke Ellington's band, for instance? In truth, the ban operated *against* union members – many of them could have played an accompanying or supporting role to the infinitely more talented visitors.

It was not until the mid-fifties, after continuous pressure from the musical press and jazz organizations, that the union relented and arrived at a reciprocal agreement with the American Federation of Musicians. Again British audiences could see as well as hear American jazzmen and the special pleasure of artist and audience communication could be enjoyed.

But, when the ban was eventually lifted many of these had died or were past their prime. A whole generation had been denied seeing and hearing a unique school of musicians the like of which will never be known again.

8

Pundits, Record Companies
and Rhythm Clubs

Rhythm was first published in October 1927 as a technical magazine principally for drummers and banjoists. The founder/editor was Julian Vedey, one-time drummer, club bandleader and small-part actor in British 'quota-quickie' films. For a time, 1930–32, he was the main record reviewer, facetiously berating most jazz records and repeatedly claiming that regarding jazz music he was 'uninitiated', although often boasting of his long experience 'in the profession' as a way of emphasizing that his strictures were justified. Few writers have made such proud and emphatic claims to ignorance and prejudice.

Later, the magazine featured reminiscences by pioneer dance-band musicians and features on jazzmen. There were articles by Spike Hughes and Stanley Nelson who, in one contribution called 'Syncopation in General', referred to 'jungle drums as the chrysalids of the art' and claimed that 'Whiteman and Hylton will go down in posterity for their wonderful virtuosity in a legitimate as well as rhythmic capacity'.

In the November 1930 issue, Bernard Tipping, dance-band trombonist, recalled hearing Sidney Bechet in the Red Devils at Rector's Club, the instrumentation comprising piano, violin, banjolin, saxophone, drums and clarinet. (This band broke up and some members, including Bechet, later joined Benny Peyton's Jazz Kings.) Tipping remembered that:

> they were a bit noisy at the time, but had a fine swinging tempo. Their greatest novelty was a chap called Berchet, [*sic*] their clarinet player. Here is Berchet's picture. I have especially included this as I know there are

hundreds of readers who, as soon as they see it, will immediately recognise him. Berchet was a real jazz artist, if ever there was one. He would conceive the most weird and clever ideas quite spontaneously whilst he was playing and out they used to come on the spur of the moment as it were . . .

Some of the ideas struck me as a little far-fetched, but as crazy as his tricks might at first appear, when one analysed them one found that they always fitted properly and were always musically correct.

One thing that tickled my fancy more than anything else was his glissando playing. I had never heard glissando played so well on a clarinet before, but here was a man who could glide and slide about the clarinet so easily as if it were a slide trombone. So it will not surprise you to know that scores of musicians of all ranks listened in amazement to Berchet playing his clarinet.

Lew Davis, writing in a mid-thirties *Melody Maker*, mentioned that he'd attended a performance by the Southern Syncopated Orchestra in London in 1919. He said it was sparsely attended, but made no mention of Bechet. The next article on Bechet, by James Holloway in the *Melody Maker*, didn't appear until December 1939. Holloway, echoing Ernest Ansermet's sentiments, asked: 'Is it just one of those freaks of fate that only now, with another world upheaval started, we should begin to appreciate this genius?'

Rhythm in January 1930 printed an unsigned review of Armstrong's 'West End Blues' – since accepted as an immortal classic. It was yet another review that reflected the critical uncertainties of the time:

The Parlophone Company have always endeavoured to foster the art of the modern rhythmic orchestra, but their latest achievements, the 'New Rhythm Style' series, is easily their *chef-d'oeuvre*.

Louis Armstrong's opening with a breath-taking cadenza in which slurring, the smear, intricate tonguing and the acme of pitch are demonstrated on 'West End Blues' is as perfect an example of rhythmic virtuosity as I have ever heard. Armstrong excels, who couldn't with such a backing?

Rock-like tempo and perfect orchestra background throw the silver tone of the trumpet into vivid relief and the vocal work, although *lied ohne worte*, strikes just the right note.

Of Earl Hines who plays the piano I shall speak later when I deal with his solo record, but on this record he gives us a few bars tinged, you might say, with a little needless chromaticism, but harmonically and rhythmically off the beaten track.

The same reviewer, probably Stanley Nelson, didn't rate Armstrong's 'Ain't Misbehavin'' from the same batch of releases, much preferring the

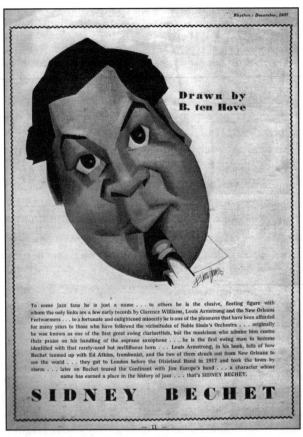

Drawing of Sidney Bechet by Boy ten Hove, published in *Rhythm* magazine, December 1937

backing, Eddie Lang's 'Freeze an' Melt'. Of the former, he wrote, 'The vocal may be the essence of Harlem but my Anglo-Saxon soul was repelled and excellent though Armstrong is there is too much prominence accorded the trumpet, especially at the close of the performance.'

The same edition contained an arresting photograph of Murray Pilcer and his Ragtime Octette, taken years earlier. This was the same Pilcer whose 'jazz band' recorded for the Edison Bell label in 1919. His drum kit in this photograph illustrates the emphasis on miscellaneous percussion in those guileless days. It included a variety of gongs, woodblocks, bells, cymbals, tambourines and klaxon horns. No doubt this assemblage was energetically struck, tapped and pumped to produce the most awful clatter!

Equally bizarre was the feat of Pilcer and his band in playing for twelve hours non-stop at the Normandie Ballroom, Margate, in the mid-thirties. This epic, or part of it, was filmed by British Movietone News.

In December 1935, *Rhythm* was acquired by Odhams' Press and published as a photo-magazine companion to the *Melody Maker*. It ceased publication in 1939, a war casualty. Before *Rhythm* was absorbed by Odhams it published some fine caricatures of British bandleaders by Slade, but after the take-over it developed into a very attractively produced magazine with a broad editorial content and strong emphasis on eye-catching design under the direction of Bernard Greenbaum. In 1938 its format was changed to pocket size, with engaging little figures spilling out of the margins. During this period the Dutch artist Boy ten Hove contributed some magnificently drawn caricatures of jazzmen, although the 'humorous' cartoons were abysmally unfunny. *Rhythm* was a credit to editor Percy Mathison Brooks and assistant editor Dan S. Ingman, and despite being a 'commercial' publication, it engaged the best jazz journalists in Britain.

During the twenties a succession of reviewers in *Gramophone,* edited by Compton Mackenzie and Christopher Stone, at first lumped jazz and popular music together, but most were kindly disposed towards the former. Major Stone was Britain's first disc jockey, playing 78s and making his comments as he wound up his portable gramophone. The major, well-spoken and gentlemanly, was a far cry from today's brash and strident DJs, seemingly bent on the debasement of the English language. He played many jazz records in his programmes, and in 1933 made a record for Brunswick called 'Jazz to Rhythm' with Fred Elizalde's band, demonstrating changes in style from 1920 to 1933.

After a very brief stint with Jack Hylton, Edgar Jackson became the *Gramophone*'s dance-music critic, writing under the heading 'Dance and Popular Rhythmic Records'. Reviewing a Paul Specht record he recalled Specht's continual pressure for reciprocity which, as Jackson put it: 'Everybody saw through as a means of flooding the country with American bands as our own were not good enough to make the exchange.' Later Jackson took over a separate jazz-record column.

With the *Gramophone* and *Rhythm* and the variety trade papers, *Era*, *Performer* and *Stage* and some well disposed and reasonably informed journalists in the lay press (Collie Knox of the *Daily Mail* in particular) all giving jazz regular coverage, the music began to assume a degree of respectability. But it was the *Melody Maker* to whom the enthusiast primarily looked for information. It was the bible for the record collector and 'members of the profession' and in 1933 became a weekly with the maverick Jackson back in the fold, but not as jazz critic. He continued in this role with the *Gramophone*.

* * *

Lew Stone and his orchestra

Britain was now into the 'Golden Age of the Dance Bands'. Their bowing, beaming, frock-coated and baton-waving leaders were household names and making fortunes – Ambrose, Jack Hylton, Jack Payne, Billy Cotton, Henry Hall, Roy Fox, Lew Stone, Debroy Somers and others. Many of these allowed their jazz-minded sidemen the occasional chorus, sometimes permitting a 'special' hot arrangement. For good economic reasons the activities of these popular figures dominated the *Melody*

Maker's pages. The jazz public was not large enough to maintain the sales and advertising revenue necessary to keep it profitable but the music was given a considerable allocation of space and the news and comments were now much more informed, thanks mainly to John Hammond's despatches from America and Spike Hughes' articles.

The paper generally showed a lot more assurance about jazz. In a gossip column called 'The Busker', under the heading 'ENCYCLOPAEDIA BRITJAZZICA!', they quoted a famous dictionary:

> Jazz is considered worthy of recognition in the new edition of *Encyclopaedia Britannica*. Illustrations are given with covering captions showing how jazz effects may be obtained by accenting beats, skipping and tieing notes, etc.
>
> The musical illustrations given include the break from W. C. Handy's 'Memphis Blues', part of Irving Berlin's 'Pack Up Your Sins' and a few bars of De Sylva, Brown and Henderson's 'Varsity Drag'. We are indebted to learn about 'jazz effects', although we were under the impression that 'accented beats' and the skipping and tieing of notes were devices as old as music itself.

The *Melody Maker* opened its correspondence columns to that emerging species, the dedicated jazz record collector. Editor Percy Mathison Brooks was not a little proud of his indulgence of these often fractious and pedantic correspondents who peppered him with acid missives. At the end of one such letter he added: 'Precisely! We have nothing to say. We wouldn't if we could. Mr Thompson has left us speechless, wordless. Besides, what other country could produce letters like this or the magazine to publish them?'

He had been spoofed. The correspondent, L. V. Thompson of Slough, was a reader with a sly sense of humour. At this time the government had launched a 'Buy British' campaign and in reply to a letter from a Mr Wilson he wrote:

> I read Mr Wilson's letter in the last issue with considerable interest and I must agree with him for several reasons. Firstly I do feel in these days of crisis it behoves all true Britishers to buy only British records by British dance bands playing tunes by British composers, thus helping to reduce unemployment.
>
> Secondly, as Mr Wilson so truly says, we still have two of the best bands in the world, Jack Hylton and Debroy Somers. How could Ellington's 'The Mooche' and 'Creole Rhapsody' compare with the delicious *morceaux* of Hylton's 'Rhymes, Parts One and Two' and 'He Played His Ukulele as His

Ship Went Down'? What comparison can there be between Debroy Somers' 'A Savoy Hunting Melody' and such trivialities as Duke's 'Mood Indigo'?

Besides, our bands are infinitely better in other departments. Which of the hot merchants can combine the good looks of Roy Fox and Jack Payne? How many negroes have such a fine and manly figure as our own Max Bacon? Can Coleman Hawkins distribute music scores with one hand whilst playing saxophone with the other as Burton Gillis with Henry Hall's band?

Can Louis Armstrong imitate Nat Gonella as well as Nat Gonella can imitate Louis Armstrong? I am afraid that on such tests as these Mike's pets compare very badly.

Unintentionally humorous was a report that the arch-enemy of jazz, Dr (now Sir) Henry Coward, had enjoyed Jack Payne's stage show. Sir Henry qualified his approval but admitted there was 'none of the bang, bang, bang, drum, drum, drum and the moaning of cows and the ripping of calico'. Surely many an addict of these noises which he thought to be jazz music must have slept easier in his bed knowing that the sounds of the orchestra led by that peacock of thirties pop, Jack Payne, had mollified Sir Henry.*

The mixed bag that was the *Melody Maker* in the early thirties provided further unintentionally comic items like the photograph of a Japanese Ladies' Jazz Band with two drummers, and an article with the headline, 'Highlights on Dark Subjects' – about black musicians working in London. But now the paper came out strongly against racism, attacking the distributor of anti-Semitic leaflets in Archer Street – the professional musicians' open-air club in London's West End – and printing an article by Rudolph Dunbar on the indignities he had suffered on account of his colour. This was a welcome change from Edgar Jackson's days as editor.

Such comprehensive press reportage of jazz was complemented by a steady stream of jazz releases. Most of the independents had by now gone bankrupt or been absorbed by the major labels now run by two main combines, Electrical and Musical Industries, issuing HMV, Columbia, Regal-Zonophone and Parlophone, and the Decca complex, issuing the label of that name, plus Brunswick, Vocalion and Rex.

---

* By 1940 Sir Henry, at the age of ninety-one, further confirmed his support of 'jazz' on a broadcast where he conducted Joe Loss and his band playing a version of Poet and Peasant, and remarked afterwards that 'jazz musicians were far superior to the type of music they played'.

During the late twenties HMV had sporadically issued jazz before commencing their 'Hot Rhythm Records' in 1932, which lasted until 1935 when they introduced their 'Swing Series' retaining much of the former catalogue. The cognoscenti were well served by both series. The catalogues included: Duke Ellington's orchestra, then boasting the greatest array of soloists Duke had in fifty years of band-leading; McKinney's Cotton Pickers, a vibrant black orchestra led by saxophonist Don Redman and second only to Ellington for compositions and arrangements; the better Paul Whiteman sides arranged by Bill Challis and featuring Bix Beiderbecke; Fletcher Henderson's orchestra with trumpeter Roy Eldridge and Coleman Hawkins; and, from the mid-thirties, Benny Goodman's big band and his innovatory trio and quartet recordings with pianist Teddy Wilson, vibraphonist Lionel Hampton and drummer Gene Krupa. Also featured were the Quintette of the Hot Club of France; the Muggsy Spanier Ragtime Band; the irreverent Fats Waller and his Rhythm; and the large swing bands of Artie Shaw, Tommy Dorsey and Bunny Berigan. HMV's cheaper sister label, Regal-Zonophone, issued sides by the New Orleans trumpeter Wingy Manone with widely varying personnels, and the thirties recordings of Clarence Williams.

Columbia's releases, too, had been irregular. The discographer/historian Brian Rust thinks they may have been influenced by Edgar Jackson's strictures but in 1928 they commenced their 'Swing Series', including records by a pick-up band organized by John Hammond especially for the British market with Joe Venuti, Jimmy Dorsey, Bud Freeman and Adrian Rollini.

Parlophone continued their 'Rhythm Style' series, later commencing a 'Swing Style' series mostly of British musicians. Throughout the thirties the Decca company continued to issue the jazz output of Ambrose, Jack Hylton, Lew Stone and Roy Fox; plus studio recording groups – the Lew Davis Trombone Trio, the Embassy Rhythm Eight (from the Ambrose Orchestra), Nat Gonella with the black American pianist Garland Wilson, solos by Wilson, pianist Billy Mason's band with trumpeter Duncan Whyte and saxophonist Buddy Featherstonhaugh, pianist Gerry Moore's Chicago Brethren, the Danny Polo Swing Stars with trumpeter Tommy McQuater, trombonist George Chisholm and pianist Eddie Macauley, and the recordings of George Shearing before he went to America to find fame and fortune.

In addition the company issued hundreds of American sides, notably by the Venuti-Lang All Stars, Louis Armstrong with the Luis Russell Orchestra, and Bob Crosby's orchestra, an outstanding white band of the thirties.

From Decca's inception in 1929 primarily as an ancillary to the com pany's main produce – gramophones – its contribution to the movement had been significant. It acquired Vocalion, from which source Levaphone/Oriole and Keith Prowse drew their specialist catalogue, but in 1936 Vocalion launched its superb 'S' series, a total of 247 sides up to 1940, when the label ceased for the duration of the war.

These releases included records of blues singers Rosetta Crawford, Rosetta Howard, Trixie Smith and Billie Holiday, all with first-class accompaniment, the last named being supported mostly by various pick-up bands led by pianist Teddy Wilson. Other Vocalion artists were Coleman Hawkins; trumpeter Red Allen; bassist John Kirby's Onyx Club Band with trumpeter Charlie Shavers; and Shavers with clarinettist Johnny Dodds and a little-known black band, Al Cooper's Savoy Sultans. White jazz was represented by New Orleanian trumpeter Sharkey Bonano, Woody Herman's first band and Benny Carter's British band,

Star trombonist George Chisholm

the first truly star-studded assembly of British jazz musicians on record.

Two of Vocalion's releases created something of a furore. They were by Jones–Smith Inc: 'Shoe Shine Swing'/'Lady Be Good' (S68) and 'Evenin''/'Boogie Woogie' (S163). Actually, this was a five-piece contingent from the large Count Basie band which, coincidentally, had its first British release in the same month – April 1937.

Both the quintet and the band sides served to introduce the name of pianist William 'Count' Basie and his principal soloist, tenor saxophonist Lester Young, who later (in post-war years) was to have a profound effect on a whole school of tenor saxophonists – most of them white – such as Stan Getz, Zoot Sims, Brew Moore and Allen Eager.

The first review of these Basie records was in the *Melody Maker*, 27 March, by 'Rophone'* who at the time was Leonard Feather:

> On 'Lady Be Good' he [Basie] plays the first chorus with his right hand only (or so it seems) with drums and bass compensating the lower frequencies. I don't want to unduly rhapsodize about this band as it has already been a victim of preposterous over-enthusiasm from certain quarters, but there is no doubt that it shows promise . . . 'Shoe Shine Boy' (alias 'Shoe Shine Swing') is taken very fast, giving Young time for two good choruses. 'Lady Be Good' is less self-conscious and the successful Quintet side, if you can forgive the bass player.

The next review, glowingly complimentary, of these issues was in *Rhythm*, April 1937, written by John Hammond, and this is, presumably, the 'preposterous over-enthusiasm' to which Feather scathingly referred – he must have heard Hammond's critique, or had some intimation of it – prior to its appearance. Maybe someone on the sister paper had tipped him off!

> I hope the editor will forgive me for interpolating these four sides into this month's column, for there is the possibility that they will not be released for another few weeks in England. I consider them so important . . . for I don't believe that the gramophone has ever captured swing so subtle and devastating as this . . . I fully realize that Hammond will once again be vulnerable to the charges of hyper-enthusiasm but I don't care what brickbats come my way. These records are solid enough to shield me from abuse. These sides were recorded in Chicago by five gentlemen from Count Basie's orchestra: Joe [Jo] Jones, drums; Tatti Smith, trumpet; Walter Page, bass; Lester Young, tenor sax; and Bill Basie, piano.
>
> Most people in England and the Continent are acquainted with Basie's piano work on old Bennie Moten records on HMV. Even in those days he was a superlative artist, but the records gave only a slight idea of his subtlety, solidity and power. He did not have Joe Jones, who is certainly one of the three great drummers in captivity, to propel him, nor did he have Lester Young to turn out some of the most exquisite phrases that ever issued from a tenor sax.
>
> 'Lady Be Good' is in many ways the most completely satisfying record I have heard since the Golden Twenties. The swing is completely relaxed, the

---

* To complement 'Mike' – obviously this pseudonym deserved a connotative mate!

rhythm section so perfectly co-ordinated that there is none of the pushing sensation one gets from almost every big band in the country today and this accomplished without a guitar or bass drum! Lester Young is an entirely original saxophonist, without so much as a trace of Hawkins in his style and with a facility and attack I have never heard the like of. Only the trumpet playing is not of the highest calibre.

'Boogie Woogie' cannot compare with 'Lady Be Good' I'm sorry to say, despite Jimmy Rushing's grand singing and Young's two memorable choruses. . . 'Shoe Shine Boy', however, is a different story. The two tenor choruses and their supreme backgrounds are not to be matched in other records of recent memory; the background to the trumpet has so much guts I can't begin to describe it.

'Evenin'', which is a magnificent tune by Harry White, is another darb, easily in the class of 'Lady Be Good'. It is my firm conviction that music like this can come only from the greatest of improvisers. We of another race can only attempt to copy as best we can.

Hammond made further mention of these records in the May issue of *Rhythm*. The Jones–Smith Inc. sides (named as such for contractual reasons) were organized by Hammond and it could reasonably be said that his strong personal interest (although, he asserts, with no financial involvement) in these accounted for this fulsome review. His praise however was fully justified. All four sides have become universally acclaimed, especially 'Lady Be Good'.

The thirteen-year-old who had become interested in jazz listening to Specht's Georgians at Lyon's Corner House in 1923 had become an *eminence grise* in American jazz, and his feat of bringing Basie to general attention was one of his major achievements.

Later, Leonard Feather (an Englishman from Maidenhead, Berkshire), in his multifarious activities in the post-war American jazz scene, was guilty of similarly 'preposterous over-enthusiasm' about the bands and records with which he was directly (and financially) connected and, as a critic, he was a fervent supporter of Lester Young when the 'bebop' clique (Feather their foremost spokesman) adopted the tenor saxophonist as one of their own, even though he was not strictly a 'bop' musician.

In his massive and indispensable *Encyclopedia of Jazz*, Feather devotes, quite rightly, 120 lines to Lester Young, referring to him as the 'founding factor in a new school of jazz thought and the original influence on virtually all new tenor men in the late '40s and '50s'.

At the end of his reviews in the May issue of *Rhythm* Hammond wrote a sharp footnote:

> To 'Rophone' [*Melody Maker*]: Critic John Hammond was no more responsible for Helen Ward leaving Benny Goodman's band than he was for her initial engagement with Goodman. Critic John Hammond disapproved violently of her singing, but the sole reason for her leaving the band was her marriage to Albert Marks. Let me state emphatically that Helen was not fired: she left of her own free will. She was a definite commercial asset to the band and no one knew this better than Benny himself.

Both Hammond and Feather were very active and influential at overlapping times in the US jazz scene, but their early disagreements were fought out in the columns of Britain's two major popular music papers.

Another Hammond footnote, same issue, was an apology for his incorrect identification of soloists on Carter's British recordings, but he remained defiantly critical of these records.

> To Benny Carter: Apologies for the slip-ups in *Down Beat* about the personnel of your English recordings and my attributing the work of McDevitt and Buddy Featherstonhaugh to you. My opinion of the discs remains the same, however: I'm delighted to see you making such a grand success, but distressed that the records should be so hopelessly lifeless. Incidentally, Benny, I hope the name is still John and not Mr.

There was a bumbling and meaningless critique of the Jones–Smith Inc. sides in the *Gramophone*, May 1937:

> I believe I said earlier that the Bill Basie band didn't have much in the way of outstanding soloists and now he is with four of his men going to town like, I was almost tempted to say, with the best of 'em. Which just goes to show how unsafe it is to judge musicians individually by their band. I am not saying, however, that these effusions by the quintet will be to everyone's taste. It depends whether one likes things fast, furious and so extravagant that even the most hard-baked jazz fan will find it hard to see what connection there is between the tunes named on the label and what is actually played.

Thus did the indomitable Edgar Jackson dismiss records which, seven decades later, are widely accepted as masterpieces of small-jazz-band improvisation and significant milestones in the music's history.

At 2/6d apiece these, and many other Vocalion issues, were gems for a song.

* * *

Brunswick also had a meritorious history in the matter of jazz releases, going back as far as 1924 with the issue of the first Mound City Blue Blowers record that led to their English trip; and the issue of King Oliver's Savannah Syncopators, Edgar Jackson's first and not too happy experience of black jazz on record. Later the label issued sides of the Nichols Five Pennies, Elizalde's university band, the Original Dixieland Jazz Band (from American Aeolian 'hill and dale' recordings) and the black bands of Claude Hopkins, Noble Sissle (with Sidney Bechet), Luis Russell, Earl Hines, Chick Webb, Don Redman and many others.

It was a Brunswick project in 1936 that was to have the most far-reaching results. This was an album of twenty-eight sides entitled *Classic Swing*, priced at twenty-four shillings and issued with a twenty-thousand-word booklet entitled *Twenty-One Years of Swing Music*, written by Leonard Hibbs, priced at one shilling and sixpence. (Hibbs also recorded three twelve-inch sides for the same label entitled *Conversations About Jazz*.)

The *Melody Maker* of 18 January 1936 gave these releases the arresting headline, 'SENSATIONAL RECORD PROJECT', and reported:

> It is well known to all readers of this paper that American Decca have been re-recording all the most notable outpourings from the old Gennett catalogue.
>
> THE VERY CREAM OF THE CATALOGUE – RECORDINGS THAT ACHIEVED FOR THIS COMPANY THE REPUTATION FOR WHAT IS KNOWN AS 'CLASSIC SWING' – WILL BE ISSUED IN TWO ALBUMS.
>
> This historic decision means, at last, the ordinary fan will be able to buy records which are discussed with bated breath at Rhythm Club meetings; and which, although only the merest handful of so-called authorities have ever heard them, are rightly regarded as the foundation stones of modern jazz.
>
> The recordings from which the twenty-eight sides have been selected stagger the imagination at the feast of good things that will soon come your way.
>
> There will be four records by Joe Oliver's Creole Jazz Band. This outfit was the original one he founded in New Orleans with Louis Armstrong playing second trumpet and singing in a style that is unbelievable.
>
> Another classic which has been unearthed is that immortal one by 'Bix and his Rhythm Jugglers', which is the very first Bix ever made to have his own name on the label. It is also the only authentic record of his composition 'Davenport Blues'.

There will be all the Wolverines in which Bix is again to be heard, including the famous 'Tiger Rag', which has never been released in any country in
the world. Bix is again heard in the Sioux City Six, a combination which has
never even been mentioned before in rhythm circles. The other members of
the six are Miff Mole, Rube Bloom, Frankie Trumbauer, Min Leibrook and
Don Murray.

But even yet the delights are not exhausted. The Friars Inn Society is a
name which hides the identity of the New Orleans Rhythm Kings and for
the first time it will be possible to hear the composer's own versions of such
masterpieces as 'Bugle Call Rag', 'Farewell Blues' and 'Tin Roof Blues'.

The remaining records include discs by Carmichael's Collegians; an early
Armstrong, 'Keyhole Blues'; some grand examples of Wingy Manone at his
earliest and best; and in all probability the little known masterpiece by Curt
Hitch's Happy Harmonists, a middle-west outfit of the same era as the
Wolverines, with whom Hoagy Carmichael made his first record of
'Washboard Blues'. Because they liked that tune Hoagy composed 'Boneyard
Shuffle' on the spot for recording.

Dubbed from records indifferently recorded by the early acoustic
process, most of the records are more significant for their historical than
their musical interest, but the Creole Jazz Band recordings, similarly
recorded and dubbed, were the revelation. Even the muddy recording
and mediocre rhythm section could not dampen the pristine exuberance
of the young Louis Armstrong blending with his bandleader and mentor,
King Oliver, with clarinettist Johnny Dodds weaving and twisting
through the ensemble. These recordings were to plant the seed of interest in New Orleans jazz, to be the models for many hundreds of young
British and European musicians a decade later.

Strangely, in view of the front-page prominence given to these albums,
no *Melody Maker* writer reviewed them, nor did the paper give the
project further editorial support. Nor did its sister paper *Rhythm*. We
shall never know the reason for these omissions.

Understandably – since its editor compiled the accompanying booklet
and perhaps had a hand in the compilation of these albums – *Swing Music*
ran a lengthy review and Brunswick placed an advertisement in the
March 1936 issue.

A John Goldman wrote:

> This series of 'Classic' swing records is something I had never expected to
> hear. Long since, I had supposed that they were lost for ever in the collapse
> of the Gennett Record Company. Thanks to the foresight, diligence and

taste of American Decca and our own Brunswick Record Company, they have been found, dubbed and in two comprehensive albums issued for the British public.

No one should pretend that these records are examples of modern jazz; they are the beginnings, frequently experimental, which sound comic to our ears . . . but no one can question their importance. My second point is to warn people that jazz was not suddenly born with the ODJB and King Oliver's Creole Jazz Band, or that they were the only groups playing at that time. The word jazz is known to have existed in 1880, but it was not until the post-war period that it reached its amazing impetus.

By 1918 numerous bands were playing – some were experimenting on new lines and some carrying on in the old ragtime manner. Among the experimenters were the ODJB, the New Orleans Rhythm Kings and King Oliver. Be warned that they were not alone. Fletcher Henderson . . . with Joe Smith on cornet was making marvellous records in 1921–22.

Goldman quickly homed in on the heart of the matter in his assessment of the King Oliver Creole Jazz Band recordings, which took pride of place in his piece. Remember: these recordings had been made in 1923 and were being heard in Britain for the very first time in 1936. There is no reference to any of the titles being heard, or commented on, before then.

The Oliver titles were 'Dippermouth Blues', 'Canal Street Blues', 'Mandy Lee Blues', 'I'm Gonna Wear You off My Mind', 'Weather Bird Rag' and 'Just Gone'. Goldman commenced his critique with views on 'Dippermouth' and 'Canal Street'.

'This record, made in 1921 [1923 in fact] possesses already that quality that distinguishes jazz from any other form of music – SWING! That your foot must, willy-nilly, be induced to beat the floor is the fundamental prerequisite of jazz.' How true! Later critics were very snooty about dancing to jazz, completely overlooking the music's original function. Peter Tanner, writing in *Rhythm* in February 1939, was scathing about the 'jitterbug' menace. In that issue, *Rhythm* ran a photo of young American jivers leaping about in a theatre aisle and another photograph, of a more sedate crowd of English people solemnly listening to jazz, with appropriately favourable comments from Tanner.

Goldman, however, didn't favour 'Weather Bird Rag'. 'I do not like this so much. Perhaps because it is broken up by "breaks". This kind of thing was outmoded so long ago that it sounds silly now . . . '

Now, well over half a century later, it would be easy to pick holes in this generally percipient appraisal; to mention that Joe Smith was not with Fletcher Henderson in 1920–21; that Henderson's records of that time were stiff and unswinging – Whiteman-inspired – that his objections to 'Weather Bird' smacked of Edgar Jackson's insistence on 'improvement being the inevitable concomitant of the passage of time'.

Goldman refers to: 'the simple negro harmonies of clarinettist Johnny Dodds . . . with many errors of taste, tricks and clichés, although, apparently doing no harm . . . the ensemble playing you listen to over and over again on account of the two trumpeters on these records – King Oliver and Louis Armstrong. They are a force . . . it seems so easy yet so aggressive in a sense that no white orchestra is . . . the way Armstrong follows Oliver is amazing . . . It is simple and hardly diverges from the melody but the swing they produce is enormous . . .'

Edgar Jackson reviewed the album in the March 1936 issue of the *Gramophone*. He wrote in Jacksonese but he arrived at a truth when he said of the Oliver sides: 'This is the combination that gets nearer to ensemble swing as we know it. This seems due to the fact that, in spite of the inevitable plinky-plinky banjo, it has the best rhythm section. The melody instruments are more advanced than other groups. They have solo swing.'

In his preamble, Jackson wrote:

Since the early Gennett days the characteristics of jazz may, or may not, have improved, but it has certainly changed. Jazz has grown up. It has become more ambitious and outwardly more finished. The charming guilelessness of its childhood has been succeeded by a worldliness which many not only accept as a natural result of its emancipation, but demand in the belief that it is only an essential symbol of progress.

If you look at it this way you may find these records outside the scope of your taste. They are naïve in the extreme. Necessarily so. Jazz was like that then. Admittedly they contain phrases, in some cases, whole passages, which are gems, even in the light of modern ideas, but one may have to be an enthusiast to feel the experience of hearing them justified. They are certainly not those who are merely looking for superficial entertainment . . . all are acoustically recorded and reproduction is decidedly inferior to today's electrical recordings. But these albums have a deep and twofold appeal. They give more than a glimpse into the evolution of the music and those who played it.

* * *

Budget records, obtainable only in Woolworth's stores, were produced under the Crown label. These records were nine inches in diameter, cost sixpence, and featured, under the pseudonyms of the Rhythm Rascals and the Swing Rhythm Boys, British musicians including George Chisholm (trombone), Tommy McQuater (trumpet), Freddy Gardner (alto saxophone) and Billy Amstell (tenor saxophone). This label was one of the refuges for those jazz-minded dance-band musicians.

The number of jazz records issued in the thirties was vast, the content extremely varied and representing almost every facet of jazz. No doubt the companies, bowing to the pressures from a minority movement, hoped to profit from this fraternity and often did. The best Parlophone 'Rhythm Style' jazz items stayed in their catalogues for forty years, but many of the issues must have sold at a loss. From this flow of releases were built the basic collections that stayed on jazz buffs' shelves for the rest of their lives, and as a testimony to their enduring value many repeatedly appeared in compendium albums after the inception of the long-playing record.

The often shrill jazz-loving minority frequently condemned the executives for not releasing the best examples of their heroes, sometimes with justification. But, with hindsight, it has become obvious that these executives were considerably more perceptive of differences in the merits of available masters than the vociferous collector would suppose. Years later, when alternative 'takes' were issued for collectors, it was shown that almost invariably the best of the available masters were those first released. One illustration of this is Paul Whiteman's 'Louisiana'. On the second take Bix Beiderbecke's irresolute solo is much inferior to the poised construction of the first, the recording initially issued. Another example is Red Allen's 'Swing Out', where Allen's fiery contribution on the first take is markedly superior and it was from this matrix that the first record was issued. Considering that those executives in the late twenties and early thirties were relying on their ears and not the 'experts', they more often than not chose well.

* * *

Such a spate of recordings, with attendant press coverage, led to the launching of a movement belonging entirely to its time. This was the network of Rhythm Clubs, gatherings of aficionados who listened to recitals and discussed the respective merits of the records played at these meetings.

In early 1933, Dave Toff, Billy Cotton's manager and later a publisher, gave informal recitals at the Majestic Theatre, Tottenham Court Road, and the City Sale and Exchange, a record shop in Fleet Street, invited enthusiasts to hear the latest jazz releases on the first Monday of every month. There was no admission charge, the invitation being open to those who had purchased one or more records during the previous four weeks. At one of these gatherings collectors Eric Ballard and Bill Elliott met and hatched the idea of an organized Rhythm Club, meeting weekly.

In the classified advertisement page of the *Melody Maker*, 1 July 1933, a notice read, 'Hot Rhythm Club. Members wanted. First class hall in Regent Street taken. Accommodation 100. Write, W. Elliott, 386 Uxbridge Rd W12.'

The following week Eric Ballard of Wakehurst Road, SW11, wrote:

> You have published a letter in a recent issue concerning the formation of a 'hot' record circle in London. I have been considering a similar idea for some time and have in mind a venue in the West End which should prove very suitable from every point of view.
>
> Providing sufficient support can be obtained, the expense would be negligible.
>
> It would not be practical to go into details here, but I would be very happy to discuss the matter with all who care to get in touch with me. Briefly, the accommodation and gramophone would be provided and recitals given by records loaned by members.

Thus the first ever British Rhythm Club, designated the No. 1, held their inaugural meeting in central London, at Victory House, 90–91 Regent Street, on a Monday, 24 June 1933. Ballard was elected the secretary, Elliott the treasurer and Jeff Aldam the chairman. Percy Mathison Brooks and – inevitably it would seem – Edgar Jackson, were made vice-presidents. Forty-five enthusiasts attended this historic meeting.

Pioneers Ballard and Elliott were very enterprising. They kept a list of people who had professed an interest following Elliott's initial advertisement and Ballard's letter but who did not appear on the opening night. One evening the intrepid pair set out – Ballard by car and Elliott by public transport – to call on these parties, urging them to

Meeting of No. 1 Rhythm Club, c.1934. Carlo Krahmer is on drums.

attend future meetings. Elliott, writing of that night in *Swing Music* in August 1935, related how they disturbed a man in his sleep who called from his window to enquire 'What the bloody hell did they want?'* Once he realized the reason for their call he invited them in and they talked 'hot' records until the early hours of the morning. Elliott expressed the hope in this article that the time would come when the club would have its own premises for seven nights a week with every amenity for members. Following the inauguration of the No. 1 Rhythm Club many other clubs were founded throughout the country, numbered in order of their appearance.

The *Melody Maker* gave the venture their full support and the comforting term 'affiliated to the *Melody Maker*' was used by club secretaries in their letter headings and advertisements. The *Melody Maker* published a weekly list of meetings free of charge, giving the names and addresses of the secretaries but rarely telephone numbers. The telephone, like the motor car, was something of a luxury in the thirties.

* This was in the relatively puritanical thirties, and the remark was rendered in *Swing Music* as 'What the – (censored – Ed.) hell did they want?'

John Hammond was a recitalist at the No. 1 Club in 1933. He played a beat-up Paramount recording of Meade Lux Lewis playing 'Honky Tonk Train Blues' a year before he returned to the USA to track down the then

IF YOU READ THIS YOU'RE INTERESTED IN JAZZ

As you're interested in jazz, come along to the No. 1 RHYTHM CLUB after this afternoon's show.

Just two minutes from here at the Bag of Nails, 9 Kingley Street, Regent Street, W.1.

Special Meeting to-night at 6.15. All star Jam Session and record recital.

Provincial visitors heartily welcomed.

Usual meetings every Sunday afternoon at 3, when you can hear

- The best Jam Sessions
- Leading recitalists
- Latest American recordings

BILL ELLIOTT AND REX HARRIS OFFER YOU THIS INVITATION

Advertisement for the No. 1 Rhythm Club. Note the reference to 'provincial visitors'.

forgotten Lewis. Frank Guarante and the Georgians at Lyon's Corner House in 1923 implanted a seed that was to germinate in a fashion which the host, thirteen years old, could never have imagined.

Among the distinguished American stars who visited the club were Louis Armstrong, Benny Carter, pianists Garland Wilson, Buck Washington, Bob Howard, Jack Russin and the violinists Svend Asmussen, from Denmark, and Stéphane Grappelli from France. Every week British jazzmen from the professional and semi-professional areas played in the jam sessions.

In 1936 the No. 1 Rhythm Club ran their first Riverboat Shuffle, an emulation of jazz on the Mississippi riverboats where Louis Armstrong and so many other pioneer jazzmen 'paid their dues'. In the jam sessions some of the No. 1 members, like Jeff Aldam and Rex Harris, took up instruments – the trombone in their case.

The usual trip, from Richmond to Chertsey, some six miles, didn't quite compare in epic length and scenic grandeur with the journey from, say, New Orleans, Louisiana to Davenport, Iowa, over 900 miles, nor was the hired craft, a Thames pleasure steamer, as magnificently baroque in its construction as a genuine Mississippi stern-wheeler, but the spirit was there and 'spirit' was often the operative word. The everyday and irritating licensing laws didn't apply on these boats and full advantage was taken of this freedom from the usual irksome restraints. Alcohol, for

No. 1 Rhythm Club 'Riverboat Shuffle', c.1936

good or bad, has always been a concomitant of jazz activity.

Rather too much, apparently, on the occasion of the club's 1943 Shuffle. This bacchanalia was covered by the *Melody Maker*'s reporter/photographer Jack Marshall. He sternly wrote: 'One lesson the organizers must learn is to curb their well-meaning but quite overdone hospitality. The amount of liquor consumed would have floated the steamer safely through any lock!'

* * *

Although jazz attracted people from all classes, the moving spirits of the No. 1 Rhythm Club were primarily middle-class. For instance, one of the club's founders, George Penniket, became finance controller of the

Electricity Generating Board and still, at the age of seventy-five, retained an adolescent enthusiasm for jazz, regularly having 'sessions' with his brother-in-law, a stripling of seventy.

The jazz-club movement, in its splendidly amateur fashion, was instrumental in furthering jazz appreciation, and a lot of credit is due to those enthusiastic young chaps with their hair parted down the middle and wearing double-breasted waistcoats, Oxford bags and two-tone shoes with pointed toes.

The clubs formed into a federation. The German-born critic, anthropologist, film-maker and author Ernest Borneman, resident in London at the time, recalled the Rhythm Club movement and the beginning of the federation in *Harper's Magazine*, March 1947:

> To understand the function of this sort of organization in the life of the European jazz fan, his utter dependence on the phonograph records will have to be remembered. Cut off from the living music by time as well as space he submits to a peculiar shift of values. The record becomes more important than the music; minor musicians who have left recorded examples of their work behind them become more important than those major musicians who for one reason or another have never got around to a recording studio; and the man who has met the musicians and knows his way through a maze of records becomes more important than the musician himself. Thus the peculiar and altogether top-heavy standing of the so-called 'critic'.
>
> At the weekly meetings of the No. 1 Rhythm Club one such 'critic' after another would make his stand before the public by putting his favourite records on a big phonograph and expecting their entranced members to nod their heads in unison to the succession of adverbs and adjectives that formed the basis of the commentary. Every once in a while a 'critic' who once had his shoes shined by Bix Beiderbecke's favourite bootblack would give a guest recital and those evenings were the highspots of the season.
>
> Some time in 1935, on a pleasant April Sunday, Bill Elliott of the No. 1 Rhythm Club, the late P. Mathison Brooks of the *Melody Maker*, Edgar Jackson of the *Gramophone*, Eric Ballard of *Hot News*, Leonard Hibbs of *Swing Music* and an enthusiastic multitude representing Rhythm Clubs from as far north as Glasgow and as far south as Torquay crowded into the neo-lavatorial splendour of the Royal Hotel, Bloomsbury, and voted the British Rhythm Club Federation into existence. Bill Elliott wanted to call the whole thing the British Federation of Rhythm Clubs, but Percy Brooks, with the nostalgic wisdom of the old newspaperman, warned sternly against the initials B. F. Thus strengthened in our knowledge, we proceeded with the

formation of 'area committees' covering the whole of the United Kingdom like a well-organized Gestapo network.

We were supposed to represent four thousand determined members, but somehow no more than one member could ever be found who was wholly in agreement with himself and in this the jazz movement continued to live up to its highest tradition.

This 'highest tradition' was its internecine strife, and in January 1937 the Federation of British Rhythm Clubs was dissolved through lack of support, despite a resolution from Mr E. Sinclair Traill, of the Leamington Spa Club, that the federation should continue to exist at least for a few more months. Traill was later to found and edit *Jazz Journal*, later called *Jazz Journal International*.

The monthly subscription expected from all club treasurers was three-pence, but even this extraordinarily small amount was often tardily settled and sometimes not at all.

The federation had, arguably, only itself to blame for its failure. It had promoted various albums, one of them by British jazz artists, that met with unanimous criticism. In February 1936 the federation's secretariat sent a collective letter to the *Melody Maker* roundly condemning 'Mike' (Spike Hughes) for savaging the album, which included tracks by his former colleague, tenor saxophonist Buddy Featherstonhaugh. In an editorial the *Melody Maker* chided the federation for its 'apathy' and criticized it for the kind of records promoted and the sort of concerts presented. Sadly – in retrospect – the federation was being condemned for presenting concerts and organizing record sessions of British jazzmen.

* * *

By the mid-thirties the gathering momentum of jazz appreciation encouraged two enthusiastic and idealistic collector-critics to launch their own magazines, each wholly specialist. They were *Swing Music*, edited by Leonard Hibbs, and, published a month later, *Hot News*, edited by Eric Ballard. Both drew from the same coterie of unpaid writers. *Swing Music* became the unofficial organ of the British Rhythm Club movement, an honour No. 1 Club founder, Ballard, would surely have wanted for his paper.

The initial issue of *Swing Music* contained among its many features an article by Bill Elliott pressing fans to support the Federation of British Rhythm Clubs. He proclaimed 'unity is strength' as the watchword needed to make headway with the BBC and the record companies. Both entities, it was heavily emphasized, needed the expert advice of the cognoscenti in the preparation of their programmes and record lists respectively, and this was certainly true of the BBC. John Reith, the Director General, was a stern authoritative man who fashioned the BBC into a 'cultural' force no other country in the world has ever surpassed, but in Reith's austere definitions real jazz had little or no place, not even on the Regional Programme, the 'light' alternative, and certainly never on Sundays until the war.

In successive issues of *Swing Music* there were articles co-authored by two remarkable women, Bettie Edwards and Mary Lytton, both extremely knowledgeable about jazz, an interest then as now seen as a largely male prerogative. Their collective pen-name was B. M. Lytton-Edwards.

Edwin Hinchcliffe, honorary secretary of the York Rhythm Club, wrote an appraisal of Spike Hughes' 'Harlem Symphony' by his British band; James Cross defended some of the journalists on the national dailies who reported on jazz matters sensibly, Hannen Swaffer not being one of this rare species; Spike Hughes wrote an article on spirituals; Leonard Feather contributed potted biographies of jazzmen; the omnipresent Edgar Jackson compiled a short list of Ellington recordings; Spike Hughes made reference to a black saxophonist who copied Buddy Featherstonhaugh's solo on Hughes' 'Buddy's Wednesday Outing'.*

The American correspondent was graphically forthcoming about the peccadilloes of American jazz musicians: unpunctuality, heavy drinking, the smoking of illegal substances, known as 'tea' or 'reefers', and violence. It was reported that clarinettist Albert Nicholas had stabbed a *Blackbirds* showgirl in a fit of jealousy.

Swing Music quoted an unusually cognisant lay critic who, reviewing Spike Hughes' ballet *High Yaller* in the *Morning Post*, wrote: 'When jazz is in question a kind of horrified shudder goes down the spine of the average English critic who seems to think that any liking for it must endanger his reputation for good taste and knowledge.'

---

* The saxophonist was Joe Garland with the Mills Blue Rhythm Band in their version of the same tune. Almost invariably the imitation was by British musicians of American solos, so this was a rare reversal of roles.

In the November/December issue Hibbs sadly announced his financial losses since he launched *Swing Music* and optimistically stated that he intended to seek capital for the formation of a company. The existing circulation of five thousand had to be doubled and Edwin Hinchcliffe made an impassioned plea for the dedicated to rally round the flag.

In the early 1936 issue Bill Elliott reviewed the achievements of the No. 1 Rhythm Club: forty-six meetings, one thousand four hundred and fifty records played, thirty-four different recitals and thirty-one other attractions, such as bands and West End musicians. The balance sheet revealed an expenditure of £170 against an income of £172.

The cover of the June 1935 issue of *Swing Music*, featuring Duke Ellington's orchestra.

Swing Music appeared irregularly throughout 1936, maintaining its high standard, and in the autumn a double issue was published with some of its pages in glossy paper and some in rough-textured sheets. It ended with a full-page advertisement for Alderton's Dress Hire Service, endorsed by the editor; on the back page was an advertisement for Levy's Sound Studios.

This was the last-ever issue of the magazine. There was no announcement of its demise. The difference in quality of paper in the same issue reflected the production problems on a cramped budget, while the advertisements represented a last, futile attempt to give the paper financial stability.

Hot News made its first appearance in April 1935, priced at sixpence: three pence cheaper than its rival. Despite the rivalry, Ballard contributed to *Swing Music* a series of articles, 'From Dixieland to Duke', which had commenced in another paper he edited (with the help of Jeff Aldam) called *Ballroom and Band*. An unworkable combination of jazz content and ballroom dancing features, *Ballroom and Band* lasted from November 1934 to March 1935 and it was from its wreckage that Ballard and Aldam put together *Hot News*.

In the editorial of the first edition of *Hot News* Ballard thundered:

> The band business is in a rotten state. You know that we want to be independent of these rackets. We want to tell the big shots of the band business just where they get off. Quite a few of the aforementioned racketeers will be smiling to themselves when they read this editorial. Well, let them smile. Maybe they will not be ready to do so in a month or so's time. It's up to you.

With the help of the pure in heart, David Jazz in Wakehurst Road, London SW11 was to pit his honesty and integrity against the rottenness and racketeering of Goliath in Tin Pan Alley, WC2. This missionary zeal was characteristic of jazz people of the thirties and forties, and while most of the converted were prepared to speak – and loudly in defence of their chosen faith – they were not prepared to spend a modest few pence in buying the magazine that espoused their cause.

Hot News featured many interesting and informative articles. Like its rival it had an intelligent approach to a music that was slowly becoming accepted in its own right, slowly freeing itself from the dance-band associations so characteristic of the twenties.

Published from April 1935, *Hot News*, edited by Eric Ballard, was Britain's first specialist jazz magazine.

Among its features was an article on the number of Scottish musicians with marked jazz ability; an article by Hugues Panassié countering Continental promoter M. Canetti's accusations that Louis Armstrong *wanted* inferior musicians on his Continental tour so that the limelight would not be deflected from him; and a long and interesting article by New Orleans trombonist Preston Jackson which lauded King Oliver and a trumpeter whose name was totally unknown to British collectors in 1935. This was Mutt Carey, who was to enjoy a totally unexpected popularity in the fifties. Jackson also claimed that the Original Dixieland Jazz Band often hung around King Oliver when he was playing and 'stole' 'Eccentric', including the breaks that imitated a rooster and a baby, and that white trumpeters Paul Mares and Louis Panico took lessons from Oliver. There was a report that Happy Blake cheerfully 'handed over the drums' to Edgar Jackson at the Shim Sham Club, a spot frequented by such jazz-minded dance-band musicians as Duncan Whyte, Alan Ferguson, drummer Maurice Burman and guitarist Ivor Mairants; a review of Hugues Panassié's *Le Jazz Hot*; a report from America that American musicians would not welcome Jack Hylton's band to New York as he had reneged on a deal to bring Fletcher Henderson's band to this country; a reference to 'spades' that read: 'Man, you've never seen those spades at the Savoy Ballroom when they're really high, just on hot music, then there's a sight you must have a gander at before you die'; and a reference to pianist Earl Hines' ego from the same correspondent, George Frazer.

On the last page of the October 1935 issue there was a note on Ballard's new address, but no mention that the paper was folding. Earlier he hinted that he was considering a broader policy that would increase the paper's selling power. This implied departure from the initially avowed policy and the paper's eventual closure was a sad indication that the economic facts of life had compelled him to consider lowering the standards he had naïvely set himself. Ballard, like Hibbs, lost money fondly nurturing the belief that the pure in heart would support a paper devoted entirely to the genuine article, one without dance-band news and 'commercial' advertisements. And, of course, it was absurd that, at that time, two specialist magazines should jostle for the same meagre support; while jazz enthusiasts held strong convictions about their chosen music, getting them to part with money in support of these persuasions was quite another matter.

The demise of both papers was unfortunate, but 'Busker' in the *Melody Maker* wrote: 'Probably one of the great disappointments from my point of view is the absorption by the *Melody Maker* of its rivals on their clos-ing down. One of the great amusements in this office was the perusal of these sheets on their publication and hearty laughter at their latest efforts to down this old rag. Now this is to be denied us and we can only talk about each other and bandleaders. Silly, isn't it?'

Indeed, and uncharitable to crow at the demise of papers that never did anyone any harm. Their thrusts at the 'big shots' were mere pin pricks, but it was unbelievably artless on the part of these brave editors to think that their efforts could survive without advertising revenue.

It was not until approximately ten years later that a stream of magazines was to flow from drawing-rooms and 'dens' throughout the country.

9

Books and Magazines

Books about jazz in the 'jazz age' had little to do with the music. Indeed, the titles were blatant misnomers. In America, Paul Whiteman published his *Jazz* and Henry Osgood *So This is Jazz*. Whiteman's book mentions one genuine jazzman – Gus Mueller – and quotes the clarinettist's trenchant remarks about 'pretty music' without realising their significance (see page 60). Osgood's book made no mention of even one accredited jazzman.

In England R. W. S. Mendl wrote *The Appeal of Jazz*. He too made no reference to any musician whatsoever. Jazz was a curious choice of subject for the author of *Revelation in Shakespeare*, among other titles.

The first book published in Britain that had any real connection with the subject was *All About Jazz* by Stanley Nelson, which appeared in 1934. Nelson, B.Sc., oboist and pianist, had contributed to the *Clarion*, *Era*, *Rhythm*, *Melody Maker* and the pre-war *Fanfare*, in which he railed against 'the pansies infecting the BBC'. The book has an introduction by Jack Hylton, whose knowledge of jazz was sketchy, even if it had been improved by the impact of Ellington's brass section by the time this volume was published.

Hylton wrote:

> From its birth jazz has been surrounded by a gloom which, even in these enlightened days, is still apparent in the attitude of the music-loving public. Since the really tentative days when I formed my orchestra I have seen the gradual moulding of public taste in popular music in the direction of the best jazz and I have done my best to follow that trend.

I believe the best jazz orchestras have been instrumental in bringing before the public much that is good in music in a manner at once entertaining, instructive and original.

Jazz has come now, as Mr Nelson says, to be a potent factor in the lives of people, for the influence of popular music on the masses today is really amazing.

Typically, Hylton was confusing jazz and dance music, which were not necessarily one and the same thing. As a bandleader he played a considerable part in fudging the lines of demarcation yet, as an impresario bringing Duke Ellington to this country, he unwittingly helped to clarify the wide difference between ordinary dance music and the vitally alive and creative music called jazz. Nowadays, Jack Hylton's own recordings have little more than period curiosity value. He probably wrote this introduction before his Ellington experience.

Nelson, in his introduction, wrote: 'In presenting this account of the rise of jazz in Europe I have been compelled to trace its origins and popularity in America, the land of its birth. That I have been able to do so is largely due to Henry Osgood's *So This is Jazz*, a most informative book which I heartily recommend to readers in search of further information.'

In his first chapter, 'Syncopation',* Nelson gives his account of the origins of jazz:

> The intervention of the war [1914–18] left the civilized world in a mental chaos and jazz was the very stimulant it required. Vulgarity was the predominating feature of 1918 jazz and 'noise' was the only word that could aptly describe it; but the passing of the years and the gradual settling down of people has brought back melody as the vital ingredient, with harmony as the furnishing and rhythm as the sauce.
>
> From a position of pre-eminence the drummer has been relegated to the background, until we have the modern syncopated orchestra falling naturally into two sections, melodic and rhythmic. The latter section, although the more important of the two, gets (as usual in life!) little of the praise, for it is the melody instruments such as the saxophones, trumpet, etc, which catch the eye of the uninitiated.

---

* Nelson cites Lafcadio Hearn as using the word forty years previously, but without a specific reference. Dick Holcroft, in *Vintage Jazz Music*, claimed to have read every line of Hearn without finding the word 'jazz'.

In describing orchestrated 'jazz' Nelson was indeed correct. But in jazz proper the rhythmic and melodic parts are, or should be, intertwined. Although Nelson states that to 'compare modern syncopation with serious music, despite the works of Gershwin, is manifestly ridiculous', reinforcing his point by referring to the over-orchestration of banal tunes, he nevertheless devotes much time and praise to the Gershwin and Whiteman alliance. He acknowledges that much early jazz emanated from New Orleans and quotes Osgood (in turn quoting the distinguished English music critic Ernest Newman) comparing early 'methods of jazz' with the concerted singing of the fourteenth century:

> In that epoch people were only just beginning to realize dimly what a jolly effect could be made by a number of people singing different things at different times. As yet they did not know how to combine different melodic strands, so that they indulged experimentally in a sort of catch-as-catch-can descant . . . the singers – amateurs like the early jazzers – used to decide upon a given canto fermo, and then all improvise on it simultaneously. Writers of the period have told us of the horrible results.

What Osgood, Newman and, to a point, Nelson, didn't appreciate was that the early jazz bands – the only one they could have heard being the Original Dixieland Jazz Band – played different melodic strands that followed a logical and compatible pattern, the interweaving being the essence of their music. But to a generation that had grown accustomed to the deliberately compartmentalized rhythmic and melodic parts of the twenties and thirties dance band, early jazz would indeed have sounded like 'catch-as-catch-can descant'. This was yet another example of misapplied phraseology addressing a subject about which the authors had a completely wrong conception.

Nelson's non-jazz material comprised potted histories of dance bands and biographies of dance musicians, crooners and songwriters. At the time he was writing (1932–33), 'jazz' was a collective term covering the manifold aspects of popular music of which dance bands, crooners and songwriters were a part. The non-jazz names in his book include singers Sophie Tucker, known as the 'Red-Hot Mama' and 'Queen of Jazz', Gracie Fields, Elsie Carlisle, Bing Crosby and, inevitably, bandleaders Jack Hylton and Paul Whiteman.

Of the so-called 'King of Jazz' he writes: 'Whiteman was (in 1923 and 1926) a revelation. The perfect balance and tone and the special orchestrations of Ferde Grofé caused the sceptics to reconsider their opinion.' The sceptics were the 'Crowhards' and again there is an implied seeking of academic approval for music that had come a long way from the 'crudities' of the original. 'He played at the London Hippodrome and Grafton Galleries, was presented to the Prince of Wales and generally created the biggest sensation since Sousa,' he goes on. The references to a London theatre, a rather exclusive ballroom, royalty and the composer of famous marches had the ring of respectability which the Whiteman disciples desperately sought and were quoted where it was thought such references would strengthen the case for making jazz 'respectable'.

Nelson made admiring references to the size of Whiteman's ensemble. 'Whereas the average band consists of about twelve men, Whiteman has thirty. In this way he was able to get a full complement of strings and this, coupled with the "doubling" propensities of the players, allows him a huge palette of tone colours to produce the most bizarre effects.'

Nelson cites the programme of Whiteman's famous Aeolian Hall concert in New York, which culminated in the first-ever performances of Gershwin's 'Rhapsody in Blue'. One of the tunes played was 'Livery Stable Blues'. In his *Jazz* Whiteman admits that he was shocked when this was well received. 'When they laughed and seemed pleased with the crude jazz of the past I had for a moment the panicky feeling that they hadn't realized the attempt at burlesque – they were ignorantly applauding the thing on its merits.'

Yet another ironic twist in the history of jazz. And, according to H. O. Brunn, the soaring clarinet of Gus Mueller was heard for the last time as five men from Whiteman's orchestra paid one fleeting tribute to the memory of pure jazz in playing 'Livery Stable Blues'. Was it on this rather overblown occasion that Mueller made his simple, pointed remarks?

Nelson refers to the Original Dixieland Jazz Band and grants that, compared with records of his own day, the Dixielanders 'are not as *démodé* as one would think'. Of black orchestras he writes: 'Much of their work is still aesthetically on the level of their forerunners in New Orleans, but from a technical point of view they can give points to Whiteman, even . . .'

It was a favourite ploy of music journalists at the time to dwell on the 'future of jazz', and this was the heading of Nelson's final chapter.

Gershwin is quoted on the 'composing' of jazz, but in a long, discursive and often contradictory chapter Nelson has this to say about black jazzmen:

> In the early days of jazz the negro exponents were usually condemned by the experts as too crude. They had undoubted technique on their instruments – some of the playing was colossal, but their jazz had a blatancy which was far from pleasing to white ears, and the peculiarly throaty type of singing affected seemed simply vulgar. Famous bands like Duke Ellington's, Fletcher Henderson's, Louis Armstrong's etc., were all very well in their way but their jazz was a poor thing beside the refined product of the best white bands.
>
> It is rather strange that this opinion has been very much modified since then. Today Ellington, Armstrong and other coloured bands have practically assumed the position of arbitrators of modern rhythmic style. Ellington is a very fine musician and a composer of real promise.
>
> It is my belief that most of the future development of jazz will come from the coloured race themselves and not from us. We have certainly played a great part in emancipating our present popular music from the crude form of the early cake-walks and we have standardized the instrumentation of the popular dance band. But our mania for order had led us into a cul de sac. We lack the spontaneity of the coloured people and their innate feel for the jazz idiom. When their bands are playing they are as absorbed as the dancers whom Beverly Nichols described as being drunk with rhythm. Their playing is characterized by its extreme fervour; instead of playing in the detached manner of white bands, these coloured artists subordinate every feeling to the job in hand.
>
> They do not seem to be influenced by any dictates of commercialism. Indeed, I should imagine that it would be difficult for them to play in any other style. I am not particularly enamoured of the style of singing adopted by these coloured bands, but I must admit that it is far more rhythmic than the luke-warm, plum-in-the-mouth style of some of the white vocalists.
>
> The work of the coloured bands is at once the acme of sophistication and extreme naivety. It bristles with instrumental virtuosity, yet has the strain of improvisation which gives it a simplicity which is more apparent than real. But they are superlatively good to dance to and that is the supreme test.

Clearly Nelson was reluctant to change long cherished views but, to give him credit, he admitted his doubts and confusion. It is obvious that he started the book (mainly based on his articles in *Rhythm*) when the genuine jazz giants had yet to play in Britain. A Whiteman admirer, he, albeit reluctantly, realized that the crown rested uneasily on his idol's head.

It is significant that Nelson's writing becomes more interesting when, even unwittingly, there is the expression of fundamental truths, and these few paragraphs render the trivia of gossip, scraps of information, half truths and contradictions that largely comprise the rest of the book of no consequence. However reluctant to jettison old misconceptions, he had reached the heart of the matter.

Between the time he started this book and its publication events had caused this change of heart. He had cried at hearing 'Mood Indigo' by Duke Ellington at the Palladium on 12 June 1933, after he had been so disdainful about the band. Now, in 1934, he, like many others, was going through a period of reappraisal, some of it clearly painful.

Nelson wasn't alone in his contradictions and wavering convictions. This was symptomatic of the period's critical dilemmas. The early influence of Edgar Jackson had been challenged by John Hammond, Spike Hughes and their fellow spirits. The visits of Louis Armstrong and Duke Ellington had drastically brought about a new awareness. 'Symphonic' jazz was beginning to be seen for what it was: a mess of ephemeral trivia; a falsehood, falsely worshipped.

At this time the jazz cognoscenti generally were at the crossroads. They were looking back to the simple origins of the music, but were also now confronted by the relatively complex music of Ellington, just two strands in jazz's rich tapestry. Criteria were rapidly changing, but they were by no means formalized. There were further eruptions to come that would drastically alter standards and attitudes.

* * *

During Ellington's 1933 visit one of the stream of 'intellectuals' who visited him, or paid him tribute in print, was composer Constant Lambert. Ellington mentions this in his *Music is My Mistress*; Spike Hughes referred to Lambert's interest in Duke in his *Melody Maker* articles.

There is not the space to quote Lambert at length, but the following extracts from 'The Spirit of Jazz' in his *Music Ho!* indicate just how woolly and peripheral his observations were:

> By jazz, of course, I mean the whole movement roughly designated as such, and not merely that section of it known as Afro-American, or more familiarly as 'Harlem'. The negro once enjoyed a monopoly of jazz, just as

England once enjoyed a monopoly of the industrial revolution, but for the negroes to imagine that all jazz is their native province is as if an Englishman were to imagine that all locomotives were built by his compatriots. Even the Harlem section of jazz is by no means so African as might be supposed.

There is a double yet opposed conspiracy to persuade one that modern dance music represents a purely negroid tradition. On the one hand, we have the crusty old colonels, the choleric judges and beer-sodden columnists who imagine they represent the European tradition, murmuring 'swamp stuff', 'jungle rhythms', 'negro decadence' whenever they hear the innocent and anodyne strains of the average English jazz band, hugely enjoying their position of Cassandra prophesying the downfall of the white woman. On the other hand, we have the well-meaning but rather sentimental propagandists of the negro race, only too eager to point out that the negroes are the only begetters of a movement that has admittedly swept all over the world and that provides an exotic influence far exceeding the localized exoticism of Cocteau and his followers. The only flaw in both these arguments is that most jazz is written and performed by cosmopolitan Jews [*sic*]. Were this fact sufficiently realized, it would hardly abate the fury of the colonels and the columnists, for from their point of view the Jew is just as much an enemy of the British and Holy Roman Empires as the negro; but it might slightly curb the hysterical enthusiasm of the poor-white negro propagandists whose sentimental effusions must be so embarrassing to the intelligent negro himself. The particular type of white inferiority complex responsible for this propaganda has been so ruthlessly dealt with by Wyndham Lewis in his 'Paleface' that one can add little to his conclusions except to point out that in music also the same game of intellectual 'pat-a-cake' is taking place . . .

If anyone doubts the essential element of European sophistication in jazz, it is a simple matter for him to compare a typical piece of jazz music, such as Duke Ellington's 'Swampy River', first with a lyric piece by Grieg and then with a record of native African music. It must be clear to the most prejudiced listener that apart from a few rhythmical peculiarities the Ellington piece has far more in common with the music of Grieg. I am not denying for a moment the racial characteristics implicit in these rhythmical peculiarities – I am only pointing out that Ellington, like all negro composers, has to use the European harmonic framework. Ellington's works are no more examples of African folk song than James Weldon Johnson's poems are examples of the Dahomey dialect; they both represent the application of the negro temperament to an alien tradition and an acquired language.

The emotional appeal of jazz depends not only on its rhythms which, though childishly simple compared with those of African folk music, may legitimately be accounted African in origin, but also on its harmonic colour, which cannot conceivably be traced back to Africa for the simple reason that harmony as we understand it does not exist in primitive African music. Hornbostel in his admirable handbook on African music records only one example of pure harmonic writing in the whole history of his discoveries, and that consisted of two chords at the end of a satirical song about the local missionary, the intention of which was obviously to parody the lugubrious effect of his harmonium.

The harmonic element in Afro-American music is an acquired element mainly due to the religious music of the Anglo-Saxon, an influence that naturally had a more powerful effect on the *déraciné* negroes of America, bereft of their language and their cultural traditions, than on the self-satisfied if not contented negroes of Africa. We find it hard now to realize not only the emotional effect but the full sensual effect of the hymns of John Bacchus Dykes and his followers.

Regarding jazz, Lambert's heart may have been in the right place but his observations and strictures were as off-beam as those of any lay press hack and all the more perplexing coming from a man who, while not exactly part of the classical music establishment, was highly respected. The ordinary collector spending his half a crown weekly on a new 78 for his collection would have been a lot more illuminating on the subject. It is surprising that as late as December 1983 the perceptive Steve Race, musician and journalist, should in his Radio 3 series 'Jazz in Perspective', speak highly of Lambert's support of jazz.

Swing That Music, published in 1937 and ostensibly co-written by Louis Armstrong with Horace Gerlach, was a very shoddy and much criticized book, and it was years later before an accurate account of Armstrong's life, *Louis*, by Max Jones and John Chilton, was published (1971).

The first truly scholarly analysis of jazz was *Hot Jazz* by the French critic Hugues Panassié, written in 1934 and published in Britain in 1937. Informed as it was, there was little mention of the New Orleans musicians who shaped the music in its origins. This was the main content of an extremely influential book, *Jazzmen*, written in 1938 by Charles Edward Smith and Frederic Ramsey Jr. It was the first volume to deal extensively with the grass roots of the music. It presented a new face to criteria and its publication led to the discovery of New Orleans jazz on record by pioneers still alive and – until this work – forgotten. *Jazzmen* was imported into Britain and received belated publication here in 1949.

The first honest autobiography of a jazz musician was Mezz Mezzrow's *Really the Blues* (co-authored with Bernard Wolfe) and published in

Britain in 1946 when the 'revival' was getting under way, and its account of a twenties white, Jewish jazz musician identifying himself with the coloured race had particular appeal. The narrative included some quite graphic accounts of his term of imprisonment for dope peddling, and of his own experiences with drugs.

In 1939, *Young Man with a Horn* by Dorothy Baker was published. This was a highly romanticized account of a jazzman's life, allegedly based on that of Bix Beiderbecke and later, in 1950, to be the basis of an unintentionally hilarious film starring Kirk Douglas called *Young Man of Music*, the producers, or censor, having decided that the original title was unsuitable for British filmgoers. It showed admirable concern for our prurient susceptibilities, but the jazz enthusiast could only wish that the makers had shown equal care for historical fact and chosen someone more musically appropriate to play the hero's trumpet on the soundtrack than Harry James.

It wasn't until after the war that, with histories, biographies and discographies, jazz books amounted to a complete library of over a thousand volumes. In the meantime there emerged a spate of little magazines, all of them home-produced, and most of them spreading the gospel according to New Orleans.

* * *

At the outbreak of war in 1939 it had been twenty years since the Original Dixieland Jazz Band had first startled British ears generally, outraged the clergy and classicists and incurred the sarcasm of the press. In those intervening years jazz had revealed itself as a music of infinitely varied nature, but at the end of the thirties the American scene was dominated by the large 'swing' bands led by Benny Goodman, Artie Shaw, Woody Herman, Jimmy and Tommy Dorsey, Bunny Berigan, Harry James, Gene Krupa and Charlie Barnet.

These bands were technically skilled, their arrangements generally repetitive and predictable, and only the solos made one distinguishable from the other. They were enormously popular and generously represented in the record catalogues. British bands widely imitated them.

In contrast, HMV issued records of the Duke Ellington Orchestra, then enjoying a resurgence. With the entry of Jimmy Blanton on the string bass the rhythm section displayed a new jauntiness; the addition of

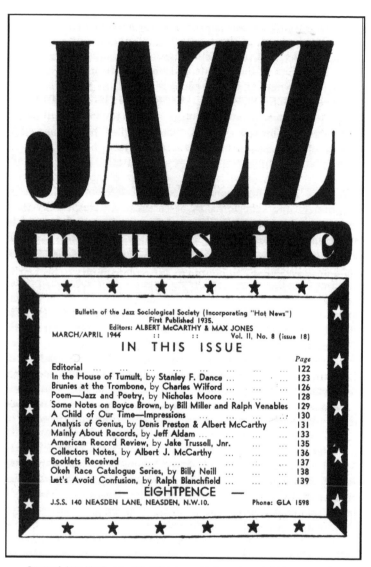

JAZZ
music

Bulletin of the Jazz Sociological Society (Incorporating "Hot News")
First Published 1935.
Editors: ALBERT McCARTHY & MAX JONES
MARCH/APRIL 1944   ::   ::   Vol. II, No. 8 (issue 18)

IN THIS ISSUE

— EIGHTPENCE —

J.S.S. 140 NEASDEN LANE, NEASDEN, N.W.10.   Phone: GLA 1598

Cover of *Jazz Music*, arguably Britain's most informed specialist jazz magazine

Ben Webster on tenor saxophone and the composing and arranging collaborations of Billy Strayhorn and Duke Ellington were combining to produce even more entrancing orchestral textures, bringing jazz a stage further in its development.

In further contrast HMV issued current recordings by Sidney Bechet's New Orleans Footwarmers, Jelly Roll Morton's New Orleans Jazzmen and Muggsy Spanier's Ragtime Band, these appealing particularly to the fundamentalist critics and fans.

Researchers into the history of jazz led to the rehabilitation of many pioneers. Morton, Bechet and Muggsy Spanier had languished in the thirties, and the time was ripe for Spanier to lead his own uncompromising jazz band instead of having to rely on Ted Lewis for his meal ticket.

Brunswick issued their *New Orleans* album with Louis Armstrong and Sidney Bechet, reunited for the first time since they recorded for Clarence Williams in 1924–25. Other contributions to the album were by fellow New Orleanians, trumpeter Red Allen and clarinettist Ed Hall. Parlophone reissued many of the old Louis Armstrong Hot Five and Seven classics, along with much other historic material.

* * *

Edgar Jackson, reinstated as the *Melody Maker*'s jazz critic by the exigencies of war-time staff shortage, castigated the Bechets, Mortons and reissued Armstrongs, but praised the Spaniers.

In 1941 the *Melody Maker*, now edited by Zahl Ray Sonin and much reduced in size with its print almost microscopic, introduced a weekly feature called 'Collector's Corner' that embraced purely jazz discographical details and arguments, potted biographies, news culled from American magazines and a record exchange and mart. It was initially edited by Bill Elliott, then still secretary of the No. 1 Rhythm Club, and Jeff Aldam.

The idea of this feature was gladly accepted by Sonin, who saw it as the opportunity to contain the earnest, disputative jazzers in one page instead of occupying the limited space he had to publish features and information about the dance bands that really sold the paper.

In 1942 'Collector's Corner' reported that a band led by trumpeter Bunk Johnson had recorded for the Jazzman label in New Orleans. The label was the brainchild of William Russell, a pioneer collector and early writer about New Orleans jazz who 'rediscovered' Bunk. 'The Corner' marvelled at the fact that the combined ages of the band totalled some three hundred and twenty years. Johnson was sixty-three, his clarinettist George Lewis forty-two. It was the first time any of these veterans, who were direct links with the very origins of jazz, had recorded. Another band, of white men, based in San Francisco and playing in the style of the King Oliver Creole Jazz Band, was Lu Watters' Yerba Buena Jazz Band.

The unavailability of these records and their historical associations gave them a glowing aura of desirability and presumed musical quality not always confirmed upon release, but this didn't prevent them from having a quite extraordinary influence, particularly on young white men, primarily in Britain, who attempted to play in this style.

These historical and revivalist records, whether issued in Britain or not, engendered and were the editorial substance of the first independent jazz magazines to be published since the demise of *Hot News* and *Swing Music* in the mid-thirties. They were run on the evangelical hope and faith of their editors and the charity of their unpaid contributors.

The pioneer magazine of this era was *Jazz Music*, first published in 1942. It was the organ of the Jazz Sociological Society, jointly edited by the society's founders, Albert McCarthy and Max Jones, and published at 140 Neasden Lane, London NW10. The portentous title of the parent organization (that had no function or activity outside the publication of *Jazz Music*) was consistent with the index and editorial of their first, duplicated, issue.

Bulletin of the Jazz Sociological Society

For Students of Hot Music

Editors: Albert McCarthy and Max Jones

Production: Charles Gustavus, Jnr

Issued from JSS, 140 Neasden Lane, NW10

Annual Subscription (valid until Dec. 1942) 1/6d

INDEX

In our preliminary leaflet we undertook to survey the jazz field and issue periodical bulletins, supported by records, to members of the JSS. This ambitious programme has been modified for the time being and we have produced our first periodical somewhat prematurely as a result of consistent demands from jazz students.

For the benefit of those who have not seen the Society's published leaflet, we reprint its aims below.

A handful of critics have formed the Society with a view to investigate and survey the New Orleans origins of jazz, the history of it and its place in society.

The Society intends to delve into the social significance of jazz, to issue records to support this point and to issue bulletins on the following points:

ORIGINS OF JAZZ

1 The urge to create jazz was purely coloured.
2 Development of the minstrel.
3 A reaction of the machine age.
4 The effect of the industrial development on slave owners and subsequent reactions on Negroes.

INFLUENCE OF ECONOMIC CONDITIONS ON JAZZ

1 Storyville.
2 Shift to Chicago.
3 Prohibition and stock boom.
4 Wall Street crash and Depression period.

In this and subsequent issues, the editorial and contents emphasized the superiority of black musicians, especially those from New Orleans; the highly popular and financially successful swing bands were soundly berated, and there was much concern about racism in the United States, particularly where it applied to the jazz musician.

After four issues on duplicating paper, *Jazz Music* was printed on high-quality paper with the layouts, photographs and typography profess-ionally organized by Ian Bradbery, MSIA. The standard of writing was generally high, the contributors including Charles Edward Smith, Jeff Aldam, Frederic Ramsey, Ernest Borneman, Edwin Hinchcliffe, Eugene Williams and Denis Preston (later St Denis Preston) in addition to those listed in the first issue.

Jazz Music, with other publications of a similar nature, ran into difficul-ties with the paper rationing authorities and in order to comply with the regulations produced individual booklets including *Chicago Documentary* by Frederic Ramsey, *Piano Jazz* by Max Jones and Albert McCarthy, *Record Information* by John Rowe, *This is Jazz* (an exposition of New Orleans Jazz) by Rudi Blesh and *A Critic Looks at Jazz* by Ernest Borneman. The prices for these highly informative documents ranged between one shilling and two shillings and sixpence.

The Jazz Sociological Society distributed what was the most enlighten-ing and entertaining of all jazz magazines, *Record Changer*, published in Washington and featuring cartoons by Gene Deitch that amusingly illus-trated some of the manic aspects of jazz researchers and collectors.

Jazz Music continued publication until 1953. It was the inspiration for many similar magazines in this now completely changed climate of jazz appreciation. New Orleans was the epicentre of the shock waves that rippled round the jazz globe. That city was the emotive as well as the musical focal point of this new awareness and articles about its jazzmen were the substance of these crusading broadsheets.

The earnest missionaries who produced these papers were mostly in occupations and professions far removed from journalism, and this was often evident in the writing. A good many were not in the armed forces. Some were conscientious objectors, many in 'reserved' occupa-tions; others were medically unfit for military service. It was another irony of jazz that individuals not actively concerned in the fight against Nazism and its racial persecution were, from the safety of their front

Max Jones (*left*) and Albert McCarthy (*right*), founders of the Jazz Sociological Society, with jazz writer and later record producer Denis Preston, 1943

rooms, fervently righteous in their objections to racism in the society of Britain's principal ally three thousand miles distant.

They attacked the 'commercialism' of the *Melody Maker* and were particularly critical of Edgar Jackson. These zealots were the first of the British 'Spade Ravers', this replacing 'Jig Chasers' as a contemptuous term for those who were held to have overly lauded the black man and emotively exaggerated his contribution to jazz.

Other organizations included the Discographical Society, whose booklets were edited by Max Jones' brother Cliff; the South of Scotland Jazz Society, whose duplicated sheet, *Jazz Commentary*, was edited by Donald Biggar (an RAF flying officer who later perished in an air raid over Germany); and the Northern Society for Jazz Study, whose sheet was issued under that title and whose 'officiators' were Vernon M. Thorne, Ernest F. Love and A. Leslie Jowett. Its title was later changed to the National Society for Jazz Study.

In 1943, the North London and Southgate Jazz Society was formed and published a sheet called *Jazz Tempo*, edited by John Rowe. In his editorial of 15 May 1943 Rowe made reference to a 'storm in a teacup' that resulted from a disparaging reference in *Melody Maker*'s 'Collector's Corner' to 'a glut of rhythm club magazines'. The editorial ended on a selectively friendly note: 'We extend our hand of friendship to the editors of *Jazz Music and Discography*.' Not to the editors of 'Collector's Corner'. Internecine strife was commonplace in the little world of jazz.

In Nottingham the Jazz Appreciation Society was founded by James Asman and Bill Kinnell, co-editors of its magazine *Jazz Records*. The early contributions were from the editors and from Graham Boatfield, Kennedy Brown and Stanley Dance, and the first editorial also caustically referred to the criticisms of little magazines in 'Collector's Corner'.

Jazz Records was notable for the anti-authoritarian views of its contributors, particularly Graham Boatfield, an ideological Quixote of the forties thrusting his lance against all manifestations of 'commercialism'. There were few purer in heart than Boatfield and only the very 'pure' artists, nearly all of these black, met with his approval.

In April 1943, the editorial advised that they had been forced to suspend regular publication until the paper-supply situation had eased, but that they would be issuing occasional booklets. Their first was one on Fletcher Henderson by discographer G. F. Gray-Clarke, and contained an editorial detailing the new system of issues to conform with instructions from the paper-control authorities.

They lamented being denied the use of the *Melody Maker*'s advertising columns:

> We ask you to insist that your local Rhythm Clubs and record shops stock numbers of our editions so that they will become available to more and more Jazz students, particularly to those serving in the Forces. If you, the British Jazz fraternity, allow the Jazz magazines in this country to stop production through your own lack of support and help, you will have killed the only real outlet for your views and interests. And, whilst we admit the service the *Melody Maker* has done to 'hot music' we also realize that it must serve a commercially minded public, too. And to a greater extent.
>
> We intend to devote our pages to the interests of the ordinary jazz fan. That is our policy and one which we believe to be fully worthwhile. But we need your ardent support all the time now, and more members. Don't let us down!

There are strong echoes of Hibbs and Ballard in these editorial cries for support. Sadly, these pleas were equally ineffective.

Later it was discovered that Edgar Jackson had reported the regular (illegal) issues of these magazines to the authorities, by way of retaliating against their sustained attacks on him. He was ever the opportunist.

The 'Society of Jazz Appreciation for the Younger Generation' published a bulletin called *Intro . . . the Younger Generation*. The founders and editors (whose combined ages totalled thirty-one years) were Michael Wadsley and John Gee. They were the main contributors, with additional articles by Brian Rust, Owen Bryce and Albert McCarthy. In the first bulletin, this duo of young experts, representing the 'Younger Generation', listed in detail the society's aims, which included the ambitious intention to 'decide the future of this most progressive art form'. The society's headquarters were at 47 King Street, Tring, Hertfordshire; an unlikely address, it would seem now, from which two schoolboys could decide the future of a progressive art form, but with the missionary zeal of those days anything seemed possible.

Pick-Up was founded in 1946 by the ex-secretary of the Leamington Spa Rhythm Club, Sinclair Traill, who had spoken against the dissolution of the British Federation of Rhythm Clubs at the Tavistock Hotel, Bloomsbury in 1936. *Pick-Up* was independent of any 'society'. The editor, patently not one to be associated with left-wing organizations, published his magazine from the palpably middle-class environs of Ladbroke Square, London W11, and sensibly opened his pages to advertisers. He adhered religiously to the economically sound tradition of jazz magazines in his encouragement of unpaid contributions.*

Albert McCarthy launched *Jazz Forum* from the Black Hut, Fordingbridge, Hampshire, in 1946. It contained, in its relatively short life, many informative and well-written articles on jazz, but suffered from a very self-conscious 'intellectuality' and was overly 'sociological'. It was printed in various colours: this issue in a royal blue, that issue in a strawberry pink. There were articles with titles like 'Clock and Song of Our Anxiety', 'The Psychology of the Hot Solo' and 'Jazz Surrealism and the Doctor', plus poems and prose by Toni Del Renzio, George Woodcock and Louis Adeane. In the first issue of *Jazz Forum*, undated, priced at two shillings and sixpence, Del Renzio contributed a panegyric on Jimmie Lunceford's orchestra, entitled 'On the Outskirts of Town', after a title recorded by Lunceford. The florid style was characteristic:

> With this perspective, instrument of feeling as much as of intellect, we are able to apprehend *actively* the blues in all its glorious mutations. Of these,

---

* *Pick-Up* later became *Jazz Journal*.

recently, perhaps the loveliest and most inspiring is that wrought by the Jimmie Lunceford band weaving their sonorous ectoplasm 'On the Outskirts of Town'. Dissatisfied with the picturesque folk-material that has so often served to hide the blues even from devoted and earnest admirers, this band has not hesitated to eschew any limiting and inhibiting factors. Skilfully they have avoided, however, destroying the quintessential jazz which alone, like an elixir, can prevent a pitiful Ellingtonian collapse into the negative and sterile hues of beige, brown-pink, primrose yellow.

On the outskirts of town we learn to appreciate the fiery flow of jazz as distinct from the watery flow of the great fatheads, Brahms, Beethoven . . . apocalyptic, the blues light up the future and its promises. On the outskirts of town man and woman each so long containing the germ of the other, melt qualitatively into the whole circle of light and dark where the intended and unexpected are reconciled, the arranged and improvised in the music of Lunceford . . .

Eric Thacker contributed a poem in tribute to trombonist Joseph 'Tricky Sam' Nanton in the Duke Ellington Orchestra:

> Now the controlled madness,
> its eyeless shapes hovering
> over the black tears'
> swamp,
> with its wide mouths
> froglike, its gnarled and
> purpled throat crying
> hopelessly in the night;
> with its intestinal symbols
> translucent in depth of depth,
> worming redly its fevered flowerlets
> in the black,
> black but white bellied dead.
> Oh, spectre of the street
> of mid-day, suspended like
> the train whistle; its adolescent
> joy, its mature despair.
> There's ink on your nose and there's
> white in your hair. Splayed toes
> of grief battering the doors of day.

The inclusion of 'literary' material in a magazine mostly devoted to jazz was indicative of the desire to give it an aura of cultural standing. Although different in approach, this desire for respectability was akin to the support Jackson and others gave the jazz prettifiers of the twenties. The race and class aspects of jazz were stressed from an anarchist point of view.

Discographer Brian Rust, vehemently right-wing in his views from his very early years, was critical of the literary exercises and of the long-haired and sandalled visionaries who wrote such prose in *Jazz Forum*. The editor of *Pick-Up* manifestly shared these sentiments and was happy to print a piece by Rust satirizing the contributors to his variously-hued rival. In the November 1946 issue of *Pick-Up* Rust became – for the first and last time – a poet.

ODE TO JELLY ROLL MORTON

by Brian Rust (with apologies to Toni Del Renzio, Louis Adeane, George Woodcock and all stations to Colney Hatch)

> Piano,
> Tinkling in the backroom of a gin-
>   palace in a hundred cities of the
>   USA,
> Wherever the capitalist writ of RCA
>   Victor may run,
> Mr Jelly Lord, the expression of the
>   down-trodden masses of the prole-
>   tariat,
> (Funny, he calls himself 'Mr Jelly
>   Lord' but there it is; you'd think
>   if we were so much against the
>   Upper Ten he'd
> Call himself something quite
>   different.)
> So much piano.
> Piano of a million notes, chords and
>   heaven knows what, ragging and
>   stomping and strokin' away,

The player is dead, but his records
    live on,
So long as there are plutocratic
    fatheads like us to collect them.
    I'm sorry,
I was forgetting; it is only Bach,
    Beethoven and Brahms – poor filthy
    old Brahms, bless his Hungarian
    Dances –
Who are fatheads; no one else
Is.
(I've wandered off the subject, but
    one is apt to do that in poems of
This sort; the more you do so, the
    greater genius
You are.)
Dear Doctor Jazz, the greatest of
    them all, why do crazy people
Malign you so? Ah, they don't
understand, no
One understands but me.
No one but I could understand the
    deep
Agony you felt in mind when you
    hollered 'Aah, hello, Central, give
    me Doctor Jazz!'
(Number engaged; will you hold the line?)
The aching tone of Omer Simeon's
    clarinet (unless of course you are
    talking about a record like 'Fickle
    Fay Creep' where it's the white
    Victor House man, in which case
    delete the following)
Proclaims a striving, struggling up-
    wards against the powers of tyranny,
    a thought, a dreamsequence, this
    tumult of images
Projected by the turn of a disc through
the Incomprehensibility of Memory-

past to the Great Unknown of
Memory-future never mind Memory-
present . . .
What the hell is all this about?
Your guess, as Mr Teagarden says on
BrE 01913 (VG sale, 6/-)
Is just as good as
Mine.

It wasn't only the pseudo (as many would have it) literary jazz publications that were lampooned. The magazine *Jazzology*, edited and published by Charles Harvey, 208 High Street, Harlesden, London NW10 was amateurishly produced. It published totally unsubstantiated claims of patently fictitious record sessions and events, fell headlong for a spoof, reproduced from the *Record Changer*, announcing the most unlikely and anomalous cast for a forthcoming Hollywood epic called 'New Orleans', and became a repository for hoaxes by waggish collectors. These flashes of humour made for welcome light relief from the usual solemn pronouncements of the mid-forties jazz journalist, but despite the pretentious literary excursions and the heavy emphasis on socio-political factors – important as they were – these little magazines played a very important role in the development of jazz appreciation in Britain and honours are due to the Jones/McCarthy *Jazz Music* for its consistently high standard of content and production.

10

Discographers

One issue of *Jazz Forum* included a discography of the Original Dixieland Jazz Band by Eric Tonks. Had the time machine been a reality and operated in 1919 to give a glimpse of the future it would have been instructive and no doubt entertaining to study the reaction of the band to this listing of the recordings they had made or were going to make, those they had made but which were unissued, and many that were made under their name with only one or two of the original members present.

Surely they would have gaped at the wealth of meticulous detail: personnels, titles, dates and places of recordings; record companies' matrix and catalogue numbers; and labels of various countries in which their records were issued. Had they read some of the more serious reviews they might have been simultaneously amused and rendered apoplectic by these often ponderous critical assessments of their 'art'. They had claimed to be the originators of jazz but had never had artistic pretensions. On the other hand they would not have been too pleased with those who dismissed them as tricksy copyists. Hundreds of other musicians who made records in the twenties and thirties were to be surprised and at times offended by later evaluation of their ABC years.

Discographies of hundreds upon hundreds of early jazz, jazz-related and blues records were printed in home-produced magazines, forming a groundbase for the major compilations to come. It was essentially a collective, widespread and continuing process of cross-checking, correction and counter-correction.

The tabulation processes were made even more difficult in that only a tiny proportion of the records listed had ever been released in Britain. A discography could do a listing of, say, fifty records, without the compiler having heard one of them. Conversely, he often had to rely on aural identification in the absence of firm data.

Even in America, land of jazz, discographers were similarly disadvantaged. The minor labels, particularly, hadn't been widely distributed; some were long deleted from the catalogues and many of the companies were defunct, their files destroyed.

The jazz record collector's preoccupation with names, dates and numbers, sometimes bordering on the pedantically farcical and frequently focusing on total nonentities, went back to 1926 when the Elizalde brothers' despatches from America to the *Melody Maker* brought the names of individual jazzmen as well as bandleaders to the notice of the readers. In 1927 Edgar Jackson, realizing the imperative need for personnel identification, wildly guessed at names. Reviewing Red Nichols' 'Washboard Blues'/'That's No Bargain' he thought the drummer's style 'reeked of [Ben] Pollock' (Pollack was the correct spelling, Vic Berton the actual drummer). In 1927 the Parlophone advertisements were listing the star names to be heard on their releases.

The intensely personal nature of jazz style compelled this interest in identity. Simple enjoyment of the music was insufficient and the surrounding data were positive aids to critical assessment, helping to establish various influences on respective soloists and to plot changes in development. It is fascinating, for instance, to compare Coleman Hawkins' style on his early Henderson recordings to his development with the same band and other groups a few years on, and to plot further changes in approach after the war when he became influenced by the new kind of jazz, 'bebop'.

In reply to a detailed list of queries from a reader the *Melody Maker*, in its 'Collector's Corner' of 30 October 1942, set out guidelines on how to negotiate the vagaries of the matrix system, the bedrock of discography. 'The Corner', as it was affectionately known, provided at least part of the answer:

> Matrix numbers have proved a stumbling block to many a collector, and Mr France is justified in his bewilderment at their vagaries and peculiarities.

First, it can generally be assumed that discs are recorded in the order of their matrix numbers, but to give a list of the numerical series used by each of the Am. and Eng. Companies and their respective dates would be a herculean and impossible task.

We can, however, say that confusion has arisen owing to the fact that two or more series have been used simultaneously by one company. Each company, however, has its own series, and any duplication of series numbers is purely coincidental.

Generally speaking, discs retain the original numbers when dubbed (that is, re-recorded from an ordinary disc because the master is lost or damaged), but when re-recorded the new copies are given the original numbers plus a suffix.

This apparently simple explanation is marred by the fact that in certain cases, where American discs were made available to British companies, the latter invented apparently fictitious matrix numbers for the English issues (probably to confuse the enemy).

Such is the case with the Original Dixieland Jazz Band issues on HMV and the Bessie Smith album on Parlophone, and many of the English Columbia discs. This sounds as though we should warn you to regard every matrix number with suspicion until you have checked it. How right you are!

The matter of the little triangles, squares, OEAs, OAs, TNYs, etc. is a private code of the recording companies concerned.

They relate not only to the place of recording – i.e. whether inside a studio or outside – but also to the method of recording.

These are referred to as studio prefix letters, and are not of account to general collectors. The A, B, I or II after a matrix number refer to the master chosen from two or more made of the same title.

Thus 82037-B for Louis Armstrong's 'Struttin' with Some Barbecue' means that two (or more) recordings of that title were made for OKeh, and the second (B) was picked as the better (or best) for issue.

Finally, the American discs available to our companies over here are as follows. EMI (with HMV, Regal Zonophone, Columbia, Parlophone) draw from Victor, Bluebird, Columbia and OKeh and Decca/Brunswick from American Decca.

The statistical method, by no means infallible, was as effective as carbon dating of geological strata, providing the discographers had the necessary basic information. If they didn't have this detail they had to rely on aural identification, this often leading to violent disputes. In these controversies many a harsh word was written, many a man's ears alleged to be made of tin.

In 1940 thousands of words were expended in the *Melody Maker* on a controversy headed 'Bix v. Secrest'. The latter, trumpeter Andy Secrest, was a Beiderbecke imitator and also a member of the Whiteman band, and was so successful in pastiches of his idol's style that many a collector was fooled into actually believing it was the master and not the pupil. The dates of Beiderbecke's departure and return to the Whiteman fold in 1930 were related to recording dates established from matrix numbers, this method proving it was impossible for Beiderbecke to have played on certain Whiteman (and Frank Trumbauer) records, thus establishing that Secrest was the performer.

* * *

It took resolutely investigative zealots to thread their way through such labyrinthine complexities. Collectors in Europe assailed musicians in America with letters enquiring about their past and the activities of their contemporaries. They plundered record companies' files for scraps of information that might provide vital clues in a complicated investigation.

Even though American discographers had relatively easier access to musicians when they were resident in clubs or on tour and visiting many cities, a stumbling block was the musicians' poor memories. When they made those records years earlier they had no idea that they would later be the subject of research and designated as part of a national culture. They played sessions for a few dollars, and often never heard, or thought of, the records again until confronted by an earnest young white man with a stream of questions and a notebook in hand.

'History revels in irony,' wrote Humphrey Lyttelton in his *Best of Jazz – Basin Street to Harlem* and, indisputably, the history of jazz is a succession of ironies. Although the music is largely African in origin and its more renowned executants African-Americans, it was white men and women (mainly men) – with not one single black writer – who delved into its history, wrote the in-depth critiques and painstakingly compiled the discographies. Furthermore, these investigative activities were predominantly undertaken by Europeans.

Many a musician was unwilling to talk about records he thought best forgotten, especially if his own style had developed over the years, but the researcher-collector-discographer was nothing if not resourceful. In the photo-magazine *Jazz Illustrated* (1949/50), drawings portrayed a characteristically solemn-looking white man with pen-at-the-scribble as he bent over an ageing black trumpeter. *Jazz Illustrated,* published by Bert Wilcox, had contributions from Ernest Borneman, Max Jones, Charles Wilford, Steve Race and Derrick Stewart-Baxter, and cartoons by Humphrey Lyttelton, Tony Grey and Smilby (later *Playboy* cartoonist and owner of Magpie Records specializing in early blues and piano and singers).

Smilby cartoon from
Jazz Illustrated,
June 1950

When, in 1956, the Musicians' Union at last lifted their ban on foreign musicians the Americans who came to Britain were variously astonished, flattered, amused or annoyed by the attentions of discographers. Trombonist Vic Dickenson literally fled from eager questioners in a Norwich dance hall where he was appearing with a British band, and locked himself in a car.

On a post-war tour of Britain Coleman Hawkins took devious routes from theatre to pub and back again to avoid 'those motherfuckers who screw me with cotton-pickin' questions about records I made in 1925'. If Hawkins had ever listened to those early records since he made them, which was highly unlikely, he would have had every reason for not wishing to be reminded of them by some ardent discographer.

Had Frank Guarante lived (he died in 1942) and returned to England when discographical research was developing and when his New Orleans associations had become known, he would most certainly have been inundated with questions, although not necessarily about himself. There would have been a much greater interest displayed in his friend King Oliver. He would have been asked for opinions and information about other pioneer black New Orleans trumpeters, like Manuel Perez, Buddy Petit, Papa Celestin, or Buddy Bolden, and contemporary white horn players like Nick La Rocca, Ray Lopez and Johnny Stein. This interrogation about *other* musicians the questioned parties found less than endearing.

Had Eddie Lang returned to Britain in the investigative post-war years he would have had precious little time to indulge in card games or impromptu sessions. Here was a man whose career was certainly the most varied of all jazz musicians'. He recorded with Bessie Smith, and sundry other blues singers; with Louis Armstrong, King Oliver, Jack Teagarden, Joe Venuti, Benny Goodman and Paul Whiteman; with Bing Crosby and numerous other popular singers. The whole spectrum of American popular music in the twenties and early thirties is represented in his discography. To escape the inevitable attentions of the determined researcher Lang would have been grateful for the sanctuary of the National Sporting Club.

* * *

In 1934 the French critic, Charles Delaunay, was the first to publish a comprehensive discography – a word he himself coined. Produced at a time when such research was in its relative infancy, it contained a multitude of errors. In 1935 the first British compilation, *Rhythm on Record*, by Hilton Schleman (with the assistance of Stanley Dance) was published. This contained much information on bands that had little to do with jazz and gave collective personnels instead of detailed listings. Each book was a basis for and the inspiration of later works of similar character.

Throughout the thirties discographies of individual artists and bands appeared in the *Melody Maker*, *Hot News* and *Swing Music*. One of the earliest researchers and prolific letter writers was Ralph George Vivian Venables, of Tilford, Surrey, whose letters were signed R. G. V. Venables and who insisted that his first name was pronounced 'Ralfe'. Venables was a fanatical propagandist of white jazz and went to extraordinary lengths to substantiate his extremely biased views.

He quoted Louis Armstrong as saying that Bix Beiderbecke was the greatest of all trumpet players. It's unlikely that Armstrong ever made such a categorical remark but, whether or not he was misquoted, Venables, no Armstrong admirer, seized upon it with a zealot's grip. In the late thirties and early forties he was uneasily aware that white jazz was being subjected to uncomfortable critical examination as knowledge of the black man's contribution was increasingly growing. When he obtained an imported copy of *Jazzmen* he was quick to pounce on a discographical error in a book that was, for him, making far too much out of black jazz, particularly when the narrative disparaged his treasured white musicians.

In the *Melody Maker*, 10 February 1940, he wrote:

> No doubt many enthusiasts have purchased the recently imported book *Jazzmen* and it is indisputably a most interesting piece of work. In places, however, it is written in an authoritative manner which naturally inclines the reader to accept all the statements as facts.
>
> I would, therefore, like to point out that it might be unwise for anyone to seize upon Red Nichols' record of 'Lazy Daddy' as one of the finest examples of Goodman and Sullivan (as affirmed on page 178 of the book) for in actual fact neither of the musicians was present when this grand record was made. Jim Dorsey takes the clarinet solo which the writer (Charles Edward Smith) rightly considers to be excellent whilst young Jack Russin is on piano.
>
> After the many nasty things we read about Dorsey's playing it is amusing to read, 'Benny's chorus on "Lazy Daddy" is creative and definitely along melodic lines; the decorative phrases that often mark his playing are absent.' It is amusing to speculate whether he would have lauded this solo in the same glowing terms had he realized that it was the 'always boring Jimmy Dorsey'.

He continued to fight a rearguard action on behalf of white jazz (*vide* his article in the first issue of the Jones/McCarthy magazine *Jazz Music* entitled 'The Same Old Story') until, in the mid-fifties, he retired from the scene altogether and became editor of a motor-cycle magazine.

In 1949 Venables was partly responsible for the first British attempt (outside of Schleman's compilation) at a complete discography. With Albert McCarthy and Dave Carey he launched *Jazz Directory*, published in instalments by the Delphic Press, Fordingbridge, Hampshire. The first issue covered bands and artists listed alphabetically from A to B, embracing the period from the earliest recordings to the (then) current releases.

Carey, in his introduction, wrote:

> The enormous scope of THE DIRECTORY may incite purists to carp, nevertheless they will find themselves better catered for than elsewhere . . . the primary concern in THE DIRECTORY is jazz. Even so, we have endeavoured to extend it to the widest realms of application. We have admitted, on the one hand, negro spiritual, gospel and race recordings (of obvious historical and sociological importance) and, on the other, an extremely liberal presentation of swing, jive and bebop, in order to reflect adequately the total picture.
>
> A word about the art of discography as such. Although one critic has disparagingly referred to it as 'musical book-keeping' and discographers as a clan are often portrayed as being more interested in the obscurity of a label than any musical merit, it is a fact that it is pleasant if one knows who is on a record and when it was made and where. The whole point is that discographers have helped to unearth some superb jazz records which might have otherwise been unknown and have assisted to make known to general collectors the work of many talented but unknown artists. The music is the thing that ultimately matters, but discographers are so often misrepresented that it seems not out of place to put in a word for a hard working fraternity who are more often blamed for their mistakes than praised for their genuine discoveries. I cannot refrain from mentioning that discographers work much more unselfishly than many of their critics.
>
> In honesty it must be said that few discographers can claim that their work is one hundred per cent individual. We all build on the work of others and with the assistance of dozens of collectors I doubt if one in a thousand of discographies is the individual work of one person.

Venables dropped out and the intrepid Carey and McCarthy managed, against overwhelming odds as more and more releases piled up, to progress throught the alphabet to L–O and then gave up the struggle. The last two editions were published by Cassells. Their price was twelve shillings and sixpence, a five shillings increase on the first editions by the Delphic Press, but small sums to pay for such monumental labour and, whatever the compilers received for such industry, it could hardly have been commensurate with their time and effort.

It was left to the doyen of British discographers, Brian Rust, laboriously to amass a complete discography – complete, that is, within the time scale he set himself. This was his comprehensive *Jazz Records 1897–1931*, which also embraced ragtime, mostly on banjo, and jazz-tinged popular music. The compilation was typed, duplicated and collated by

Doyen of discographers, Brian Rust.

Rust in loose-leaf form, held together by a snap ring; five hundred copies were published in 1961. Subsequent editions took the compilation up to 1942, consistent with his firm belief that little recorded after 1940 was of any merit. The discography, in its much-revised and enlarged two-volume form, lists approximately 60,000 recordings; some 10,000 American and British bandleaders, musicians, arrangers and vocalists, sometimes with relevant notes; plus an index of names and 16,000 songs. It is an extraordinary work, quite epic in its conception, a tribute to the compiler's almost superhuman diligence and application, and has been of enormous guidance to the collector and radio jazz presenter. It represents scholarship of a high order.

Jazz Monthly, edited by Albert McCarthy, was the successor to *Jazz Forum*. In its October 1956 issue, collector-critic Michael Wyler wrote of Rust:

> It is fashionable in the world of poetry to refer to Auden, Isherwood, MacNeice, Spender and Day Lewis as the spokesmen of the thirties. The jazz world too has its representative figures – Leonard Hibbs, Percy Pring, John Fryer, Stanley Dance, Albert McCarthy, Hilton Schleman and Spike Hughes are some of the names that might conjure up the mid-thirties to you . . . The late thirties saw the emergence of Charles Fox, Max Jones, Sinclair Traill, Bill Elliott, Langston-White, Ralph Venables and others. Then came the war. Out of the midst of this rather venerable array of father-figures piped the eager tones of Brian A. L. Rust, self-styled 'The Sage of Edgware'. His elders and betters viewed this child prodigy with something like dismay. Who *was* this brash young man who knew such a confounded lot?

As far as seniority goes Brian, I suppose, must qualify for the right to be included in the pre-war generation of writer/collectors, but 'Father Figure' seems an absurd description for one whose manner and rather owlish appearance suggest rather the excited schoolboy, agog to swop cigarette cards with you. Brian . . . reminds me more than anything of an illustration from the pages of the *Gem* or *Magnet*. (The likelifulness is, as it were, terrific.) Like Bob Cherry of the Greyfriars Remove, he doesn't *say* things, he *breezes* them. Every announcement is vital. Nothing is unimportant. And like Billy Bunter, he is always expecting something. 'I say you fellows,' you can imagine him exclaiming, 'just you wait until my parcel comes!' And indeed, the parcels *do* come, crate after crate, across the Atlantic Ocean. Gennetts from Indiana, Herwins and Harmographs from St Louis, Autographs from Chicago, all bound for Brian Bunter . . .

Brian Rust was born in 1922, which, as he points out, makes him pre-electric. Everything in his life is related to recorded music in one way or another. He is apt to remind you that his telephone number can conveniently be recalled by remembering that it is the same as the catalogue number of the CoE [English Columbia] issue of 'Nightmare' by the New Orleans Owls. He looks contemptuous when I tell him that I find it simpler to write his telephone number in my diary.

. . . There is, as Aldous Huxley asserts, a magic in numbers and, in the jargon of the consulting room, Brian would speedily be recognised as 'obsessional'! In other words, he is the sort of person who is unable to pass a row of railings without rattling his walking stick along them; the sort of person who is fascinated by tabular presentations, cross indexing, definition and pigeon-holing; with a lust for pedantic accuracy and hunger to acquire 'sets' of things. Obsessional people are remarkable for their concentration on symbols, their passion for orderliness. From their ranks come fussy little bank clerks (and great scientists), neurotic misfits (and distinguished archaeologists), the pedantic professor who must have things just right and the metaphysician who will argue how many angels can dance on the head of a pin. And, it must be added, that strange twentieth-century phenomenon, the discographer.

An extremely simple example of Rust's investigative nose for discographical truths is a note to his listing of the Mound City Blue Blowers records:

New York, February 9th 1925
14872/4 'Gettin' Told'   Br. 2849
14876/6 'Play Me Slow'   „

The following session is generally believed to have taken place in London in November 1924, during the season when the Mound City Blue Blowers were playing in the Grill Room of the Piccadilly Hotel, but by the matrix numbers, issue number and appearance of the disc it would seem to have been made as shown here.

In the same section there is a typical Rustian interjection.

NOTE: UHCA and Columbia 36281, C-6180 and DB 500 as RED McKENZIE AND THE BLUE BLOWERS; all Parlophone (except A-3339, correctly labelled) and Odeons as RED McKENZIE AND THE CELES-TIAL BEINGS; Australian Regal G-2 1480 as MISSISSIPPI JAZZ KINGS. Only the OKehs bear the correct artist, credit and matrix numbers as shown. All the others have a 351000 series matrix number. Despite the gap in the OKeh numbering these four sides were all made on the same day.

The relative simplicity of this correction to an erroneous belief and the interjection contrast with some highly detailed discourses from Rust, one example of which is his furious retort to a Clarence Williams listing in *Record Changer* in which his name was mentioned:

Throughout the discography, though generally accurate, the diverse records listed under one date suggest that Mr Williams must have got around quite a bit on certain days to be able to record with so many companies with so many different artists.

To which, for example, does the first date given refer – 70210–C ('If You Don't Believe Me') or 70240–B ('Pullman Porter Blues')? Both these are reported to have been recorded at the same session. One is led to believe that on October 11th 1921 OKeh's New York studios recorded over thirty sides at least. Yet this amazing feat of engineering has never been approached at any time in the company's history.

Two items below, we see that Irene Gibbons is accompanied by a jazz band including no mention of Williams, but with Fletcher Henderson at the piano. Are we sure it could be Henderson? I mean, could it have been Jelly Roll Morton by any chance? or King Cole, or George Webb? or Ignace Paderewski? If it was Henderson what is it doing in a Clarence Williams listing?

There follow three pages of indignant disentanglement of the erring discographer's compilation.

The indefatigable Rust, apart from writing to American companies and musicians, raided the files of the English combines and endeavoured to track down the files of defunct companies. He optimistically visited Lugton's wholesale record distributors in London's Tottenham Court Road, who distributed the Guardsman label in the twenties, to glean what information he could. Any scrap of memorabilia would have been prized and noted. Nobody at Lugton's had even heard of the label and the only interest they showed in the questions from this earnest, bespectacled young man with the professorial air was bewilderment as to why he should be interested in scratchy old 78s. Rust realized it would have been hopeless to attempt an explanation.

The interest in vintage jazz aroused by the early discographers' listings produced yet another phenomenon, a sort of archaeologist, not excavating ancient sites for pottery, bones or coins, but scrabbling his way through a tangle of old sinks, broken chairs, dog-eared books and reproductions of 'Monarch of the Glen' in junk shops to seek out records deleted from the catalogues, some with only minimal jazz content – a few bars here and there – or – a coup! – an American label that had somehow found its way to this country.

When these were first purchased and played on wind-up gramophones with goose-necked horns in British drawing-rooms there was no realization that they had durable content, that they would be the subject of intense discussion two or three decades later. Once they had been played they were thrown away or disposed of to the rag and bone man, eventually finding their way into tatty emporia where they were sought by intrepid collectors who surrendered two or three old pence for their prize.

Invariably they were chipped and cracked and scored by the heavy sound arm irreverently dropped on the record's surface when first played, and if there was any reaction then to the 'hot' content it was probably annoyance that instrumentalists were departing from 'the melody'. But the happy finder of such an item, once home, would play the solos over and over again (often until that part of the record was worn grey). The solos transcended the din of surface noise, making the listener happily forget the usually antiquated arrangement from which they miraculously sprung – usually after an excruciating vocal. 'Gems in the quagmire' as Stanley Dance put it. In the late thirties and early forties when 'jazz junking' was at its height, the collector might well have made use of the Linguaphone repeater device advertised in a 1926 copy of the *Gramophone* that had the plangent cry 'PLAY THAT BIT AGAIN' as its heading.

In 1956, collector Arthur Gainsbury published *Junkshoppers' Discography* listing British labels in order of their catalogue number to guide the forager. It cost five shillings. Brian Rust was scornful about the inaccuracies he found therein, and tartly mentioned them in his *Jazz Records 1897–1942*.

There were many critics of those grubbing about in the bric-a-brac. The collectors were frequently accused of being more concerned with rarity value and accumulation of the obscure than the music itself. The somewhat comic aspect of this exercise was illustrated by the fastidious R. G. V. Venables, who would not have dreamt of venturing into those dusty marts without gloves!

There may have been a few junk-shoppers who deserved the censure of their less adventurous critics, but to make the physical effort to find these records and suffer the tedium of collating the information revealed a genuine love of the music and the sum total of jazz knowledge in a multitude of books now available owes much to the junker-discographer.

(A personal recollection of 'junking'. In 1942 I was serving aboard an armed trawler in the Indian Ocean and called in at Cape Town. There I stumbled across an Aladdin's cave of rare 78s on an assortment of magical US labels in a hardware shop. I bought as many as I could afford at a shilling a record and they travelled some thousands of miles on convoy and somehow I got them back to England. These years later there is still a tug at my heart strings recalling those I had to leave behind me. I suffer the same sort of pangs remembering that to counter one of my financial crises I sold them for a song.)

11

Archer Street Jazzmen
and the BBC

While the debates about criteria in discography raged between (mostly) non-playing buffs, the British jazzman, invariably a dance-band musician, was uninterested in emotive discussions conducted in a rarefied atmosphere of musical aesthetics far removed from the economic realities of his existence.

The Archer Street man rarely had any historical perspective, was a limited buyer of records, never contributed to discographical arguments or compilations and rarely wrote impassioned letters to the musical papers. If he wrote at all he would be likely to complain that the volume and intensity of the non-playing buff's strictures were commensurate with that buff's inability to read a note – the professional's favourite counterthrust. If he ever read the specialist magazines his reaction would be one of mild amusement or sardonic comment.

When he and his *confrères* met at their open-air club, Archer Street, a narrow thoroughfare not more than fifty yards long connecting Coventry Street and Great Windmill Street in central London's Soho, they would be looking for work in dance halls, holiday camps, hotels and recording studios. They would be quite unconcerned with the matters of grave artistic import occupying the minds of the dedicated who, cheekily, had no hesitation in telling others they should starve for the art they believe in. Many of those pointing the finger were happily ensconced in professions and occupations where such artistic and moral dilemmas didn't apply.

Archer Street: the dance/jazz band musicians' 'labour exchange' and open-air club, c.1950. The Harmony Inn, where Ronnie Scott's nine-piece was conceived, is on the right-hand side.

Even if the British dance-cum-jazz musician had exchanged this mess of pottage, giving up playing in nightclubs and dance halls to play jazz exclusively, there would have been precious few opportunities to follow his brave decision and equally few people would have attended to give vital financial support at the door. The jazz buffs, denied hearing American musicians in the flesh, stayed at home to listen to the records of their far-away heroes. Indeed, attempting to play jazz for a living in the twenties and thirties was to court starvation and public support was insufficient even for semi-professional bands to undertake the exercise. Many a prisoner of commercialism wished it were otherwise.

There was quite a furore when Gerry Moore, a fine pianist who tried hard to earn a living playing jazz, mostly in drinking clubs, joined Victor Sylvester's ballroom dancing orchestra for 'the money'. He stood it for a few years but, unable to tolerate its stultifying monotony, he departed with a blistering attack on the format in the *Melody Maker*.

The bitter correspondence that ensued reflected the extremes of a situation where the musician wanted to express himself in a colourful language but cruel economics limited him to making trite utterances.

Ironically, Moore was succeeded by another jazzman, Eddie Macauley, whose solo, for instance, on Danny Polo's 'If You were the Only Girl in the World' on the Decca label was craftsman-constructed and exhibited a genuine swing lacking in most British pianists.

But paradoxically the thread of jazz was interwoven throughout the whole fabric of this despised commercialism, most of the bandleaders giving their soloists opportunities to improvise and to record wholly jazz instrumentals.

Bert Ambrose led the most technically proficient and jazzworthy of the West End restaurant bands. He was a mediocre violinist who knew little about jazz, but employed the best of jazzmen and made several memorable records for the Decca label in the thirties, one of which, 'Cotton Pickers' Congregation', a Sid Phillips composition and arrangement, was quite outstanding. A surging brass 'choir', led on cornet by Tommy McQuater to give it an unusual timbre, provides a fitting back-cloth for Lew Davis' growling and wailing as the 'preacher', Billy Amstell's lilting tenor and Danny Polo's skipping clarinet, with the rhythm section laying down a firm beat. It's a gutsy sound, a world away from the Embassy Club where these musicians nightly churned out cloying arrangements to a chattering, chowing and shuffling clientele of hearty Guards officers, simpering debutantes and provincial mayors doing the town. The band *must* have preferred to play jazz but the time had yet to come when a British jazz musician could earn a living playing the music he most liked.

Another leader of a West End restaurant band, pianist and arranger Lew Stone at the Monseigneur, Piccadilly, made several jazz recordings for Decca after he took over the orchestra from the quintessential bandleader of the thirties, Roy Fox. Fox, an indifferent cornettist, was far more concerned with the cut of his frock coat than music; he worried how its tails dangled as he turned his back to the audience directly to face the orchestra and superfluously 'conduct' a brass flourish or bring them to the end of a number with a dramatic wave of his baton.

The star soloist of the Fox/Stone band was trumpeter Nat Gonella, who was the first British trumpeter to play in the Armstrong style at a time when all his contemporaries were emulating Beiderbecke and Nichols. It was another paradox that a player in the tough Armstrong manner should be allowed his head, albeit occasionally, in the gilt and plush milieu of an 'exclusive' restaurant. Gonella later toured the variety halls with his Georgians, featuring his Armstrong-influenced solos and vocals. His brother Bruts, also on trumpet and the better of the two jazzmen, and his pianist Harold Hood, were both underrated.

In 1942 Stone made his best records ever with a band selected for recording purposes only (for Decca, the friend of the British jazzman in the thirties) issued as by Lew Stone and his Stone-Crackers. They featured the West Indian Dave Wilkins and Scotsman Archie Craig on trumpets, with fellow Scot George Chisholm on trombone and Canadian Jack Penn on piano. Chisholm was then developing into an impressive soloist and contributed the excellent arrangements.

Jack Hylton, whose 'Riverboat Shuffle' was the first 'jazz' record reviewed in the very first issue of the *Melody Maker* in 1926, had primarily a stage band and featured live and on record the Frenchman Philip

Valaida Snow, trumpeter and singer, recorded with numerous musicians in Britain in the 1930s, including George Scott-Wood and Johnny Claes.

Brun, Jack Jackson and Tommy McQuater (trumpets), Lew Davis (trombone) and Dave Shand (alto saxophone). After Duke Ellington's visit Hylton recorded a tantalizingly convincing pastiche of the Ducal style in a medley of Ellington tunes titled 'Ellingtonia', with Freddy Schweitzer performing an uncanny imitation of Hodges. It has been alleged that when this was played to the Ellington band 'blindfolded' they recognized each other, but not themselves.

Titan of the tenor saxophone, Coleman Hawkins, left America in 1934 to live and play in Europe. Somehow Hylton bypassed the ban on American musicians working in Britain and recorded two tracks with Hawkins in 1939: 'Darktown Strutters' Ball' and 'My Melancholy Baby'. The band was obviously uplifted by the experience of accompanying 'the Hawk'. Hawkins returned to America that year to make his classic 'Body and Soul', regarded as one of the greatest jazz records of all time.

Another orchestra recording on the HMV label and led by composer-arranger Ray Noble also had only an occasional existence outside the recording studio. This contained, at various times, all the recognized British jazzmen and brought to notice a young multi-saxophonist, Freddy Gardner, who recorded eighteen titles for the Rex label between 1937 and 1939. '10 am Blues', featuring Gardner and a trumpeter named Norman Payne (who was really Tommy McQuater) with a rhythm section was the memorable session. Payne plays with true blues feeling.

Nat Gonella in his famous Parlophone Records pose

Collectively, the names that appeared and reappeared in these recordings throughout the thirties and early forties were trumpeters Max Goldberg, Norman Payne, Tommy McQuater, Archie Craig, Frenchy Sartell, Duncan Whyte; trombonists Ted Heath, Lew Davis, George Chisholm; saxophonists Buddy Featherstonhaugh, Billy Amstell, Harry Hayes, Freddy Gardner, Danny Polo, Sid Phillips, Jack Miranda, Harry Hines; pianists Eddie Macauley, Gerry Moore, Jack Penn, Bert Barnes; drummers Joe Daniels, Bill Harty, Max Bacon; bassists Tiny Winters and Dick Hall; and guitarists Alan Ferguson, Albert Harris and Ivor Mairants.

In 1933, coinciding with the Ellington visit, Madame Tussaud's Dance Band, led by tenor saxophonist Stanley Barnett, recorded twelve titles, mostly Ellington compositions played in the Ellington manner. Much of the jazz played by the Archer Street men was in the recording studios under pseudonyms like the Blue Mountaineers, the Embassy Eight, the Swing Rhythm Boys, the Rhythm Rascals, Joe Paradise and his Music, the Rhythm Revellers and the Rhythm Gangsters. Sometimes actual names were used: George Scott-Wood's Six Swingers, Joe Daniels' Hot Shots, Phil Green's Busketeers, Mario 'Harp' Lorenzi, Jack Miranda and his Meanderers, Leonard Feather and Ye Olde English Swynge Band, Danny Polo and his Swing Stars, Tiny Winters' Bogey Seven and others.

The repertoire of these pick-up groups was a mixture of jazz standards and Tin Pan Alley tunes, many of them indifferent vehicles transmuted by the ability of local jazzmen freed from the constraints of their normal employment.

With a series of intermittently and grudgingly issued work permits, multi-instrumentalist and arranger Benny Carter worked as staff arranger for Henry Hall's BBC Dance Band in 1936. It was odd that one of the world's most talented jazzmen should be employed by a leader who rarely allowed solo improvisation in his arrangements, but during this atypical employment Carter recorded twenty-six titles with British musicians for the Vocalion label. He composed many of the tunes and wrote all the arrangements, playing trumpet, clarinet, alto and tenor saxophone and piano with the pick of British jazzmen. Writing in *Swing Music*, Carter praised the British musicians who recorded with him, compliments that contrasted with John Hammond's dismissal of these sessions in *Down Beat* and his unequivocal repetition of his strictures in *Rhythm*.

In 1938 Carter was actually granted permission to appear in public. In *Melody Maker*, 16 January 1938, Leonard Feather reviewed the 'Swing Music Concert' promoted by that paper at the London Hippodrome on 10 January:

> Of the sixteen hundred fans at Sunday's concert, at least half must have been feeling like Tantalus at the banquet of the gods. That poor sufferer you may remember had the choicest of fruits placed just out of his reach and his star-vation was tortured by the sight of them.
>
> For a year the jazz fraternity of England has had Benny Carter in their midst but never until last Sunday was an opportunity afforded to everyone to feast on the musical delicacies he had to offer. So, the curtain went up to reveal the broadly smiling, fast moving figure with a baton leading thirteen musicians. These hundreds of Tantaluses were unfettered and their saviour prepared to entertain them in the flesh. Benny acted as ringmaster . . . his alto playing was all one expected – limpid, free and expressive. His solos on trumpet and clarinet brought him no less applause and I fancy he could have added another string to his bow had he cared to take a chorus on piano.

In 1939 a musicians' co-operative called the Heralds of Swing was formed with the avowed intention of being an uncompromising jazz unit, but this lasted for only a few months. The Heralds were Tommy McQuater, Archie Craig (trumpets), George Chisholm (trombone), Dave

Shand, Benny Winestone, Norman Maloney (reeds), Bert Barnes (piano),
Tiny Winters (bass), Sid Colin (guitar) and George Firestone (drums).
Many of these were to be in the war-time RAF dance orchestra, the
Squadronaires, recording many jazz-slanted sides for the Decca label.

The black contribution to British jazz at this time was slight. The
West Indian-born Reginald Foresythe, composer and arranger, wrote

Drinking-club session, possibly at Jig's: Charlie Short, bass; Frank Deniz, guitar; Carlo
Krahmer (*standing*); Kenny Baker, trumpet; Freddy Grant, alto

'arty' pieces with titles like 'Dodgin' a Divorcee' and 'Serenade to a
Wealthy Widow', the latter recorded by Paul Whiteman. Foresythe
recorded four titles with an American band that included Benny
Goodman and arranged for Earl Hines' orchestra at the Grand Terrace
Ballroom, Chicago, but added nothing to British jazz. Ken 'Snakehips'
Johnson, a dancer from Georgetown, British Guiana, formed an all-black
band in 1937. In 1938 he took this band into the Café de Paris, and
declared, 'I'm determined to make them like swing at the Café or die in
the attempt.' Later he said: 'Boy, I nearly died.' His policy at the Café de
Paris was primarily 'commercial' and out of all the records he made only

were jazz-orientated. The jazzmen in his unit were Dave Wilkins and Leslie Hutchinson (trumpets), Carl Barriteau and Bertie King (saxophones), Errol Barrow (piano) and Joe Deniz (guitar).

These frequently joined a coterie of black musicians working in the warren of one-room drinking clubs in London's West End, notably in the red-light district of Soho. The living was precarious. Following police investigations into infringements of the jumbled licensing laws these establishments changed hands, names and addresses at a rapid rate, but in this sub-world of night people the preference was for jazz rather than

Sunday session at the Feldman Club, 27 July 1947. The band is Campbell's West Africans.

formal dance music, a situation not so different from Chicago speakeasies in the roaring twenties. The list of these clubs is endless, but those offering employment to jazzmen included the Big Apple, Gerrard Street; the Nest Club and Bag O' Nails, Kingly Street; the Shim Sham and Cosmos, Wardour Street; the Blue Lagoon, Frith Street (the present site of Ronnie Scott's Jazz Club); the Rhythm Club, Old Compton Street; and the Unity, Dean Street. Besides jazzmen these often shady places booked entertainers like pianists Hetty King and Sticks Freeman and dancers Black Bottom Johnny and Sonny Thomas; again not dissimilar to the vaudeville tradition in Harlem's nightclubs.

One of the longest-lived establishments and probably the most fre-quented by jazz buffs was Jig's Club, Wardour Street, its entrance in St Anne's Court.

'Jigs' had long been a US slang term for negro, and the word, although usually referring to a dance of that name, was used in many song titles. Louis Armstrong, in his 1931 recording of 'Just a Gigolo' (with Les Hite's Orchestra) impishly changes one of the lines in the lyric to 'Just a Jig I Know'. Armstrong visited Jig's with Nat Gonella in 1932 and found the atmosphere much to his liking. Run by Alec and Rose Ward, the club had a name appropriate to the predominantly black membership drawn from the then relatively small West Indian population, with a sprinkling of visiting black US seamen gravitating to Wardour Street from Dockland.

That not so large room had a charged atmosphere with, one suspects, 'charge' contributing to the pungent fug that was so much a part of the ambience. The usual denizens of this establishment were not all ordinary, respectable, law-abiding citizens!

It was probably the most frequented of the West End 'dives' by white jazz buffs. Palefaces from the suburbs, immersed in the historical and racial background of jazz, came to Jig's naïvely believing that they were entering an approximation of one of the lower level Harlem 'joints' like Smalls' Paradise, Monettes or the Lennox Grill. On reflection, Jig's probably was that approximation, and because we were all so determinedly pro-black we gave the band, very rough and out of tune, more credit than it deserved, but this posture would be symptomatic of the year, 1941, in which I visited the club.

The 'house' drink was rum and peppermint, a heady concoction, and that may be clouding, these many years later, the recollections of this particular paleface, then eighteen, who travelled to this 'little Harlem' via the mundane Dartford Loop from Sidcup to Charing Cross on the Southern Railway, thrilled at the prospect at entering a haunt so atmospheric, and becoming quite proud of the fact that Dreamer, the enormous black doorman, would recognize me.

Signed photographs of visiting musicians, including that of Louis Armstrong, adorned the grimy walls. In the middle of this pressurized room stood a billiard table where preoccupied cue-holders sized up their shots, quite oblivious to the energetic and graceful jitterbugging going on around them. Steve, a diminutive black waiter, wheeled and ducked through the swirling dancers triumphantly holding his tray of drinks high. The jazz buffs, crowded round the tiny bandstand, had little to do with the regulars and they certainly disapproved of the jitterbugging; 'jitterbug' was then a dirty word in the serious buff's vocabulary.

There was nothing 'racial' in this non-communication. The buffs were there to listen to the music – the regulars present for drinking, 'smoking', billiard playing or, in some instances, doing business, probably of an illegal nature – considering the place it was and the wartime rackets. One or two ponces and their charges were regulars. To these people the music was just incidental, or providing the inspiration for their intricate and animated jiving.

During its long run – which was strange perhaps, in view of police interest in these shady establishments – many Archer Street jazzmen visited the club (and others like it) 'after hours', escaping from the gilded fleshpots of their normal employment. In these less acceptable (socially speaking) environs where the air was undoubtedly fouler they (musically speaking) could breathe more freely.

It would be typical of these Archer Street men – all union members – to charge the rate for *one second* of overtime they worked at restaurant or hotel, fretting during this paid overtime, and yet to hie themselves to a spot where they would blow all night for no financial reward whatsoever!

This was also typical behaviour on the part of many US dance-band-cum-jazz musicians in big cities of America, an endearing characteristic of the jazz-minded professional. The American Federation of Musicians, however, put a block on this important cross-fertilization in after-hours jam sessions. Narrow-minded interference was not just a peculiarity of the British Musicians' Union – even they, then restrictive in so many other ways, never attempted to put such a ban on their members.

The usual, black, personnel of the Jig's Club band was Cyril Blake (trumpet and leader), Freddy Grant (clarinet), Lauderic Caton (electric guitar), Clinton Maxwell (drums) and Brylo Ford – who later played with Chris Barber – on bass. The '88 duties', as the *Melody Maker* would have put it at the time, were sometimes performed by Errol Barrow, but more often by Colin Beaton, a white pianist.

Four records of the band were made 'live' at the club in December 1941 and issued on the Regal-Zonophone label.* Outstanding is the guitar playing of Lauderic Caton and the records capture the raw excitement of

---

* 'Cyril's Blues', 'Frolic Sam' and 'Rhythm is Our Business' have been reissued on CD on *Black British Swing*, Topic TSCD 781 (2001).

a 'black' nightspot in London's sinful square mile. Probably because of the nature of the area the windows of the club were protected by iron bars, which had to be removed to allow the recording engineer's cables into the premises.

Feldman Club, October 1947: Derek Neville, clarinet; Carlo Krahmer, drums; Russ Allen, bass; Reg Arnold, trumpet; possibly Monty Feldman, piano

* * *

Apart from the Jig's Club band very few of the groups that worked in these often shady establishments ever got on record. Drummer Carlo Krahmer recorded with his Nut House Band on the Parlophone label, but the majority of his recordings were made on acetates last heard of lying in an East Anglian garage. Much of the aural history of this little documented area thus remains unheard.

Krahmer was the most prominent figure on the club circuit. Born 13 March 1913 he, unlike most professional musicians, was an avid collector of records, amassing thousands of 78s and, later, LPs. He led bands at innumerable clubs including: the Nuthouse, Regent Street; the Cuba Club, Gerrard Street; the Cabaret Club, Beak Street; the Gremlin, Archer Street; the Top Hat, Coventry Street; Merry's, Baker Street; the Jamboree, Wardour Street; and the Panama, Knightsbridge. Only partially sighted, Carlo moved around London without stick or glasses and often was playing three residencies in a night. He, in his quiet way, was the nightclub gig king and it was mostly jazz his various bands played.

* * *

OUR 7-YEAR-OLD KRUPA GOES TO TOWN !

Victor Feldman received huge publicity as a child star. This photo was taken at the No. 1 Rhythm Club.

The war was to become the catalyst of many social changes reflected in jazz and to result in a situation where Britain produced probably the greatest number of accredited jazzmen outside the United States of America.

Conscription had reduced the size of the big dance bands – *and* the authoritarianism of their leaders. If one of them was lucky enough to obtain the services of an 'ace stylist' – to use one of the *Melody Maker*'s favourite terms for a skilled soloist – for a band he was leading in one of the socialite 'niteries' still open in war-time London, he wasn't in too strong a position to argue if the said ace stylist wanted more than the eight or sixteen bars solo that had been customary in pre-war conditions. The smallness of the bands made them more hospitable to improvisation. For the time being at least, some of the stodgy arrangements were put aside and in the mood of desperate gaiety lively jazz was more acceptable.

The most active musicians emerging in this changing climate were trumpeters Kenny Baker, Leslie Hutchinson and Arthur Mouncey; saxophonists Aubrey Franks, Ronnie Chamberlain and Kathleen Stobart; clarinettists Carl Barriteau, Harry Parry and Frank Weir; pianists Art Thompson and George Shearing; and drummers George Firestone, Krahmer and Jock Cummings.

In November 1941 HMV recorded the First Public Jam Session, in association with the No. 1 Rhythm Club and the *Melody Maker*, and issued four twelve-inch records under that title with mixed personnels that included Dave Wilkins, Kenny Baker, Buddy Featherstonhaugh, Harry Parry, Frank Weir and Carl Barriteau. One of the organizers – and this is no surprise – was Edgar Jackson. It would seem that his presence at every British jazz event was by divine right. One of the stewards (unpaid) was the author.

These musicians were the hard core of the weekly jam sessions held at the Feldman Club, 100 Oxford Street, on Sunday evenings from 1942.

The club was founded by Joseph Feldman, a furrier, to promote his three sons, Robert on clarinet, Monty on accordion and Victor on drums. Victor was a child prodigy, playing the drums in public at the age of eight and dubbed the 'Kid Krupa'.

*   *   *

From the beginning of the forties a series of purely jazz recordings was made for major studios. In 1940 the BBC tardily acknowledged the existence of jazz sufficiently to present a programme, 'Radio Rhythm Club', for all of half an hour weekly. It was

Harry Hayes

produced by Charles Chilton, an amateur guitarist and keen buff, and its resident band was led by clarinettist Harry Parry who, from January 1941 to October 1949, recorded 102 titles for Parlophone, nearly all under the name of the Radio Rhythm Club Sextet. Parry, an accomplished – if predictable – player, featured excellent musicians such as Roy Marsh (vibraphone); Lauderic Caton, Frank and Joe Deniz (guitars); Yorke de Souza, George Shearing, Tommy Pollard, Eddie Macauley (piano); Dave Wilkins, Pat Barnett, Stan Roderick (trumpet); Reg Dare, Derek Neville (tenor saxophone); Bobby Midgeley, Danny Craig (drums) and Jack Fallon (bass).

Parry's successor for the BBC's weekly half-hour allocation was tenor saxophonist Buddy Featherstonhaugh, with a sextet comprising himself, Don Macaffer (trombone), Vic Lewis (guitar), Jack Parnell (drums), Harry Rayner (piano) and Frank Clarke (bass). Trumpeter Kenny Baker was later added to some sessions. They recorded twenty-nine titles for HMV between June 1943 and February 1945. Lewis and Parnell formed their Jazzmen in 1944 and recorded thirty-one titles for Parlophone between February 1944 and January 1946. While the Parry and Featherstonhaugh sides were primarily a string of solos with the minimum arrangement and the Lewis–Parnell sides were in loose dixieland style, another series of recordings in a different vein were being made by alto saxophonist Harry Hayes.

Hayes then already had a long professional career behind him. The

February 1926 *Melody Maker* includes a photograph of him in Julian Vedey's band taken at the Cosmos Club, Wardour Street, that year. In 1928 he played and recorded with Fred Elizalde; in 1930 he recorded with Spike Hughes and was a member of Louis Armstrong's only British band in 1932. Hayes was a quintessential Archer Street jazzman who earned a strong reputation as lead alto saxophone with a variety of dance bands, including Maurice Winnick, Sidney Lipton, Bert Firman and Geraldo, but retained a strong interest in jazz throughout his life.

Popular drummer Freddie Crump (*centre*) worked for bandleader Johnny Claes (right of Crump with trumpet) in the early 1940s. Ronnie Scott can be seen just above Claes' trumpet.

In 1941–42 Hayes recorded eight titles with trumpeter Johnny Claes, writing the arrangements for trumpet, four reeds and rhythm. Claes' playing is coarse (particularly when duetting with Nat Gonella on two sides) but Hayes' scoring for the saxophones and his own crisply articulated solos distinguish these recordings. The thirty-nine sides he recorded between November 1944 and July 1947 for HMV were influenced by the small-band Ellington groups, usually under Johnny Hodges' name. Again his scoring and solos – with some delightful compositions of his own – make them worthy of a place in the buff's collection.

The playing of jazz anywhere outside America was at this time an essentially imitative exercise (albeit that much American jazz could also be fairly described as similarly derivative, depending on the ages of the players). Yet the British endeavours were made in a spirit of genuine regard for the genre and most of the recordings mentioned in this chapter, however variable, reveal how surely the British musicians were coming to grips with the idiom. The solos were played with so much more assurance, the arrangements more subtle, the melodic and rhythmic parts so much better integrated. And all this absorbed from gramophone records with only sporadic and inspirational appearances of the better-equipped Americans.

It is, of course, purely conjectural as to whether British jazz musicians would have improved more quickly had American bands and soloists appeared in Britain in greater numbers. In Benny Carter's case, for instance, his employment with Henry Hall's BBC Dance Orchestra didn't noticeably alter their sound and Hall's contract with that august organization would certainly have been terminated had Carter's influence given the orchestra a more pronounced jazz flavour. Also, it is likely that individuals given work permits might have had the same fate as Danny Polo – an excellent jazz clarinettist generally playing a saxophone part in cloying arrangements.

In ending this summary of the contribution of the Archer Street jazzmen it has to be acknowledged that while their living was derived from Tin Pan Alley ephemera they expressed themselves in the jazz idiom whenever they could, but some were sensitive to inevitable comparisons between their efforts and those of their American mentors. Nat Gonella was one of those who protested that he and his fellow Brits should have received more praise on patriotic grounds. 'Give the British chaps a break,' he declared in one interview, but Harry Hayes, in a conversation with the author, put it very simply: 'After all, good or bad, we were only copyists.'

* * *

It was years later, in January 1961, that Steve Race, in *Jazz News*, put the matter of British jazz absorption very bluntly:

'Something that is peculiarly Anglo-American in jazz.' The phrase comes from Cy Laurie, describing clarinettist Acker Bilk's style in the January 7th issue of *Jazz News*.

I like that phrase 'Anglo-American jazz'. At least it's halfway to the truth which, unaccountably, so many people find so bitter.

The truth is that there is no such thing as British jazz. There is only American jazz played by British musicians . . . or Swedish or French, or any other nationality that chooses to imitate the American model.

There is nothing particularly British in Henry Ormonroyd and his Batley Stompers playing 'Ilkla Moor': one might as well claim that a bottle of

Australian Burgundy is French. As long as the instrumentation is modelled after New Orleans or 52nd Street; as long as the tone or vibrato is copied from Dodds or Getz; as long as the phrases are culled from Lester, Diz or Louis, there'll be no British jazz.

I put it in a nutshell: as long as our jazzmen learn their trade from American records, they'll go on playing American jazz.

I don't write this with any regret. Mind you, as a patriotic Limey, descended from a long line of proud islanders, I'm no more delighted about the present cultural invasion from America than my distant forbears were when the Latin milestones started springing up along the Dover Road. But the plain fact is that if I want jazz I must accept America, just as one must look to Holland for Dutch paintings, or to ancient China for the Ming vase.

Strong, pertinent words! But if imitation was the essence of British involvement with jazz some very good imitators came to make records of enduring value, many of which the author, for one, rates it his pleasure to have in his collection, and not on any spurious patriotic grounds.

* * *

From the beginnings of jazz appreciation in this country, even from the time, 1933, when the Rhythm Clubs gave the movement a unity and a voice, even when, during the thirties, there was a spate of records being released to show that the record companies acknowledged the existence of the jazz community, even when the lay press showed an intelligent interest, the British Broadcasting Corporation remained aloof and its announcers and commentators were allowed to make facetious and irrelevant remarks about the idiom. One young woman announcer in 1940 made a disparaging comment about a Muggsy Spanier Ragtime Band

Pianist Dill Jones with saxophonist Kathy Stobart

record before playing it and the howl of protest from the *Melody Maker* actually forced an apology from the corporation's press office.

The faded dons and unsuccessful writers who occupied the mysterious planning regions of the corporation gave scant time to jazz, live or recorded. Only occasionally did buffs hear their music on 'the wireless'. In the thirties Christopher Stone from London and Robert Tredennick from the Midland Region gave infrequent fifteen- or thirty-minute recitals. During 1936 members of the No. 1 Rhythm Club, including Leonard Hibbs and George Penniket, were granted a half-hour each to talk about a particular musician or band, Penniket choosing Fred Elizalde as his subject, with that doyen of BBC announcers, Freddie Grisewood, intoning the opening introduction.

Any jazz activity in Portland Place in the thirties was due mainly to a couple of sympathetic employees – Leslie Perowne and Charles Chilton. Perowne was educated at Winchester, and Chilton was slum-born and educated at a Kings Cross elementary school, a fact mentioned in view of a subsequent comment about this enlightened partnership. He joined the BBC in 1932 as a messenger boy and graduated to become producer

Feldman Swing Club, 27 July 1947. Under various names, the basement at 100 Oxford Street has been a popular jazz venue for more than sixty years.

Perowne's assistant. Between them they were responsible for the historic transatlantic hook-ups for live broadcasts from jazz spots in New York and a series called 'Swingtime' going out from 1937 to 1939 at the late hour of 11.30 pm.

The number of letters and telephone calls received about this pro-gramme surprised the big-wigs; so much so that some of them actually tuned in and were horrified by the cockney accent of presenter Chilton. He was summarily replaced by a duty announcer, any one of whom could have been a household name in the thirties when radio reigned – Freddie Grisewood, Stuart Hibberd, Lionel Gamlin or Alvar Liddell, all with per-fect elocution but probably sounding a little stiff in their pronunciation of 'Tricky Sam' Nanton, Cootie Williams, Meade Lux Lewis, Big Sid Catlett, Butterbeans and Susie, or grappling with titles like 'Gimme a Pigfoot', 'Nobody Rocks Me Like My Baby Do' (should such a title have ever been allowed), 'Don't Give Me That Jive' or 'Flat Foot Floogie with the Floy Floy'.

There was considerable opposition within the BBC's portals to jazz of any sort being played on air and on one occasion the matter was referred to one of the Board of Governors, Sir Henry Walford Davies, then Master of the King's Music. How Davies was persuaded that jazz was acceptable is not known, but it may well have had something to do with the fact that the person who approached him on this thorny matter was Perowne, whose father was the Bishop of Winchester and brother the Governor of Aden. Such connections helped!

Perowne and Chilton formed the Radio Rhythm Club in 1941, the forerunner of what became an almost continuous BBC jazz slot under various names, later presented as 'Sounds of Jazz' by Peter Clayton.

* * *

Chilton's humble origins were remarked upon by Commander Campbell RN, a member of the famous BBC 'Brains Trust', in his book *You Have Been Listening to . . .*, contrasting these with the more favoured Perowne, of whom Charles Chilton, decades later, spoke very highly. This was far from being the only jazz-related comment from the 'Brains Trust' panel.

The 'Brains Trust' was a programme with an extremely high listener rating, and the panel included Professor C. E. M. Joad, 'popular' philosopher and writer of many books now totally forgotten. A witty and cogent speaker, if not an author of any enduring value, he could always be relied upon to make a pithy anti-jazz riposte. One of his comments was about 'jazz bands dispensing negroid music for the benefit of tired sportsmen and their wives', in a context not recorded.

Jazz people had long been accustomed to lurid descriptions of jazz and its practitioners, and its allegedly corrupting effect on youth; but that it, according to Joad, was for tired sportsmen and their wives was imagery of a quite different order. Joad was the Dr Crowhard of the forties.

Guitarist and concert promoter Sid Gross ran a series of concerts under the title of 'Swing Shop' at the Coliseum Theatre, Kingsway. For one of these he issued invitations to various notables, including several 'classical' musicians – 'long-hairs' the *Melody Maker* called them in those days – and sat back to await the response, rather expecting comments anent 'cacophonous jazz', 'primitive discords' or the like but, generally, the reaction was favourable. The silly dichotomy of 'classical' and 'jazz' was then happily vanishing – both forms of music were being judged by their separate merits – but one of the invitees, Professor Joad, typically lived up to expectations. His reply, not without its humour, was quoted in the *Melody Maker*.

> I have very little acquaintance with either jazz or swing, but that little has rendered me most reluctant to renew or enlarge it. You don't say what you are prepared to pay for this painful experience you propose to me but, no doubt, if you made it sufficiently worth my while I would come to your concert.
>
> I cannot conceive, however, what possible interest the opinion of musicians on a non-musical subject such as swing or jazz could have. You have completely conquered the public. Why not leave the musicians alone?
>
> (Signed) C. E. M. JOAD

In 1947 'Radio Rhythm Club' became 'BBC Jazz Club', produced by Mark White, a keen jazz enthusiast. In 1949 he supervised eight titles for the Decca label with pick-up groups of musicians who regularly appeared on his programme, these including old hands like Harry and Laurie Gold (saxophones), Jack Jackson (trumpet), and relative newcomers such as Dill Jones (piano), Bruce Turner (alto saxophone and clarinet) and Freddy Randall (trumpet). White later described their efforts as 'modern dixieland music'.

White subsequently put together two compilation albums of Decca 78s called *Scrapbook of British Jazz* that included Fred Elizalde, Spike Hughes, Jack Hylton, Lew Stone, Nat Gonella, George Chisholm, George Webb, George Shearing, Harry Gold, Chris Barber, George Melly, Wally Fawkes, Sandy Brown and Ken Colyer. They provided evidence of Decca's long-standing employment of British jazzmen in their studios.

White, like Perowne and Chilton before him, was an enthusiast who had long struggles with the planners even to maintain this half an hour given to jazz. Now the total allocation on all networks has been substantially increased. It is still not sufficient, but it is a great improvement on the position in the barren thirties.

12

Peckham Pandemonium
and Humphrey Lyttelton

The Lewis–Parnell Jazzmen's dixieland style employed collective improvisation and, the purists insisted, capitalized on the retrospective interest in early jazz that was spreading round the world. They recorded for a major label, appeared at West End concerts and played regularly at the Feldman Club; but in a milieu fifteen miles distant and very different in character a band of amateurs played every Monday evening in a pub called the Red Barn at Barnehurst, Kent, making this drear, dull, thirties-built suburb the source of an explosion that was to reverberate throughout the country. This band, George Webb's Dixielanders, comprised Reg Rigden (trumpet) and Owen Bryce (cornet), Eddie Harvey (trombone), Wally Fawkes (clarinet), Art Streatfield (tuba); George Webb (piano), Roy Wykes (drums) and Buddy Vallis (banjo). The band started playing at the Red Barn, home of the Bexleyheath and District Rhythm Club (No. 130) in 1943, and were billed as Spider Webb and his Cobs, a titling as joky as the apparent antiquity of the music they played. This was regarded by most members as no more than a novelty interlude between the conventional jam sessions.

Wally Fawkes was the first jazz clarinettist in Britain to be wholly preoccupied with the instrument.* Professional players of the clarinet were typically obliged to be saxophonists first, using the clarinet only as a 'doubling' instrument. Fawkes, moreover, modelled his style on the

---

* Harry Parry mostly played clarinet but in the rapidly changing climate of opinion he wasn't rated by the purists.

George Webb's Dixielanders at Decca Studios, 1946. *Left to right*: Art Streatfield, tuba; Buddy Vallis, banjo; Wally Fawkes, clarinet; Eddie Harvey, trombone; Reg Rigden, trumpet; George Webb, piano.

New Orleans master, Sidney Bechet. While the Archer Street jazzman-clarinettist invariably based his style on Benny Goodman or Jimmy Dorsey, Fawkes emulated Bechet's broad tone and marked vibrato and played with a volume necessary to compete with (eventually) four brass: two trumpets, trombone and tuba. He had a convincing, single-minded passion to play in the New Orleans style and possessed natural talent, but his playing was marred by faulty intonation, a fact remarked upon by the local semi-professionals who played in the jam sessions at the Red Barn.

Eddie Harvey was Britain's first genuine 'tailgate' trombonist: his style was in the classic ensemble tradition of Kid Ory and George Brunies, with touches of J. C. Higginbotham. The Lewis–Parnell Jazzmen initially had no trombone in their instrumentation, primarily because there was no professional musician who would countenance, much less be able to play, the 'rips', 'smears' and 'slurs' that were part of the art. These crudities were considered dreadfully old-fashioned in Archer Street.

Owen Bryce played in a staccato fashion and with dubious intonation, but initially he was the band's 'school' musician. He was able to read music and sketch out the arrangements which, interspersed with the collective improvisation, distinguished the band from the now despised jam-session groups performing what purists then called 'sterile riffing', usually as a background to 'interminable' tenor saxophone solos. Later Eddie Harvey studied seriously and contributed to the arrangements. Reg Rigden, an erratic but more impassioned player, joined to play first trumpet and Bryce took the second part.

In attempting to emulate the Louis Armstrong–King Oliver two-trumpet partnership in the Creole Jazz Band, Rigden and Bryce took upon themselves an impossible task. It was one of the band's many weaknesses. Rarely has the two-trumpet lead in an otherwise free-wheeling ensemble been successful and certainly not here. When one or the other dropped out, the band immediately assumed a freer and looser sound. In harness they stifled each other.

In its attempts to break away from the formless jam-session style, the band imposed upon itself a severe restraint to the essential looseness in a jazz band. In the rhythm section the initial guitar, played by Dick Denny, was replaced by the banjo, played by Buddy Vallis. His insistent thump on the instrument became the talisman of the trad craze in the fifties and sixties.

In May 1945 the band entered the *Melody Maker*'s South East London Dance Band Championship held at Peckham Baths. Judging the five entrants were bandleader Lou Preager, tenor saxophonist Johnny Gray, pianist Billy Penrose and – inevitably – Edgar Jackson.

In the *Melody Maker*, 3 June 1945, under the heading 'PECKHAM PANDEMONIUM', it was reported that the winners Fred Hedley and his band were met with boos and catcalls. Members of the audience thought the award should have gone to the band in second place, the Eltham Studio Band. Third place went to George Webb's Dixielanders, who received their first write-up in the *Melody Maker*:

> Special award for best 'small' band. Hon. mention for clarinet (Wally Fawkes) and trombone (Ed Harvey). A genuine old-time dixieland-style band who showed not only quite astonishing understanding of this type of jazz but also the ability to put it into practice. Nevertheless it was the lack of the finer points of musicianship which forced it down to third place – as proved by

the poor waltz, made no better by the clarinet playing continually sharp and bad balance due to lack of microphone technique.

Edgar Jackson, the originator and organizer of these contests, was undoubtedly the reporter. The report was hardly noticed; the paper had published hundreds of similar notices since the contests began and nobody in 1945 could have foreseen that this 'genuine old-time dixieland-style band' was to create a degree of pandemonium that extended far outside the environs of Peckham or Barnehurst, where they played every Monday evening for the next two years.

The Dixielanders were employed in various occupations. Fawkes was just revealing a rare talent as a cartoonist, Bryce was a shopkeeper, Rigden a librarian, but Webb, Harvey, Streatfield, Vallis and Wykes had worked in the local Vickers-Armstrong factory. Sociologically-minded critics with various left-wing and anarchist associations saw this as an expression of working-class culture and likened the band's endeavours to those of the early US black jazzmen, whose art flourished despite their subservience, socially and economically, to the white boss. The Young Communist League promoted the Dixielanders in a series of concerts in central London at the Memorial Hall, Farringdon Street under the banner of the Challenge Jazz Club. In their paper, *Challenge*, they heavily emphasized the socio-political overtones of this phenomenon.

Despite the band's limitations the overall sound was communicated to a small, enthusiastic gathering at the Red Barn every Monday evening, where the jam-session musicians were no longer engaged but some of them returned only to scoff. It was the dixieland stylistic conception that in the spirit of the time had an emotive appeal. A hard, brutal war against the forces of evil was coming to its close. Many social, political and artistic doctrines were being demolished. The bastions of commercial swing music were being stormed by these proletarian jazzmen in the Arcadia of Barnehurst.

Their letter headings proclaimed 'Jazz and Only Jazz' and they meant it. They represented the clear shining light of purity and conviction. Like Eric Ballard of Wakehurst Road, SW11 these Quixotes from Subtopia were tilting their lances against the evils of commercialism in a social milieu vastly different from that of Fred Elizalde at the Savoy Hotel or Ken Johnson at the Café de Paris, where both had foundered trying to bring jazz to the affluent. It was also different from Spike Hughes, not only in style, but in playing to an enthusiastic live audience responding to their endeavours.

Unlike all those leaders and their musicians, the Dixielanders didn't rely on music for a living. They were true dilettantes, overtly and aggressively intransigent in their policy, and they believed that learning to read music would rob them of the jazz 'spirit', a sentiment reminiscent of Gus Mueller's thrust about his contemporaries who took this path in the Whiteman band thirty years earlier.

George Webb's Dixielanders recording for Decca, 1946

Their repertoire included a tune of negro spiritual origin, called 'When the Saints Go Marching In'. It was to become the traditionalists' anthem, the rabble-rousing finale for bands on both sides of the Atlantic. The only record of the tune available in this country until 1946 was by Louis Armstrong's 1938 Decca band with trombonist J. C. Higginbotham essaying the declamatory role of the 'preacher'. It was introduced into the Webb band's repertoire by Eddie Harvey, a 'Higgy' enthusiast. The title was symbolic of changing attitudes: the new jazz saints were marching into public consciousness! Their models were the black jazzmen and not, as with most British jazzmen before them, the white musicians; this was the vital difference. But Higginbotham's influence on Harvey was viewed with suspicion by some of the Dixielanders. Higginbotham, although black, was not from New Orleans, not an ensemble – a 'tailgate' – player. Furthermore, Harvey was reported as having been seen listening to the Eltham Studio Band and, it was rumoured, actually played with them. Harvey's style had certainly changed since first joining the band and it was darkly alleged that his flirting with a *dance band* was responsible.

He was called to a kangaroo court,* the Dixielanders the judges and the jury, at Owen Bryce's shop at 23 Thomas Street, Woolwich, London SE18. He was asked to explain his deviation, to stop it forthwith and return to the verities of New Orleans jazz.

The Dixielanders came to be associated with the Challenge Jazz Club through James Asman, himself a member and the first to give the band a mention, in one of the Jazz Appreciation Society magazines. In one of the undated JAS booklets he wrote: 'We think any *sincere* local efforts to play jazz should be encouraged. We have some worthwhile British hot music other than the heavily publicised Parrys and Featherstonhaughs – and we will do our best to publicise it. We have no intention, however, of plugging any little jivey group who base their efforts on the latest swing trends. Only musicians who take an *intelligent* interest in hot music will receive our support.'

Thanks to Asman and partner Bill Kinnell, Decca recorded the Dixielanders and in another JAS booklet they boasted: 'Our recent efforts to promote British jazz received a tremendous boost on the morning of May 5th 1945 when the editorial staff of the JAS brought Tony Short, their pianist discovery, and George Webb's Dixielanders to Decca's studios.'

Also present was Edgar Jackson, who was quoted as saying he thought Short's record, 'Milton Street Moan', would receive a five-star rating from himself in the *Melody Maker* on its release. Jackson was also quoted as saying that the Webb band 'played the best dixieland I have heard in twenty years'.

---

* I was present at this meeting. George Webb led for the prosecution. I shudder in recollection of its absurdity . . . Eddie Harvey later taught music at Haileybury College and was the author of a very successful book, *How to Play Jazz Piano*.

Furthermore, Asman's report flattered Jackson – with, no doubt, an eye on a favourable review for the Dixielanders' recording – by praising him for help on 'certain technical matters', a shamefully blatant case of joining hands with the enemy if it suited the book. The pure in heart were no less guilty of the opportunism they so roundly condemned in others. However, Asman had no support for Jackson's appeal that the band play with less volume. Decca did not release these recordings and in *Jazzology*, November 1946, Owen Bryce, with admirable candour, admitted that it was he who 'blew out', that his pitching throughout militated against their release.

The JAS recorded the Dixielanders at a studio in Derby in December 1945. The titles were 'New Orleans Hop Scop Blues'/'Come Back, Sweet Papa', released on Jazz 0001. The records cost fifteen shillings, nearly five times the price of a commercially produced shellac record.

In a subsequent booklet the editorial naturally mentioned Jazz 0001, claiming that the record received a universally enthusiastic reception, but also emphasizing their financial problems: 'Frankly, it was a question of fifteen shillings per issue, or no private label and considering present-day conditions we consider the price to be reasonable. If jazz enthusiasts support our efforts on their behalf for a private label untrammelled by commercial interests we will be at their service . . .'

Again, the heartfelt cry for support. Again the enthusiasts didn't rally to the cause and JAS folded, its entire record output limited to four 78 rpm issues. Asman was later to edit *Jazz Record*, at 18 Timbercroft Lane, London SE18, not far from where he first heard Webb's Dixielanders, but in the June/July 1952 issue appealed, yet again, for support: 'We are looking for 500 more readers. Just 500! With that additional number we could concentrate on producing a first-class magazine, without having to chase people for money.' The eternal cry . . . and it fell on deaf ears, although Jazz 0001 was sufficiently liked for buffs to spend what was then quite a large sum for a gramophone record and it was favourably reviewed by Sinclair Traill in *Pick-Up* and Max Jones in the *Melody Maker*.

One critic, Stanley Dance, was less enthusiastic about Jazz 0001. In a JAS booklet, No. 1, Volume 3, undated, he made a few uncomfortable observations about the concept of revivalism:

I have said my piece often enough (to the dire discontent of most of my readers) about my mistrust of an artificial return to original simplicities.

To begin with, it is quite evident that if the record were presented with an old Gennett label and the band given a fictitious unfamiliar name the masses of fig types* throughout the world would be deliriously happy with it. My own interest would be greater if I knew this record had been recorded by an obscure New Orleans group. This wouldn't make the music any better, but would make it natural to its time, and would give it historical interest and a position in the last creative surge before this jazz style reached maturity. However, I am aware that many newcomers to jazz have only a sentimental conception of period . . .

The thing that does please me about records like this, and by [American revivalist] Lu Watters, is that young musicians should take pleasure in playing this lusty old style. The fact of *their* enjoyment is the greatest possible justification for the music resulting. I can imagine, too, that there is pleasure in listening to them in the flesh. At the same time their performance should not be compared with masterpieces of the genre, the records by the Hot Five, Oliver, Dodds and the current Kid Ory–Omer Simeon combination. In that way some sense of perspective would be acquired and some abatement in the current hysteria achieved.

Apart from these reservations I have tried to listen as objectively as possible.

Left to right: Revivalists George Melly, Peter Hull, Mick Mulligan and Bob Dawbarn

* From 'Mouldy Fygges', a term coined by Leonard Feather to express his contempt for the revivalist faction.

Dance praised Wally Fawkes' playing and, understandably, favourably compared him with the inept Lu Watters clarinettist Ellis Horne. He liked Harvey's trombone but was less happy with the trumpets and the rhythm section and he saw the inclusion of the tuba as a 'silly affectation'. He ended on a waggish note: 'But how about all those solos on "Hop Scop"? What about the old polyphony? And them there polyrhythms? Play the game you cats.' This thrust referred to the revivalists' grandiose use of such words.

Jazz 0001* represented a noble failure to reproduce jazz of another era. Dance was right. It was pastiche; it was artistically futile; the performance was far below the technical standards of the musicians who had inspired it. But, contradiction that the record is, Webb's Dixielanders were, in their time, a force and often tremendously exciting 'live'. They were to become the inspiration for many similarly styled bands throughout the country: an emulation of an emulation that led to the massive 'trad' boom of the fifties and sixties.

The revivalist bands that sprang up through the country included Sandy Brown and his band, Edinburgh; the Yorkshire Jazz Band, Leeds; Mick Gill's band, Nottingham; the Merseysippi Jazz Band, Liverpool; the Avon Cities Jazz Band, Bristol; and in London, Mick Mulligan's Magnolia Jazz Band with singer George Melly; Mike Daniels' Delta Jazz Band; John Haim's Jelly Roll Kings; the Crane River Jazz Band; Eric Silk's Southern Jazz Band; Chris Barber and his band, and many, many others. All were amateurs but some were to become professional once the trad boom became established.

A band contemporary with the Dixielanders, led by trumpeter Freddy Randall, played at Cook's Ferry Inn, Edmonton, north London, every Sunday evening. Their style was based more on the Muggsy Spanier Ragtime Band, but the purists found them less acceptable than the Dixielanders, even though, like the Lewis–Parnell band, their musicianship was superior and in Bruce Turner, on clarinet and alto saxophone, they had a player of considerable talent and imagination.

---

* When my book *All This and 10%* was published in late 1976 I appeared on several radio programmes and invariably Jazz 0001 was played as an appropriate record. My reactions were a mixture of nostalgic pleasure and musical embarrassment at such a lumpen performance. It is a testimony to its historical importance that it should be in the BBC archives.

The Dixielanders acquired a steady and enthusiastic following. The staff at Barnehurst Station became used to an odd assortment trooping up the stairs from the platform on Monday evening – sober-suited professional men, art students and long-haired, bearded bohemian types. The band received frequent mentions in the *Melody Maker*, and appeared on the BBC 'Radio Rhythm Club' produced by Sheila Fryer, but actually run by Denis Preston. They appeared at the Feldman Swing Club and in several concerts in the West End.

The Dixielanders severed their association with the Challenge Jazz Club and promoted their own concerts under the banner of the Hot Club of London at King George's Hall, Tottenham Court Road, London. Their format was a record recital by an 'expert' followed by the Dixielanders' session. Among the guest speakers were that highly eccentric Irish peer the Marquis of Donegall, Max Jones, Mark White – later producer of the BBC 'Jazz Club' – Jeff Aldam, Sinclair Traill and Robert Goffin, the Belgian author of *Jazz: From Congo Square to Swing*, written in 1946. Goffin harangued a bemused audience in violently fractured English, but they listened politely. In one of the issues of *Jazz Music* Denis Preston reviewed *Jazz: From Congo Square to Swing* and his opinion of the book was such that having discovered the author was also an expert on rodents he tartly suggested he 'stuck to rats'.

In the essentially amateur spirit of the revival the guest players at the Hot Club had to be stylistically akin to the Dixielanders, and were not that easy to find. The Archer Street man, even if he had passable jazz credentials, was not, in the prevailing mood, made welcome. Similarly, he did not wish to be any part of an exercise that was so old-fashioned in conception and technically faltering.

However, there were sufficient young collectors-turned-musicians to add a little variety to the format of a recital and the Dixielanders' session. These included trumpeters Freddy Randall and John Haim and their bands, clarinettists Ian Christie and Gerry Collins, trumpeters Johnny Rowden and Alan Wickham, trombonists Keith Christie and Tony Russell, guitarist Bill Bramwell, and the original Blue Blowers, a comb and paper, washboard and guitar group.

By now 'Archer Street Jazz' had become a term of contempt among supporters of revivalism and the drubbing was particularly severe for those playing 'Archer Street Dixie' – another derogatory epithet. This applied to Harry Gold and his Pieces of Eight, Sid Phillips and his band, Joe Daniels and his band and the Lewis–Parnell Jazzmen. It was believed that their playing lacked the requisite conviction, and that their sudden interest in 'true' jazz was purely financial. It was the 'sincere' amateurs who captured the imagination and the market.

George Melly

The nub of the matter was the sincerity or otherwise of the approach. The amateurs were weak on technique but strong on conviction, and this got over. Their patent sincerity made the niceties of execution, or rather the lack of them, seem unimportant. Played now, the Lewis–Parnell records, for instance, make for infinitely more enjoyable listening than the Webb issues. The ruthless test of time overturns earlier and – it has to be admitted – muddled and emotive assessment based on vaguely 'ideological' rather than musical considerations.

But at the time Webb's Dixielanders dramatically outstripped the Jazzmen in popularity and critical acclaim, and this from a band that had just managed to win third place in a *Melody Maker* dance-band contest and had entered simply for the fun of it.

Vic Lewis particularly was aggrieved by this acclaim. He had visited New York in 1938 to record several titles with famed American jazzmen Bobby Hackett (cornet), Pee Wee Russell (clarinet), Eddie Condon (guitar), Dave Bowman (piano) and Zutty Singleton (drums). In this respect he had the most impeccable credentials for running a dixieland band and yet his Jazzmen were not making any real impact.

At one of the Hot Club concerts, he and Harry Gold were in the audience. Lewis met Max Jones in the foyer and complained bitterly about the poor musicianship of the Webb band and particularly about the leader's piano playing. He was obviously astonished that such technical inadequacy should have been so enthusiastically applauded. His bewilderment was genuine though, no doubt, his uppermost feeling was one of resentment. (The author was present and can clearly recall Lewis' criticisms and how he abruptly terminated his strictures at the sudden appearance of George Webb returning from an interval drink, Webb being known to react strongly to criticism.)

In his puzzlement and resentment Lewis unintentionally put his finger on the pulse of the prevalent situation. His 'Archer Street' revivalism had been treated with suspicion by those collectors who really cared about jazz. What he heard at King George's Hall that night was seemingly a closer approximation of the genuine article and highly regarded because of this.

(An illustration of just how purist were some of the Hot Club audience: I, the secretary, made announcements between sessions and recitals. We held raffles with records as the prizes. On one occasion the prize was 'Drop That Sack' and 'Georgia Bo Bo' by Louis Armstrong's Hot Five (the label read Louis Armstrong with Lil's Hot Shots), then only recently released on the Brunswick label and, due to the shortage of shellac, difficult to obtain. 'Drop That Sack' was played over the PA and faded as I started to make the announcement. I was shouted off the stage! I had butted in when God was speaking! Such was the intensity of purist feeling at the height of revivalist fervour.)

Typically, Lewis was soon leading a big band, himself imitating American bandleader Phil Harris' vocalisms. Later he was the self-styled 'Britain's Stan Kenton', leading a vast band in a series of concerts grandiosely entitled 'Music for Moderns', the title having strong echoes of Paul Whiteman's 'Innovations in Modern Music' twenty years before and proving just as contrived and ephemeral and, it transpired, financially disastrous.

* * *

By far the most impressive of the guests was trumpeter Humphrey Lyttelton, soon to be a highly significant fixture on the British jazz scene as musician, bandleader, critic, author and broadcaster. He made his first-ever concert appearance, at the Hot Club of London, on Saturday 18 January 1947 with a pick-up band that included Eddie Harvey, recently drafted into the RAF but on leave that weekend, and a brilliant Welsh pianist, Dill Jones.

Without rehearsal they played a somewhat discordant set that had the strong purist element among the audience up in arms. Wasn't this the scorned 'jam session', the very antithesis of what the Dixielanders and the Hot Club stood for? They were stridently vocal in their protests, but Lyttelton's contribution was a revelation. He played with a convincing authority, his physical height – six feet four – giving him an Olympian bearing that matched the power of his playing. He later sat in with the Dixielanders at the Red Barn, and after certain events and a little machination within the ranks, he replaced Reg Rigden.

Humphrey Lyttelton and his band. *Left to right*: Les Rawlings, bass; Keith Christie, trombone; Dave Carey, drums; Lyttelton, trumpet; Neville Skrimshire, guitar; Wally Fawkes, clarinet; George Webb, piano

The band that had shone in their sincerity and application now had a player of genuine class. Their popularity improved dramatically, but this shot in the arm brought with it many problems, musical and temperamental. Lyttelton was irked by the second trumpet and Bryce couldn't match the phrasing or the strength of his new team-mate. This change in personnel strongly emphasized the truth that an additional horn in an ensemble of this kind was a limiting rather than an enriching factor. Bryce soon left, leaving an unbridled Lyttelton effectively to fulfil the role of lead trumpeter.

Jack Jackson (then enjoying a revival on the BBC Jazz Club), Norman Payne, Tommy McQuater, Max Goldberg, Duncan Whyte or Kenny Baker never made the same kind of impact that Lyttelton did on the jazz buff. His conception and ability apart, one of the reasons for this was that he was known only as a jazz player and not one buried in the brass section of a restaurant or stage band, allowed just the occasional solo. His first book, *I Play As I Please*, reflected the happy situation he enjoyed. In terms of publicity his aristocratic background was a tremendous advantage, with many professionals sniffing at the unfair extra-musical press interest in an old Etonian and ex-captain in the Brigade of Guards blowing hot trumpet. Lyttelton was unhappy with the management (the author) and certain members of the band and left after eight months, taking Harry Brown (Harvey's successor) and Wally Fawkes with him. It was the end of George Webb's Dixielanders.

Wally Fawkes, clarinet; Humphrey Lyttelton, trumpet; Harry Brown, trombone, at the Red Barn, spring 1947

It was inevitable that someone of Lyttelton's stature and temperament should lead his own band, even if such a career would have seemed highly unlikely for someone expected on demobilization to follow in his father's footsteps and become an Eton master. He has continuously led bands since his departure from the Dixielanders in November 1947.

Jazz was to take some unlikely children into its fold over the years but it was yet another irony in the history of jazz in Britain that this member of the upper class was propelled by fate into jazz-band leadership by being introduced to a bunch of proletarians whose stylistic beliefs and intransigent determination he firmly embraced and put into practice with his own band. Later, however, he was to stretch himself musically – and not without arousing much controversy.

The technically limited Brown soon left and was replaced by the seventeen-year-old Keith Christie. He was another musician of genuine class with a full jazz-gruff tone and was equally adept as a soloist and ensemble player. With Christie, Fawkes and himself in the front line Lyttelton had a star trio, but he was constantly hamstrung by the problem that had always plagued British jazz, the rhythm section. In one desperate move to rectify the situation he engaged the veteran dance-band drummer and teacher Max Abrams. This inclusion of an Archer Street man caused eyebrows to be raised and vocal cords to be exercised in protest. Typically, Lyttelton was unheeding of these protests. This was one of the many snooks he was to cock at purist (and other) conventions and his short-spell employment of Abrams prefigured a less rigid attitude and a breaking down of watertight musical compartments in the fifties.

Members of Graeme Bell's Australian Jazz Band. *Left to right*: Jack Varney, banjo, and his wife; Pixie Roberts, clarinet; Russ Murphy, drums; Adrian Monsbourgh, trombone; Roger Bell, trumpet

Lyttelton, Fawkes and Brown agreed to play as part of the Dixielanders for the last Hot Club concert and the Dixielanders' final appearance. For these last rites in January 1948, the Hot Club booked Graeme Bell's Australian Jazz Band for thirty pounds, the exact sum the BBC paid Duke Ellington for the one broadcast they gave him in 1933.

The Australian Jazz Band were breezy adventurers who had toured Europe in hazardous post-war conditions and sought work in Britain en route back home. The manager was Mel Langdon who looked, in his wide-brimmed light-blue trilby and belted raincoat of a similar hue, like a tall Alan Ladd. He solemnly addressed me on the subject of billing and publicity generally: 'There's something I've got to make quite clear to you, son. The billing is Graeme Bell and his Australian Jazz Band and in your publicity they're to be described as a New Orleans band, not dixieland. You got that, son?'

This firm instruction highlighted one of the current linguistic-cum-ideological nuances that reflected the revivalists' desire for righteous categorization. 'Dixieland', redolent of the white man's jazz, hadn't the same emotive associations as 'New Orleans', this usually relating to the black man's music, although many white jazz men came from the Crescent City. It was a puzzling maze of terminology that could undoubtedly confuse a partially interested onlooker in those turbulent days. The Bell band wanted the stylistically stronger appellation, although chauvinistically insisting on the 'Australian' tag as well. Had George Webb in 1943 realized that black jazz was to become so fashionable and so critically acceptable it is likely that he would have decided on a different tag than 'Dixielanders'.

It transpired that the Australians were extremely 'dixieland' in their conception and execution, but they were well received on their stay in Britain. As Empire citizens they had no problems in obtaining the work permits denied to the American musicians with whom they most wanted to be associated and whom a legion of enthusiasts wanted to hear. Irony upon irony.

The concert included speeches from Rex Harris, Mark White, the Marquis of Donegall, George Webb and the author. The bands combined for the 'Saints' anthem. I announced this as 'When the Saints Go Marching Out'. The entire proceedings were recorded on acetate discs, these now scratchy mementos of a noble venture's last moments.

It was to be the start of a new era in British jazz and subsequent events owed much to that out-of-tune band of pioneers from the Bexleyheath and District Rhythm Club at the Red Barn, Barnehurst, Kent.

* * *

In February 1948, the Bell band opened at the Leicester Square Jazz Club above the Café de l'Europe, Leicester Square, run by Ken Lindsay, Peter Martin and Ray Jackson, formerly of the Challenge Jazz Club.

The Australians were not as hidebound in their repertoire as the English revivalists. They embraced tunes from the entire pop spectrum,

Graeme Bell and his Australian Jazz Band in Britain, 1948. *Left to right:* Pixie Roberts, clarinet; Lou Silberiesen, bass; Roger Bell, trumpet; Ade Monsbourgh, trombone; Russ Murphy, drums; Jack Varney, banjo; and Graeme Bell, piano.

including songs by Noël Coward and Graeme Bell who, unlike most of his British contemporaries, wrote his own material. Overall, their sound was rather polite, but they had in Ade Monsbourgh a multi-instrumentalist with a strong and recognizable style on the alto saxophone. In their general presentation an Antipodean cockiness was cheerfully and successfully projected, but their main contribution was to introduce jazz for dancing, an innovation with far-reaching financial and social results that favourably affected the entire jazz-club movement.

Dancing in pre-war rhythm clubs was as unthinkable as a female in the Long Room at Lord's. Dancing was for those people who went to palais where dance bands churned out the commercial hokum!

No; jazz called for serious attention! The revivalist buff, often with pipe in mouth, metronomically nodded his head to the 'contrapuntal interplay', 'Afro-American accents', 'cumulative tension' and 'resolving climaxes' (and other mumbo-jumbo phrases the like of which Stanley Dance gently mocked in his review of Jazz 0001).

This tradition of overlooking the music's original function was continued throughout the years, except at the Feldman Club, one of the few venues where American servicemen instructed locals in the art of jitterbugging, which became the general practice on the floor of the Leicester Square Jazz Club a few years later. Such antics attracted a fascinated lay press.

The Bells' much publicized policy of dancing to jazz drew many of both sexes whose admission fee at the door was to be instrumental in a situation where, for the first time, a musician could earn his living playing jazz and only jazz. Happily, the interplay, (if not contrapuntal), cumulative tension and resolving climaxes were more frequently found between the sexes on the dancefloor than on the stand.

The Bells introduced a weekly *Puffo*, a duplicated sheet with a selection of tunes the band would play, often tagging improbable names as the alleged composers. There were also light-hearted contributions from the band who called themselves 'Dags', and announcements of future events.

Humphrey Lyttelton wrote a piece for the *Puffo* in which he created a blues singer called 'Loose Legs Broganza' who, Lyttelton implied, made a record entitled 'Fetch Me a Stomach Pump'. It was a pointed joke at the expense of the purist and his obsession with real blues singers of similarly bizarre appellations, such as Bogus Ben Covington (an actual artist) who made a record called 'I Thought I Heard the Voice of a Pork Chop'. (I can vouch for this. It was one of the mint-condition Paramount records I found in my Cape Town treasure trove.)

All the joviality and jitterbugging made for a far more enjoyable atmosphere generally. Jazz had become fun, but the *Puffo* had the occasional solemn and pontifical contribution, usually from James Asman, tilting his lance at the windmills cluttering the purists' landscape – the BBC, Archer Street and 'swing' music.

The Lyttelton and Bell bands combined to make four sides, for the Parlophone label, of compositions and arrangements by Graeme Bell. These were extremely successful and presaged Lyttelton's eventual breakaway from strictly traditional modes. The saxophones were played on these records by Ade Monsbourgh and Pixie Roberts, much to the chagrin of the fundamentalists, who alleged that the instrument violated the purity of jazz.

In a few short years the scene had dramatically tilted. Old values were being questioned and established players, like the Archer Street Jazzmen, were being put down. New idols were surging into the public eye and there was to be yet another dimension to the jazz scene leading to further internecine strife, although the opponents thought themselves to be so separate from each other that the word 'internecine' could hardly apply. The hostilities that broke out were bitter and prolonged.

13

Heebie Jeebie Boys

By the middle of the late forties the revivalists thought they had won the day. Traditional jazz was in the ascendancy. In the USA veteran musicians, black and white, were returning to the recording studios after a long absence. They were appearing regularly in public. In America young white men were emulating the New Orleans pioneers, but more successfully so in Europe – in France, Germany, Sweden, Denmark, Holland, Norway, Britain (particularly) and also in Australia. Much of this activity was entirely attributable to the persistence and ideological faith of the writers and discographers who passionately believed in the early forms of jazz, but at the same time a new conception of jazz jarred their equanimity. This was called bebop, or rebop, and had been evolved almost clandestinely in New York, primarily at a musicians' club called Minton's Playhouse, on West 118th Street, Harlem, managed by Teddy Hill, Dizzy Gillespie's one-time employer. It was purely the black man's creation. Whatever the arguments about the racial and geographical origins of jazz, this new development was indisputably his.

In 1933 Spike Hughes had referred to the use of mutes by 'Tricky Sam' Nanton and Charles 'Cootie' Williams in Duke Ellington's band as 'something personal and moving'. In the mid-1940s the black musician's manner of expressing something personal and moving was in the harmonic and rhythmic (and tonally harsh) pyrotechnics of bebop, with trumpeter John Birks 'Dizzy' Gillespie and alto saxophonist Charlie 'Bird' Parker the high priests of this strange new cult. The angularity in the phrasing and rejection of conventional modes emphasized that it was also a music of social protest in a white-dominated society undergoing post-war changes and facing threats to the racial status quo.

The music, played by individuals given to the eccentricities of wearing black berets, dark glasses and goatee beards, many of whom were addicted to hard drugs, was made with the avowed intention of frustrating the white man's plagiarism. Black musicians had long believed that their birthright had been stolen by 'the white man', whose better social and economic status gave him ample opportunity to benefit by his theft. This is a simplification of a complex social and musical situation but a case in point was the enormous success of the white swing bands when compared with black orchestras of similar size. Benny Goodman commissioned arrangements from Fletcher Henderson for records that sold in their thousands. Henderson used the same kind of arrangements for his own band with an infinitely superior array of soloists that, by comparison, sold minimally. Indeed, whites succeeded more in a field of activity where blacks were generally the superior artists. Leonard Feather, in his *Encyclopedia of Jazz*, wrote:

> A bunch of young rebels gathered when their regular jobs were through and worked out new ideas. Among the innovators were a trumpet man from Cab Calloway's band, Dizzy Gillespie, a pianist, Thelonious Monk, a drummer, Kenny Clarke and many others.
>
> In 1940 Oscar Moore, guitarist with the Nat King Cole trio, ended the group's first Decca record, 'Sweet Lorraine', on a ninth chord with a flatted fifth, an unheard of departure then. At the Café Society, New York, pianist Ken Kersey found his way from a tonic to the dominant chord through an unconventional progression of minor sevenths. Jazz was fighting its way out of a harmonic and melodic blind alley. Rhythmically it was fighting too. Little by little the steady punching four-to-a-bar that had seemed necessary to the rhythm section of every band gave way to a subtler more varied punctuation in which musicians implied the beat instead of hitting the listener over the head with it.
>
> Eventually all these ideas and these people converged in Harlem and 52nd Street and these characteristics were slowly woven together. As musicians gathered together they would use an onomatopoeic expression to describe a typical phrase played by these musicians: rebop and bebop were accepted as the names for the new branch of jazz that had been born out of the desire for progress and evolution.

Inevitably it was to be played by whites once it was recorded and British whites were in the vanguard of these new departures.

The first bebop records issued in Britain were by Gillespie and appeared on two major labels, Parlophone and HMV. The first to be released, in 1947, were in Parlophone's 'Rhythm Style Series' and had been made only a year earlier, but the HMV issues didn't appear until 1949, three years after they were made, although HMV had the rights from the day of their availability. Perhaps there was an executive at HMV who, like his stiff-necked predecessor confronted with the ODJB recordings in 1917, decided against releasing the Gillespies. Understandably, perhaps, he may have thought there would be little support for music so outrageously non-conformist.

Carlo Krahmer issued Gillespie and Parker records on his Esquire label from 1948. He held informal record sessions at his flat in Bedford

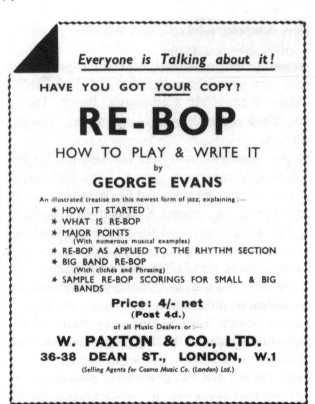

Advertisement for a 're-bop' instruction book, c.1948

Harry Morris, eleventh member of the Club Eleven

Avenue, Bloomsbury, in central London, on Sunday afternoons and there, some time in 1947, tenor saxophonist Ronnie Scott, in the company of bassist Lennie Bush, guitarist Pete Chilver, drummers Tony Crombie and Laurie Morgan and pianist-trumpeter Denis Rose, heard for the first time Charlie Parker – on a record he made with guitarist Tiny Grimes in 1944 called 'Red Cross'. Scott recalls: 'I was totally stunned. I'd not heard jazz like this before. After that experience I could only "hear" Parker when I was playing. He made me realize what musical direction I had to take from then.' Scott was one of many young British musicians attracted to the complexities of the idiom, who saw it as a challenge to their technical skill, the form allowing them greater freedom and escape from the harmonic and melodic cul-de-sac. It was an exciting challenge to which they enthusiastically applied themselves in a genuine spirit of artistic endeavour and they were as fervent in their beliefs as any revivalist.

Like the innovatory black musicians in Harlem the young British apostles gathered in one particular hotbed of activity. In 1948 the Club Eleven was formed, its enclave Mack's Rehearsal Rooms, Great Windmill Street. There were two resident bands. One featured Hank Shaw (trumpet), Ronnie Scott (tenor saxophone), Lennie Bush (bass), Tommy Pollard (piano) and Flash Winston (drums). The other consisted of Johnny Rogers (alto saxophone), Leon Calvert (trumpet), Tony Crombie (drums), Bernie Fenton (piano) and Joe Muddell (bass). The groups were interchangeable and were often joined by others, including trumpeter-pianist Denis Rose. The eleventh man – hence the club's title – was Harry Morris, the club's manager, a one-time sundries salesman specializing in American ties. This wasn't a band a 'professional' manager would handle, any more than George Webb's Dixielanders.

The erudite English critic Brian Davis recalled the club's early days in *Jazz at Ronnie Scott's*, the club's house magazine, February/March 1980 issue.

I first heard of the Club Eleven via that late and most under-rated drummer Benny (Dave) Goodman, then a resident of Southend where a group of us eager youngsters were struggling to master instruments. Benny enthralled us with tales of happenings in a fantastic London basement. 'It's all the gear there, man. It's all happening there, man.' I was in the RAF and hitch-hiked to London and we met at the club's entrance, which was a narrow doorway at 41 Great Windmill Street, opposite the Windmill Theatre 'which never closed'. Immediately to the left of the entrance was a steep bare wooden stairway painted a dull red around its well, descending to basement level. An upturned box served as a cash desk and behind this stood Harry Morris who collected 3/6d admission fee in between other duties. The stairs led to a bare room and I do mean bare! The floor; the walls; naked electric lights enhancing the starkness of the decor.

Immediately to the right of the entrance was a small stand with an upright (just about!) piano. There were a few hard chairs in front of the stand with space for dancing either side of the room. However, there was a touch of luxury – two or three off-grey, moth-eaten Victorian sofas alongside the stand and down the side of the wall. These sofas could tell a few tales of the famous who have sat on them, and of the shapely posteriors of the girls who used to frequent the club, all looking cool and attractive and performing an unhurried type of jive with dirndl skirts a-swirling: so much more sophisticated than the frantic antics of the trad club and dance-hall jitterbuggers . . .

Sometimes, if he felt like it, 'the teacher' Denis Rose would have a blow. Denis was a bit older than the others and didn't view things with the same youthful fanaticism. I recall one occasion when I was listening in my usual state of euphoria (which always overcame me from the first few notes of Tony Crombie's septet), he was seated on sofa 'No. 2' leafing through a magazine. This appalled me. It seemed almost sacrilegious, such was my uncritical acceptance of what, in hindsight, was pretty raw stuff at times. Nevertheless Denis' attitude early on was at variance with most of the others, who all seemed to concentrate intently on what the other fellow was putting down and were obviously playing for themselves, giving scant attention to the audience (who were equally serious about the proceedings) packing the place every time I was there.

Once I asked trumpeter Hank Shaw from my (as always) front seat who an unknown (to me) tenor man was: 'Schhh man,' replied Hank, eyes tightly closed, 'I'm listening – isn't he great? . . .' I never did find out who that tenor man was.

This indeed was the special aura of the Club Eleven – both participants and listeners alike lived the music. Its 'exclusiveness' fired the imagination of the young and impressionable and assuredly one was never the same after catching the heady atmosphere of that basement, not only in one's jazz outlook and appreciation but in one's everyday behaviour, which must have been insufferable to those on the 'outside' – which was almost everybody!

Another vivid memory is the sight of a thin, cropped-haired young alto player with an ancient-looking silver instrument whose playing turned everyone around. Everything is relative, but even today I still think back on that thin stranger's playing as being the closest to Parker I have ever heard. I caught Ronnie Scott in a non-playing moment to enquire who he was: 'He's Spike Robinson.' I also received an unsolicited follow-up comment from the normally taciturn Scott. 'He's an American merchant seaman. Really fantastic, isn't he?' At least Spike is preserved on an Esquire LP.

Thirty years later this is a somewhat tentative and gauche set to listen to but redolent of the tremendous excitement always to be found in that dingy, sweaty and smoke-filled basement where British bop was spawned and legendary figures began their careers to become top names in the British jazz scene (and Vic Feldman in America) although some, like alto saxophonist Alan Doniger, a fine, fiery player, have remained in undeserved obscurity.

The Club Eleven's guiding spirit was Denis Rose, who analysed the intriguing new records from America in much the same way that Al Davison had analysed the Paul Whiteman twelve-inch record of 'Sweet Sue' in a 1929 *Melody Maker*, except that Davison's task was dealing with a flatulent and showy but harmonically simple arrangement. Rose's analytical brain was applied to a totally different music played 'underground' by angry young black men of another continent who spoke in a bewildering argot.

Ronnie Scott and his contemporaries, including Denis Rose, often patronized an East End cafe called Barney Fella's in Aldgate Avenue, off Middlesex Street (Petticoat Lane). The counter assistant was known as 'Talkie'. Talkie, a Jewish man of about sixty, gained his sobriquet on account of his loquacity. He had an immense pride in his knowledge of the English language. 'Give me any word in English – any word – and I'll give you its meaning,' he would say, but probably the most telling phrase he ever uttered was an Americanism.

'Talkie' had seen local boys, many of them Jewish, rise to fame in the dance-band business. All the big leaders – Geraldo, Ambrose, Sidney

Kyte, Joe Loss, Harry Gold, Harry Roy and many more had been born and raised nearby – and he was familiar with the language of the business, but was quite bewildered by the new terminology used by Scott and company; puzzled by the names of Bird, Diz, Klook, Monk and Tadd. One evening when Scott and his friends came in to the cafe he came out with his Americanism. 'Aye, aye! Here come the heebie jeebie boys!'

At the Club Eleven, c.1948. Pete Pitterson, trumpet; Johnny Rogers, alto; Nat Gonella, trumpet; Tommy Pollard (standing); unknown vocalist and Ronnie Scott (tenor).

One of the meanings of 'heebie jeebies' was mental instability, or nervous agitation, and to most traditionalists it was singularly appropriate to describe the bop abomination that so painfully assaulted their ears. The very unfamiliarity of the style with its (seemingly) abrasive phrasing and pinched tonality caused a furore on both sides of the Atlantic. It split the jazz world into two rancorous camps: traditionalists and modernists. Controversies abounded. The traditionalists railed against the 'weird' and 'screwy' phrases. The modernists pointed to the retrogressive character of revivalism, and the rudimentary musicianship of the older American players like Bunk Johnson and George Lewis, and almost all the British and Continental exponents of the early jazz.

The traditionalists' hostility to the new wave was strident, bitter and unyielding. It would be impossible, these years later, adequately to describe the feelings of revulsion towards this new development. Brian Rust raged against it in *Pick-Up* and later asserted that Charlie Parker records made his baby daughter cry. Most of the established critics – Max Jones, Sinclair Traill, Rex Harris, Denis Preston and Humphrey Lyttelton – savaged bop. Lyttelton, reporting from the first International Jazz Festival at Nice in 1948 for *Jazz Music*, Volume 3, No. 8 (undated), wrote:

> Bebop was in almost total eclipse. It was featured in a mild form by Jean Leclerc's band from Belgium. Some of the little sawn-off melodies with which bebop numbers invariably open and close are harmlessly attractive at first and second hearing and this band did them full justice. But the solos had little to commend them. Funny little pigmy phrases came dribbling out of the instruments, with hardly the force to carry them into the attendant microphones; I was forced to conclude that this new progressive music is at present too feeble to stand on its own feet without the support of technical virtuosity. Starved of all depth of feeling and emotion, the child has got rickets; but it will take more than the cheap patent medicine of Dr Gillespie to bring it to healthy manhood.
>
> At Nice the audience reacted mildly to the Belgian bop, but it must have been a disappointment to the players to find themselves so politely received when the Master, no farther away than Paris, had only recently set a stirring example by bringing his audience to blows.

This was a reference to an earlier part of his report of the not-so-civil war which the American musicians had left behind them and which had broken out in France in no less violent form.

Some time in 1948 the BBC staged an 'outside' broadcast of their 'Jazz Club' from Leicester Square Jazz Club with Humphrey Lyttelton's band and a bebop group that included trumpeter Reg Arnold, formerly with the Lewis–Parnell Jazzmen. The club was then the home of the Lyttelton band and naturally their supporters arrived in great numbers. The bebop band was loudly booed, an unmannerly but typically 'ideological' gesture in those turbulent days. The audience was particularly rough on Arnold – a player in the 'old' style now jumping on the bebop bandwaggon.

In this bitter sectarian war the fundamentalists thought that theirs was the *real* jazz, that the boppers' pyrotechnics had no connection with 'the music', a phrase that now had strong emotive overtones. They argued the merits of 'feeling' and 'sincerity' as superior to mere technique and rationalized traditional musicians' lack of technical ability with the jargon phrases 'contrapuntal interplay', 'inner rhythms' and the like.

The 'retrogressive' endeavours of the traditionalists and the 'progressive' exercises of the modernists were equally bewildering to the dance-band leaders of pre-war vintage hoping to re-establish themselves now that hostilities were over. The revivalists in their pub backrooms and dingy basements they ignored, but they had to contend with the young beboppers who, whatever the strength of their bop convictions, depended on dance-band employment for their main income. If they could negotiate the complex chord changes of bop played at breakneck speed the modernists could easily manage the relatively simple dance arrangements to earn their 'bread'. Also the bandleaders had astutely reckoned that bop might attract a few customers so that it would be expedient to include some of its practitioners, although many came to rue their opportunism.

One of these rueful figures was Ambrose. The leader of Britain's most praised and successful pre-war dance band had fallen on hard times but could not bring himself personally to book the musicians he required for tours of the corn exchanges, palais and town halls up and down the country in which he was now compelled to play. Many of his pre-war men had retired from the business or were too old for touring, some of them now studio musicians he could no longer afford. His 'fixer' had to book the young bebop bloods who thronged 'The Street' on Monday afternoons.

Ambrose, like many other leaders, didn't take kindly to the demeanour of these tearaways* or the bebop phrasing in their solos, nor the chord inversions the rhythm section interjected. The post-war atmosphere compared unfavourably with the plush Embassy and Mayfair Restaurant days when his musicians knew their place, and when he would have convivial chats with HRH the Prince of Wales. He objected to the new-style drumming with its heavy emphasis on the top cymbal and once tartly enquired where the 'frying noise' was coming from.

Trumpeter Jack Jackson led a band at Churchill's, a plush dining and dancing establishment in New Bond Street, in London's West End. He also employed new-wave musicians, including Ronnie Scott, and the story goes that one evening Jackson was seated at a table chatting to a customer in the pre-war tradition of socializing bandleaders when he

---

* In a conversation with the author he bitterly referred to them as 'savages'.

became uncomfortably aware that perplexed dancers had stopped trip-
ping in much the same way that the Savoy clientele twenty years before
were halted in their tracks by Elizalde's band suddenly changing tempo in
one of their fancy arrangements.

It wasn't symphonic-type arrangements that were having this effect at
Churchill's. It was aggressive bebop with drummer Laurie Morgan 'dropping bombs' in characteristically explosive fashion and Ronnie Scott
on his eighth or ninth steaming chorus, and this, no doubt, merely
the exploratory beginning of an extensive development of the theme's
possibilities. One of the characteristics of bop was the extensive use of
'passing' chords enabling the soloist fully to extend himself. These young
lions required more than the eight-bar solos their trumpet-leader had
been allocated by Jack Hylton twenty years before, nor was the same simple harmonic foundation sufficient. Scott, eyes closed in the euphoria of
this new-found freedom – or rather the freedom he gave himself – was in
full flight.

A disturbed Jackson strode up to the bandstand to remonstrate with
him. Scott, totally absorbed, was utterly oblivious to his employer's
anguished entreaties. Barely able to make himself heard above the clatter
of Morgan's cymbals, Jackson testily enquired of Pete Chilver: 'What the
hell's going on?' 'Shhh,' Chilver is alleged to have replied, 'Ronnie's got
the message!' 'Give him one from me!' retorted the outraged Jackson.
'Tell him he's got the bloody sack!'

This anecdote, apocryphal or otherwise, serves to illustrate a situation
typical of the time and presaging the end of that now almost extinct and
unlamented animal, the baton-waving bandleader.

The traditionalists were quick to point out that the beboppers were
essentially *dance-band musicians*, an occupational description still con-
temptuously applied. Ronnie Scott recalls that he and his contemporaries
felt no animosity towards those who would have denied them their liveli-
hood but remembers their amazement that men of relatively tender years
should want to play 'old' music. A few veteran musicians essayed the playing of bop. One was Harry Hayes. His later recordings in that run of
thirty-nine titles for HMV included bop inflections and two titles were
'Ol' Man Rebop' and 'The Bebop'. Later Hayes developed a 'modern
style' and can be heard in this vein on several recordings in the fifties, but
later admitted that, 'Although I became known as a bop player it wasn't

really my style. In fact I sort of lost my way.'

Not all of those who flirted with the idiom were so frank. Two others who tried their hand at bop were the trumpeters Duncan Whyte and Nat Gonella, both staunch Louis Armstrong disciples. In a 1977 BBC television programme devoted to himself Gonella said that what he played during this strange interlude in his career was 'truly a horrible noise'. Any aficionado of bop

Agent Harold Davison's advertisement for an early bop band

could reasonably comment that it was Nat Gonella's contribution that was horrible and revealed his total inability to play in the idiom. The traditionalists, although surprised that he and Whyte* with such a stylistic history should even want to play bop, saw the attempt of it as yet another example of Archer Street opportunism.

The differences between the protagonists of the old and the new were not just musical. There were many others, particularly in clothing. The unkempt traditionalist wore shaggy sweaters, baggy corduroy trousers and rumpled duffle coats. He wore his hair relatively long. The modernist was a snappy dresser: an outfitters in Charing Cross Road, Cecil Gee,

---

* Whyte was the first musician I heard playing bebop and I recall the utter astonishment I registered watching an admired jazzman ineptly spluttering 'funny little pigmy phrases'. If a young modernist could only feel amazement at young people wanting to play 'old' music, I had similar feelings watching a man of forty (which I then thought old), play in a manner inconsistent with his known style. In truth he was not really an Archer Street man. For years he performed in drinking clubs so that he could play jazz, but like a few other veterans he was too steeped in an older tradition effectively to change style.

catered for him. He wore his tie straight, his trousers were always creased and his hair crew-cut. At the back it resembled what was irreverently described as the 'duck's arse'. He was 'cool', meaning unruffled, casual, relaxed.

Jazz Illustrated featured George Melly's parody of Lewis Carroll's 'Jabberwocky', from his *Through the Looking Glass*, that brilliantly summed up the differences between the traditionalist and the modernist. He named his piece 'Jazzawocky'.

'Twas bopping and the jivey toes
Did Gee and Cecil as they bopped
All bobby were the sex-a-glow
And the hairstyles outcropped.

Beware the Jazzawock my son
The beat that's two, the note that's whole,
Beware the Jazz-club bird, and shun,
The Cornier Jelly-Roll.

He took his flatted fifth in hand,
Long time the Mouldy Fygge he sought,
So rested he by the tom-tom tree,
And bopped while in thought.

And as in boppish thought he stood
The Jazzawock with ties aflame,
Came battering down the Sinclair Trail,
And Harrised as it came.

Co-ba, Ba-co, and through and through
The flatted fifth struck white and black,
He left them high and Dizzyly
He came Dankworthing back.

And hasn't thou 'sent' the Jazzawock?
Come to mine arms thou boppish boy,
Oh bopsters boast, you are the most
He Titoed in his joy.

'Twas bopping and the jivey toes,
Did Gee and Cecil as they bopped
All bobby were the sex-a-glow
And the hairstyles outcropped.

('Titoed' was a reference to accordionist Tito Burns, who led a band with a watered-down bop policy enjoying commercial success, but some of his records, like 'Bebop Spoken Here' now sound more than faintly comic.)

Many Jewish people were attracted to bop as practitioners and fans. Very few came to traditionalism, the clarinettists Monty Sunshine and Cy Laurie the notable exceptions. Traditional jazz attracted no more than two or three black players. There were slightly more in bebop – trumpeters Dizzy Reece, Shake Keane and Pete Pitterson and saxophonist Joe Harriott being the most notable. The modernist wasn't much of a drinker and, if Jewish, barely at all. The traditionalist was a beer guzzler. He smoked a pipe, while the modernist mostly smoked cigarettes. Sometimes he indulged in 'Naughty Type African Woodbines', which many thought helped facilitate their progress through the complex chord sequences – unlike the befuddling effects of too many pints of beer sunk by the Louis Armstrongs, Sidney Bechets and Kid Orys from Barnehurst, Ealing and Wallasey.

The illegality of the beboppers' indulgences attracted the attention of the police and the Club Eleven was raided at its new premises in Carnaby Street on 15 April 1950. Harold Robinson, Asaugus Eyo, Lennie Bush, Cecil Jacob Winston, Mario Fabrizi and Ronald Schatt (Scott) were charged with being in possession of cannabis. This censure was as much a reflection on antiquated laws as on the indulgence of the accused. Not that far from Carnaby Street, the Blue Posts in Eastcastle Street, the drinking habitat of the tradders from 100 Oxford Street, was frequently packed with drunks who had over-imbibed the legally acceptable anodyne.

In court the excuses and explanations of the accused bordered on the farcical. One said he had no idea how one of the 'cigarettes' was found lying at his feet; another said he thought he was smoking an ordinary fag; another that he took the drug for his toothache; another solemnly pleaded that he was quite unaware that the smoking of this particular substance was illegal and would the court please accept his firm assurance that he would never again touch the stuff.

There was an added comic touch when the magistrate, Mr Daniel Hopkin, inquired: 'What is bop?' For once the query wasn't magisterial facetiousness. It was, after all, a question that was bothering many in the jazz world. A detective inspector replied: 'It is a queer form of modern dancing – a sort of negro jive.' Mr Hopkin appeared satisfied with the explanation although, no doubt, was none the wiser for it. Alas, the use of hard drugs by some of the foremost American bop musicians was practised by a few British with tragic results. This was sensational fodder for many a Fleet Street Lunchtime O'Booze who had long fed on jazz and the sorry addiction of the few who made the headlines.

Revivalism had many writers and collectors protesting the virtue of the old over the new, but beleaguered bebop was short on propagandists. In America Leonard Feather, who had been resident in the United States since the outbreak of war, was an early advocate of the new jazz. It was tartly alleged by his enemies that his sentiments were not unconnected with his activities as a songwriter, pianist, arranger, manager, recording executive, session fixer and publisher, in which multi-capacity he served the new wave. He was also assistant editor of *Metronome*, a glossy US musicians' trade paper, then heavily promoting the new jazz. He was persistently attacked by the 'Mouldy Fygges' who wrote in the little specialist magazines, *Record Changer*, *Jazz Finder* and *Jazz Record*. Gene Deitch drew a cartoon published in the *Record Changer* of him offering a bemused-looking jazz musician all his services, for a consideration . . . Muggsy Spanier knocked him to the ground at a Chicago nightclub one night and later recorded a piece called 'Feather Brain Blues' in his 'honour'. L. G. Feather was said – with a degree of hyperbole typical of the time – to be the most hated Englishman in America since George III, and the Mouldy Fygge magazines constantly vilified him.

Feather had as much right as anyone else to capitalize on his musical talents and business acumen but it was his blatant propaganda for the bands and artists with whom he was financially concerned that earned him so much criticism – not to mention his anti-traditionalist postures.

His critics have generally overlooked his part in furthering jazz interest as a critic in the thirties and his organization of many British sessions including the fine Danny Polo Swing Stars recordings for Decca. He was also responsible for Benny Carter becoming staff arranger with the BBC Dance Orchestra, albeit that, in a jazz sense, this was hardly worthwhile.

Feather made a truly important contribution to jazz literature with his *Encyclopedia of Jazz*, an indispensable reference tome containing over 2,000 biographies, a mass of personal histories, a discography of LPs, a scholarly historical survey and many examples of notated jazz. In addition it included addresses of musicians, where known, among other data. It was, at the time, the most comprehensive work of its kind.

As with the work of Schleman, Rust, Chilton, Venables, Carey, McCarthy, Delaunay and Panassié, the immense labour involved could hardly have been commensurate with the financial reward – despite the accusations of entrepreneurial opportunism frequently levelled against Feather by the traditionalists. An interesting man: a Britisher from a county town (his first letter to the *Melody Maker* was in 1933) who made such a mark on the jazz scene on both sides of the Atlantic and particularly in America when bop was in its infancy.

In Britain, Maurice Burman, a dance-band drummer from the late twenties with a variety of bands including Roy Fox and Geraldo, had a column in the *Melody Maker* in which he stoutly defended the new development. Steve Race was another who protested its virtues, in various publications. In *Jazz Journal*, January 1950, he wrote:

> Louis Armstrong's description of bop as 'one long search for the right note' has caused much satisfaction among experts who wouldn't know the right note if they heard it. Unfortunately, it has also served to show that Louis, whose greatness as a player I would be the last to dispute, is just about as strong on criticism as Rex Harris used to be on trombone . . . If Louis had said that he just didn't like bebop, or that he found it neurotic, busy, unrhythmic, discordant or soulless, he might have returned to America something of a critic, as well as one of the world's greatest trumpet players. What a pity he hit upon a childish statement that cannot be seriously applied to any accepted music. We are not all fools: Parker, Gillespie, Hawkins, Bigard, Feather, Delaunay, a few million others and me. Neither are Duke Ellington and Benny Goodman, to name but two, who have allowed a certain amount of bebop to find its way into their orchestras . . . The average purist is genuine enough in his mistrust of bop. He has found his level in the simplest form of contemporary music. The music itself is none the worse for being restricted and elementary – no-one decries the music of Handel because it lacks the harmonic richness of Brahms – but the purist is lacking if his narrow powers of appreciation prevent him from grasping anything more complicated than 'When the Saints Go Marching In'. I ought not to make complexity my God, nor should the purer brethren make simplicity theirs.

Many anti-bop statements were attributable to Louis Armstrong, some of them probably misquotes, but there is no denying that he expressed his dislike in a record he made as late as 1954 of the 'Whiffenpoof Song' in which he sent up the boppers very forcibly:

> Up at Birdland where Dizzy dwells . . . with their beards and funny hats they love so well . . . all the boppers are assembled and when they are really high . . . they constitute a weird personnel . . . all the riffs them cats are playing . . . Crazy, Cool, Gone . . . Scoobie Doobie . . . So let them beat their brains out . . . until their flatted fifths have gone . . . they are poor little cats that have lost their way . . . like little lost sheep that have gone astray . . . Lord have mercy upon them . . . BYE BYE!

Understandably, Armstrong was getting his own back on Dizzy Gillespie for a record Gillespie made two years earlier on his own Dee Gee label called 'Pop's Confessin''. On it, singer Joe Carroll mercilessly parodies Armstrong's vocal mannerisms (and with this a thrust at Armstrong's alleged 'Uncle Tom' stage behaviour) and Gillespie apes his trumpet style, even pretending not to make a top C.

Both records are highly amusing and, more than any words can, they reflect the hostility between the traditional and modern camps.

Armstrong's record appeared on British Brunswick but was quickly withdrawn not because of objections from lovers of bop but at the request of the Kipling Society! The lyrics of the song had undergone many changes over the years but had their origins in Kipling's 'Gentlemen-Rankers', part of *Barrack Room Ballads*, written in 1892. Thus it was that an organization operating in Northumberland Avenue, London, dedicated to the memory of a rank imperialist, played its small part in the history of jazz in Britain.

Defence of the new style also came from the most unexpected quarter – Edgar Jackson. Steve Race, in a broadcast on Radio 3 in October 1983, claimed that only Jackson and himself (rather overlooking Burman) stood up for bop. In *Jazz Express* the following month the columnist 'Old Scarlett' reminded Race that Jackson used Charles Fox as his ghost-writer, but it was not until the early fifties that Fox and Alun Morgan, among others, were Jackson's 'ghosts' in the *Melody Maker* and the *Gramophone*. The music struggling for recognition against the implacable hostility of the traditionalists had an unexpected ally in Edgar Jackson, then writing his own copy.

Reviewing a Decca record by vocalist Alan Dean and his Beboppers with Johnny Dankworth, Ronnie Scott, Pete Chilver, Laurie Morgan,

Bernie Fenton and Joe Muddell in the *Melody Maker*, 22 June 1949, headed 'BRITISH BOPPERS PROVE THEIR WORTH (100 PER CENT)', he wrote: 'What this bright bunch hasn't tumbled to about bop probably isn't worth worrying about. In fact, the whole performance is conspicuous [a favourite Jackson word from the early twenties] for an ease and relaxation which are not always found even in the better American bop records.'

The defenders of bebop, in Britain and America, heartily disliked the nomenclature of the music they defiantly, almost desperately espoused. They considered the common term childish and pressed for the more stately designation 'modern jazz'. It was indeed ironic that a music which rejected

many of the accepted rules of jazz should have its apologists pleading for use of the word applying to the music it seemingly challenged. In a sense, this recalled Edgar Jackson's rejection of the word 'jazz' back in 1927 when Columbia advertised their 'Hot Jazz' series and he cried: 'It's worse than ragtime!' Jackson, it will be remembered, wanted the formal description 'modern rhythmic music' to give an aura of respectability to this music of smoky dives and sinful brothels.

Fundamentally, the bebop defendants had the same craving for respectability for a music associated with sartorial and hirsute eccentricities and ravaging drugs, but its general title and its side associations made the intelligent devotee quite uncomfortable, even paranoid.

The revivalists, well aware that the bebop musicians and devotees hated the current description of their music, deliberately and gleefully harped on it. The boppers reciprocated by rubbing in the term 'dix-ieland', knowing how much their critics hated that term, with its 'white' jazz connotations. They knew that the fundamentalists desired identifi-cation with black music.

In *Jazz Journal*, November 1950, Steve Race wrote:

> With a sigh of relief I record that this is the last article under my name which will make use of the word 'bop'. Having tried for some years now to make the word respectable, I hereby give up the battle, in face of bebop dancers, bebop outfitters and bebop drug addicts. We can no longer hope to make the word respectable in such direct competition with our worthy national press, so, remembering 'crewcut' with a shudder we must find a new term and make the low-lifes a present of the old one.

Race suggested 'Minton's jazz', since bebop originated from Minton's Playhouse.

Bebop, eventually to receive its more sedate title of 'modern jazz', achieved an unexpected degree of public acceptance. The first under-ground meetings of the heebie jeebie boys grappling with the harmonic and rhythmic compexities of the new jazz in a grubby West End rehearsal room were to lead them to the comparative respectability of the average palais and thence to a situation where they could earn a liv-ing in the many clubs that sprang up to accommodate the growing demand for modern jazz. The dance bands that remained featured bop-orientated arrangements and gave the soloists greater freedom.

This was indeed unexpected, even to its practitioners. Despite its improvisational nature, traditional jazz had an acceptable simplicity. Bop, on the other hand, required more intensive listening, not normally expected of palais audiences. The bebop bands that toured compromised to a degree by employing a female singer and playing the mandatory set of waltzes and current hit-parade numbers, but in the main they played the music of their choice, continuously developing along the lines instituted by Gillespie and Parker in the mid-forties. Not, of course, without opposition from the more conservative ballroom proprietors and managers. The plangent comment from one of this genus in the north of England went the rounds: 'Tha's naw goin' ter play t'bop lad, is tha'? Me coostomers doan like t'bop. Play something decant for crissake, won't ye?'

The heebie jeebie boys, unlike their pre-war counterparts who made a point of flashing their dentition, did not often show their teeth – except, perhaps, to bare them in a snarl in the confrontations with those who didn't much like the ninth chord with a flatted fifth.

Kenny Graham (tenor saxophonist, composer and arranger), pianist Ralph Sharon, Johnny Dankworth and Tito Burns led the first British

Kenny Graham (left) with John Dankworth

bop groups to tour the dance halls. All, excepting Burns, who had a more commercial policy, just about scraped a living at first. Dankworth's group (the Johnny Dankworth Seven) included Eddie Harvey, the first well-known traditionalist to embrace the new concept of jazz, and later both he and Keith Christie, another renegade traditionalist, were members of Dankworth's high-powered big band in the mid-fifties.

Ted Heath's large band featured many of the new-wave players, but their talents were largely buried in mechanical swing arrangements, its sound a far cry from Jack Hylton's Kit Kat band on whose 'Riverboat Shuffle' Heath played a 'red-hot' solo in 1926 – the first 'jazz' record Edgar Jackson reviewed in the first issue of the *Melody Maker*.

After their belated release of the first Gillespie disc in this country, HMV issued a spate of his recordings, but it was the Esquire label, run by Carlo Krahmer with his wife Greta and the drummer, recording engineer and film producer Peter Newbrook, which ensured that (often at financial loss) a steady flow of bop records reached the shop counters. Esquire were the first to record Ronnie Scott, Johnny Dankworth and Vic Feldman, and the label issued the first Charlie Parker records in Britain.

Steve Race made four recordings in 1949 for the Paxton label with Leon Calvert, Johnny Dankworth, Pete Chilver, Norman Burns (drums), Jack Fallon (bass) and himself on piano, and four more with another group called the Bosworth Modern Jazz Group on the Bosworth label that included multi-saxophonist Freddy Gardner, who was utterly out of his depth in attempting the bebop idiom.*

Generally the best early bop recordings were made by younger musicians with the necessary flexibility and freshness of approach to embrace the new concepts, and most of the records they made stand up better than many traditionalist recordings of the same period. Their superior musicianship has survived the ruthless test of time.

The heebie jeebie boys had triumphed and from the early fifties traditional and modern jazz coexisted, and the rancour subsided. Even the traditionalist magazines included material on the beboppers, *Jazz Illustrated* being one of the first to take this step. Bop became respectable and acknowledged as a language in its own right and traditional jazz benefited in that its rhythm sections learned from the modernists the 'subtler more varied punctuation to imply the beat instead of hitting the listener over the head with it'.

The casualty of the coincident emergence of traditional and modern jazz forms was the Archer Street jazzman of old. He returned to the anonymity of the studio and before long his employer, the bandleader, became an anachronism and faded from the scene.

Between them the warring factions, although constantly at each other's throats, sounded the death knell of these baton-waving frock-coated mountebanks.

---

* These eight titles were reissued on CD in 2003 as part of *Bop-In' Britain*, Vol. 1 (Jasmine JASCD 637).

14

Jazz Comes to Britain
by Stealth

From the mid-forties onwards a few American musicians serving in the US forces 'sat in' with British bands, mostly at the Feldman Swing Club, and Esquire Records recorded trumpeters Jimmy McPartland, Johnny Best and Dan Jacoby and tenor saxophonist Sam Donahue (all servicemen) with British musicians in 1945. In 1949 Jimmy McPartland and ex-Duke Ellington trumpeter Rex Stewart played with Humphrey Lyttelton's band at the London Jazz Club.

The first American jazz musicians 'officially' to play in Britain after the war, in 1948, were Duke Ellington and, with him, trumpeter/violinist/dancer/singer Ray Nance and vocalist Kay Davis. They were backed by local musicians Jack Fallon (bass), Malcolm Mitchell (guitar) and Tony Crombie (drums). Ellington appeared at the London Palladium and some provincial halls. Benny Goodman (bringing with him bop pianist Buddy Greco) also appeared at the Palladium in 1949. The Skyrockets Orchestra was the pit band in both cases.

Permits were granted by the Ministry of Labour as the Variety Artists' Federation had given their approval, although not, in the case of Benny Goodman, without strong objections from the union, which blocked the appearance of three musicians originally picked to appear with Goodman on the grounds that they were in arrears with their dues – guitarist Dave Goldberg, drummer Laurie Morgan and trumpeter Leon Calvert. Eventually the Goodman package was completed by Tommy Pollard (vibraphone), Charlie Short (bass), Pete Chilver (guitar) and Flash Winston (drums).

The hassles continued. When permission was sought for Goodman to appear in certain BBC programmes the outcome was that he played in a variety show called 'Hi Gang' with the comedians Bebe Daniels and Ben Lyon but was denied a hearing in 'Jazz Club', a programme infinitely more suited to his talents.

Although universally accepted as one of the greatest of all jazzmen, Goodman, in this period when traditional and bop jazz were commanding all the critical attention, was – to use critic Alun Morgan's phrase – 'stylistically stateless'. Those who admired his previous work, especially with small bands in the late twenties and early thirties, were cool towards his swing band and unhappy about him bringing with him a bop pianist. His disputed status was symptomatic of the critical turbulence of the period.

In June 1948 another body was formed to protect and further jazz interests in Britain. The founders gave it the grandiose title of the National Federation of Jazz Organizations of Great Britain and Northern Ireland. Later, mercifully, it became known simply as the NFJO. Its first officers included Rex Harris, Ray Sonin, Joseph Feldman, Bert Wilcox, Ken Lindsay and Sinclair Traill.

The weight of the title failed to impress the Musicians' Union when the organization protested that the union's members would benefit from the entry of American musicians by employment as supporting musicians. The *Melody Maker*, 10 November 1949, ran a front-page story reporting that a deputation from the NFJO had met Tom Driberg MP, on the steps of the House of Commons, to put its case and that Driberg had promised to raise the matter personally with the Ministry of Labour and the Musicians' Union.

Twenty-six years earlier Captain Grady, MP for Nuneaton, speaking on behalf of the Actors' Association, had queried why permits for black artists (including Will Vodery's Plantation Orchestra) had been issued for them to appear in the show *Plantation Review* and asked if their issue had been consistent with the Aliens Order, 1920. Now there was pressure from an elected representative of a later generation to *admit* American musicians, particularly black ones.

Significantly the banner headline of the same issue of the *Melody Maker* ran 'BECHET PLAYS IN BRITAIN!' A buccaneering individual had illegally pierced the cultural iron curtain that the NFJO deputation had sought to have removed through the 'normal channels' and that bold buccaneer was a member of that deputation, although acting independently. In *Jazz Illustrated*, December 1949 (then edited by Stan Wilcox and Kenyon Jesse)* with pictures by Richard Johnstone, the main feature was a photo-story of Sidney Bechet's concert appearance in London, his first visit since deportation twenty-eight years previously.

This feature was unique in the entire history of jazz journalism, its ramifications directly involving the Wilcox brothers, Bert and Stan, because Bechet's appearance, on 13 November, was illegal and not publicly advertised. It led to the prosecution of Bert Wilcox for contravening sections of the Aliens Order. He was heavily fined for these misdemeanours and for a similar offence which he did not commit.

The ban, on foreign musicians generally and Americans particularly, was still being enforced, but before and after the war a more enlightened official and union attitude on the Continent saw the appearance of many American jazzmen there. This was even more galling to British enthusiasts. Their idols were so near and yet so far. It was also infuriating to British entrepreneurs, who realized that, had the same artists been allowed to play in this country, the high travelling costs could have been defrayed. An exasperating situation, but one which Bert Wilcox faced in characteristic style. With the help of a nimble-minded employee he spun a web of stratagems to defy the ban.

The feature in *Jazz Illustrated* told the story of how Bechet came to Britain and the circumstances under which he actually played. Or rather, it was part of the story and the one that Wilcox would have had the authorities believe. Even if they didn't, it was just plausible enough for them not to take action. He was very nearly proved right, but an unexpected turn of events less than twenty-four hours after Bechet's arrival and the subsequent, illegal, performance of another famous American jazzman eventually led Wilcox to face charges in court.

The background to the story was that in May 1949 several American stars, including Charlie Parker and trumpeter Hot Lips Page, pianist Tadd Dameron and Bechet had travelled from the US to appear at the Paris Jazz Festival. Five hundred British enthusiasts visited Paris to see and hear the galaxy of stars denied them in their own country by the unyielding Musicians' Union.

* For two issues: the further six issues were edited by the author.

Bechet returned to Europe in November that year and Wilcox made formal application to the Ministry of Labour to present him at six concerts throughout Britain with Humphrey Lyttelton and his band. In fact, Wilcox made several applications to the *official* body, the Ministry of Labour, but it was the Musicians' Union who effectively made the decisions. The negative answer to the final application wasn't given until 14 November, one day after Bechet had actually played in London. (In the meantime the persistent Wilcox had made application to the Variety Artists' Federation who gave their blessing, but under union pressure the necessary go-ahead from the Ministry of Labour was refused.)

The *Jazz Illustrated* story commenced with a photograph of Bechet, Wilcox and Charles Delaunay. The caption read:

> It was a story of failure that Bert Wilcox had to report to Bechet and his agent Charles Delaunay. The three men found the attitude of the union difficult to understand in view of the fact that Bechet, a solo artist, would have created work for British musicians. A viewpoint that 100,000 British fans share. Jazz lovers would also like to know why Anton Karas, the man with the zither, also a foreign musician, is granted a six weeks' contract to play in this country whilst the ban is put up to Bechet and other jazz musicians.

Jazz Illustrated could also have enquired why it was that Ellington and Goodman had been given permission to appear as 'variety' artists while Bechet had not been similarly classified. The story continued that Wilcox then invited Bechet to Britain as his guest the following weekend and Bechet accepted. Photographs showed Bechet at Heathrow Airport with the Wilcox brothers, Max Jones and Delaunay, and Bechet handing his saxophone case to an immigration official for examination.

By quirky coincidence Anton Karas travelled on the same plane. Here the world's most popular zitherist (he had provided the soundtrack for the film *The Third Man*) was travelling with a permit to work for six weeks. Meanwhile, the world's most renowned soprano saxophonist and immeasurably the superior artist had, it transpired, to be manoeuvred through immigration officials with Wilcox making false declarations that he, Bechet, would not play his instrument in public. *Jazz Illustrated* didn't carry a photo of Karas, but in the *Melody Maker* Max Jones remarked on the symbolic aspect of the zitherist leaving the airport in a smart limousine and Bechet, Wilcox and company returning to London in Wilcox's battered old Rover.

The *Jazz Illustrated* feature continued with photos of Bechet at the London Jazz Club, where he listened to the band and signed autographs. The caption told how the doors had to be closed at 8.30 pm as news of his arrival quickly spread and fans jammed the basement hoping he would play.

The magazine's middle spread was devoted to the actual appearance at the Winter Garden Theatre. The text read:

> To the 1,800 members of the London Jazz Club who packed London's Winter Garden Theatre on November 13th, the first presentation of the 'Humphrey Lyttelton Show' will stand out as an unforgettable occasion, for little did they know that theirs would be the privilege of seeing and hearing the great Sidney Bechet. Seated in the box, Bechet was quietly enjoying the music of the Lyttelton band when compere Rex Harris came to the microphone and announced his presence. The spotlight swung round as it picked him up; there was heard the most tumultuous welcome ever given to one man in the whole history of the British theatre. It was terrific! To long and repeated cries of 'Play for us Sidney' the great veteran of jazz could do little else but take the stage and, accompanied by the Humphrey Lyttelton band, commenced to treat the excited audience to the most wonderful session of jazz ever heard in this country. 'Weary Blues', 'Summertime', 'Careless Love' and many others that we all know and love poured forth from his golden instrument in a glorious cascade of sound. It was the most thrilling experience of a lifetime. Thank you Sidney Bechet!

The true story, which couldn't then be told, was infinitely more complex: bizarre even, and involving more actors in the drama than the *Jazz Illustrated* feature deemed it prudent to mention.

In November 1949 Bert Wilcox was in Paris for the purpose of covering the appearance of Louis Armstrong's All Stars at the Salle Pleyel for *Jazz Illustrated* and on Thursday the fourth he and Richard Johnstone visited Charles Delaunay, critic and discographer turned entrepreneur, to ask permission for them both to attend the concert on Saturday the fifth. Sitting in Delaunay's office was Sidney Bechet and this quite accidental meeting was the beginning of an astonishing odyssey. After Wilcox had explained that he'd tried to get official permission for his, Bechet's, appearance in England, Bechet said: 'Why don't you invite me, anyway?'

Wilcox insists that this was Bechet's actual phraseology. In the light of subsequent events this report has the ring of truth. It was the sort of direct comment that would establish a rapport between two individuals who were buccaneers in their different ways. One had been a wild man in youth, as his criminal record, both here and in France, confirmed; his playing had a soaring, eagle-like majesty surpassed only by Louis Armstrong. The other was an individual similarly adventurous. Shrewd and calculating, although often naïve and gullible, Wilcox was also a gambler. The gambler responded to Bechet's simple query. He immediately thought of his concert, already advertised at the Winter Garden Theatre, Drury Lane, featuring the Humphrey Lyttelton band on Sunday 13 November. To avoid bureaucratic restrictions he decided to invite Bechet to London, have him seated in the audience at the Winter Garden and let Humphrey Lyttelton invite him to play with his band.

It was an idea that held the advantage of sheer simplicity. No permits would be required for a 'spontaneous' action in a crowded theatre. True, the authorities would have to be persuaded that it had not been premeditated, but that was a hurdle to be cleared after the main event. Bechet left the office and Delaunay, on Bechet's behalf, arranged terms and method of payment with Wilcox.

He returned to England and informed his staff at the radio and record shop in St John's Wood, north London, that Bechet was going to appear at the Winter Garden Theatre the following Sunday, although he couldn't have been entirely certain that Bechet would actually come to the country and if so actually play his instrument.

Jim Asman, then managing Wilcox's record department, wrote a circular which was typed, roneoed and enclosed in two thousand envelopes addressed to the London Jazz Club membership and the record-shop mailing list. They were all posted that night to catch the first post Monday morning. It was the only printed material advising of the appearance. The recipients must have felt cast in the role of the chosen few, selected to witness the second coming. Wilcox was taking a chance, hoping that news of the circular would not reach the ears of officialdom or perhaps an ordinary union member who felt it his duty to report the proposed appearance.

His gambler's luck held. Perhaps the Musicians' Union got wind of the appearance and decided to give Wilcox enough rope with which to hang himself, but this seems unlikely. It would have been typical of them to inform the Ministry of Labour.

On Thursday the tenth, three days before the concert, the Wilcox brothers were part of a large party that called at Heathrow Airport to pay homage to Louis Armstrong and his All Stars en route to America after their success in Paris. One of the party was Les Perrin, Wilcox's part-time publicity representative, who would be the nimble-minded accomplice in the events that were to follow. While this mixed party talked to or merely gaped at the artists denied to them as performers in Britain, Bert Wilcox was summoned to the telephone through the tannoy system.

Conspirators to beat the Musicians' Union ban: Sidney Bechet (*left*) with Bert Wilcox (*centre*) and Charles Delaunay.

The call was from his secretary. She had the chilling news that Delaunay had rung from Paris to say that Bechet wouldn't appear in England unless he had an official permit. *That* buccaneer, probably mindful of his past record in England and aware of the Musicians' Union's implacable opposition to the entry of Americans, had obviously thought the matter over since 'inviting' Wilcox to invite him to London.

Wilcox, aware from the spate of telephone calls and letters to his office that his circulars had made their impact, was committed to Bechet appearing at the Winter Garden on the thirteenth and, typically, decided on immediate action: to fly to Copenhagen and plead with Bechet to honour his word. He asked Stan and Perrin how much money they had with them for him to buy the ticket.

The more cautious Stan advised against this hasty action and left. Bert Wilcox and Perrin were musing over the problem in the former's Rover on the way back to London when Perrin whooped out the answer. He worked in the Foreign Office and knew where certain notepaper and official stamps were kept, on which they could type their own permits. This extraordinary solution appealed to the now desperate Wilcox and Perrin was dropped at Whitehall to take this action. Fifteen minutes later he emerged from the Foreign Office with several sheets of the vital paper with the necessary stamp on them.

On their return to Wilcox's shop Perrin typed out the 'permission' in officialese for Bechet to enter the country and scrawled an indecipherable signature. To blur the stamp's impression Wilcox suggested the old serviceman's trick (he had served in the RAF) of utilizing a sliced potato to make a copy.

Any author would have been laughed out of his publisher's office had he presented an outline of a story with a plot as demonstrably preposterous as this, but truth is indeed stranger than fiction . . .

To contemporary jazz listeners, it may seem incredible that such machinations could have been conceived and executed simply to bring to a London theatre stage a musician who, in 1937, found it so difficult to obtain work in America that he and another famed New Orleanian, trumpeter Tommy Ladnier, opened a tailoring shop in Harlem to subsidize their meagre earnings as jazzmen. But in 1949 the desire of British jazz aficionados was fanatically strong to see as well as hear the people they knew only on record. Miraculous as the system of gramophone reproduction is, it does not compare in its emotional impact with the physical presence of the performer. Aware of this, Wilcox was determined that Bechet should appear in person. He succeeded, but as previously indicated, it was to cost him dearly.

On Friday the eleventh, Wilcox phoned Delaunay to advise him that he had obtained the necessary 'permit' and that he would be in Paris on Saturday the twelfth to produce this and take Bechet back to London.

On the Saturday morning Wilcox made a dawn flight to Paris. It was appropriate to the occasion that he took off in the murk of morning light in another act of this cloak-and-dagger saga. When he arrived at Delaunay's office he was stunned to hear that Bechet had phoned from Stockholm to say that he would not be making the trip to London. He was suffering from stomach trouble and had broken his dentures. Later he arrived at Delaunay's office looking genuinely unwell and Wilcox, at this eleventh hour, privately despaired of Bechet making the promised appearance.

Delaunay, apparently a very persuasive individual, gave Bechet an Alka-Seltzer and – even on a Saturday morning – found a dental mechanic prepared to work on the dentures. Bechet agreed to make the trip. The properties of anti-flatulence salts and the emergency workmanship of a dental mechanic were the two mundane but vitally important factors in the dramatic unfolding of a unique day in the history of jazz in Britain. Wilcox reported that a large glass of cognac also played a part in the saxophonist's decision.

Wilcox, Bechet and Delaunay took the 4.30 pm flight from Paris and arrived at Heathrow about an hour later. On landing Bechet asked for the 'permit' he had been shown in Delaunay's office but Wilcox said he would have to retain this as he was responsible for his, Bechet's, entry into the country. Wilcox signed the declaration that Bechet would not play, unpaid or paid, in Britain, but had an anxious moment when an immigration officer asked Bechet to open his saxophone case. Bechet declared that it was a valuable instrument that never left his side. 'You're not going to play it, I hope,' said the official. Wilcox quickly answered for Bechet in the negative and they got through. The 'permit' that had been shown to Bechet wasn't produced and one of Wilcox's first actions on returning was to burn this incriminating evidence at his shop in a posh inner London suburb. Shades of Graham Greene and sinister conspiracies in respectable environs!

Ill-advisedly, as it transpired (at least for the sake of his story), Wilcox booked Bechet and Delaunay into the Kingsley Hotel, Bloomsbury Way, near Holborn, instead of taking them to his own home in Finchley, Middlesex. That evening Wilcox drove Bechet to the London Jazz Club, 100 Oxford Street, where he listened to Humphrey Lyttelton's band for the first time, signed autographs and was besieged with compliments, questions and requests to play. At Wilcox's insistence he hadn't brought his saxophone to the club, but he could easily have borrowed (but did not) either Wally Fawkes' or Ian Christie's clarinet, his prowess on that instrument being as great as on the soprano saxophone. After hearing Fawkes he murmured: 'There goes my shadow.'

The caption in *Jazz Illustrated* said: 'Sidney settled back to enjoy the performance from Humphrey Lyttelton and his band, but fully conscious of the ban did not sit in with them – but the following day, well, just turn the pages.'

Bechet, then about fifty-three, and described in *Jazz Illustrated* as a 'benign old man',[*] was tired after his flight but Bert Wilcox took him for a drive through parts of London which Bechet recalled, including the site of the Rector's Club in Tottenham Court Road where he had played with the Red Devils. Wilcox returned Bechet to the Kingsley Hotel and arranged to call for him and Delaunay at midday on Sunday to take them to lunch and thereafter to the Winter Garden to rehearse with the Lyttelton band.

At approximately ten o'clock on the Sunday morning Bert Wilcox received a telephone call from a member of the London Jazz Club asking for the address where Bechet was recording with the Lyttelton band that morning. Wilcox told him there was no such recording. The caller was insistent, naming the company Melodisc. A dumbfounded Wilcox phoned his brother and dashed to the studio in Denmark Street, which he knew was used by Melodisc. His apprehension was heightened by the sight of bandleader Mick Mulligan at this time of the day. The Rabelaisian Mulligan, an animal of the night, was certainly not one for early rising and could have been there for only one reason, a reason that confirmed Wilcox's worst fears.

Mulligan and the Wilcox brothers were soon joined by others who wanted to attend this recording but they couldn't obtain entry into the studio. It was packed so early that the doors had to be locked. From the pavement they heard Bechet's unmistakable playing and the familiar sound of the Lyttelton band. The Wilcoxes were stunned, but there was nothing they could do, even had they been able to gain entry. There was nothing in the contract with Bechet to say that he should not record. It was a *fait accompli* on the part of the Melodisc company to capitalize on Bechet's unexpected appearance without having to expose themselves to any of the consequences which Wilcox had risked, and they may have thought that what they were doing was perfectly legal, as a 'permit' had

---

[*] Then, in 1949, to be in the fifties was 'old'. As the years passed most jazzmen continued playing until death finally retired them. Bechet himself continued playing right up to his death at the age of sixty-five.

been obtained. Subsequent investigations, however, revealed underhand machinations to get Bechet and band into the studio.

Wilcox realized that once these records were issued it would shatter the validity of the story he was going to offer the authorities *after* Bechet had played at the Winter Garden Theatre that night. No one was going to believe that Bechet, instrument in hand, happened to be strolling through London and came across a recording studio with engineers working on the Sabbath and, just at that moment, all the members of the Lyttelton band, also improbably strolling round London on a Sunday morning with their instruments, miraculously converged on Denmark Street at the same time. This might suffice in a thirties Hollywood scenario, but not in reality.

The Wilcoxes knew they couldn't remonstrate with Bechet. He had still to play the Winter Garden Theatre and any unpleasantness might have made him change his mind once again.

On the night, the Winter Garden Theatre was packed, and hundreds had to be turned away. Had the performance simply been by Humphrey Lyttelton and his band a two-thirds house, at best, could have been expected, but the circulars posted only that Monday and the jazz bush telegraph ensured a full house. The atmosphere that night must have been as tense and electric as at the Palladium on the night of 12 June 1933, when the curtain went up on Duke Ellington and his Famous Orchestra, number thirteen on the bill, playing 'Ring Dem Bells' with a nineteen-year-old Bert Wilcox one of the audience. The author was privileged to be present at the Winter Garden and can testify that it was an almost unbearably fraught occasion.

After the band played four numbers, the spotlight turned on Bechet in the royal box. Wilcox, with his flair for the dramatic, had decided on this elevated position, rather than have the guest of honour seated in the audience to be 'spotted' by Lyttelton.

So, the 'very fat black boy with the white teeth and narrow forehead' who had been deported thirty years previously was about to make an illegal appearance on a British stage. Compère Rex Harris read Ansermet's appraisal (although tactfully omitting the references to his pigmentation, physical and facial characteristics) and invited him to play. There were cries from the audience of 'Play for us Sidney', exactly the response that Wilcox, Harris and the band expected. Bechet quickly covered the short distance from the royal box to the stage and tore into 'Weary Blues'. An ecstatic audience roared their approval, drowning the first few bars.

While it was a great moment, musically, to hear a giant of jazz in the flesh in England for the first time in years, there was audience awareness that authority had been flouted. Two fingers had been thrust up in the faces of the failed or retired theatre pit musicians who dominated the union's policy; there was the vicarious thrill of being present at this joyous outcome of a cloak-and-dagger exercise. The forbidden fruit tasted even sweeter!

In the excitement and joy of actually seeing a jazz giant in the flesh the audience didn't seem to notice a nervous and stumbling Lyttelton band, some of whom were nowhere near the standard of the man they were accompanying, and the rhythm section, at times, floundered helplessly. The performance of a genuine original with a band of different race, generation and country, who had largely received jazz music through the agency of gramophone records in their front rooms and, in this instance, the Eton dormitory, highlighted the difference in stature. It demonstrated sharply the inadequacies of the British revivalists, and what should have been a happy day for these young men proved to be something of an ordeal.

Humphrey Lyttelton, in his *I Play As I Please*, wrote about the concert and the recording session earlier in the day.

> The circumstances of the recording session were nerve-wracking. As Bechet was the most celebrated and important jazz musician to set foot in England during the last ten years at least, every critic, collector and man-about-jazz in London who knew of the event turned up to see him. At one end of the small recording studio the atmosphere was like a cocktail party, with people milling about excitedly and chattering to each other. At the other end Bechet and the band were busy trying to make records. There were times when he and I, discussing the arrangements, were forced to shout at each other in order to make ourselves heard.

In addition there were complications in balancing the sound, but six records were eventually made. As was customary, the band wanted to hear the playbacks, but Bechet, to their shocked surprise, showed no interest. 'Why should I?' he said. 'That don't do me no good.'

Of the theatre performance Lyttelton wrote:

Winter Garden Theatre, London, 14 November 1949. Historic concert involving (*left to right*): Sidney Bechet, Ian Christie, Wally Fawkes and Humphrey Lyttelton.

The concert in the evening remains blurred in my memory. The band jittered through a few introductory numbers and Sidney Bechet came on playing to a roar of greeting from the audience which drowned the strident notes of his saxophone even for us standing a few feet away. It was a great honour and distinction for us to be on that platform playing with him, but sometimes I wish I could have relaxed in the stalls and just listened . . . As for his own playing, I can only say that it almost swept us right off the stage at the Winter Garden into the orchestra pit. For me, its energy and power are symbolised in my memory of the knot in his tie, which jumped up and down like a piston-head over his Adam's apple as he blew.

The illegality of the appearance must have worried Lyttelton, especially after the strain of the day and his characteristic irritation with every 'man-about-jazz' cluttering the recording studio. It was easy for the audience to indulge in the thrill of law defiance from the safety of their seats, not likely to suffer any of the consequences, but a principal in the drama like Lyttelton knew he could have been accused of aiding and abetting.

In his *I Play As I Please* he asserts he was determined to play the engagements with Bechet even at the risk of imprisonment. He had a few sticky interviews with a Scotland Yard detective inspector, who reprimanded him and then asked him for his autograph to present to his daughter, a fan of the band.

Nervousness apart, the performance suffered from too many musicians on the stand. Two clarinets, as well as the dominating soprano saxophone, produced a tangle of lines and Ian Christie voluntarily retired from the stage.

Stanley Dance, in *Jazz Journal*, January 1950, wrote:

> There has been a great deal said about the benefits which would accrue to stagnant British jazz from visits by American artists and Bechet provided audible and visible proof of this as he instructed and encouraged Lyttelton on stage. A lot of beautiful theories about collective improvisation must have been shaken, too, as he demonstrated the value and importance of the riff. Again and again he had the rest of the band playing a riff to back a soloist with the happiest of results. It is arguable whether collectively 'improvised' ensembles do indeed provide the most exciting jazz sound, especially since today they must conform to the pattern of the originals.
>
> Certainly, the solo can often sound like the most wonderful thing of all when a good rhythm section provides inspiration and the other horns furnish the kind of extra propulsion by means of a well chosen riff.
>
> Of course, Bechet is unique in that he nearly always plays well, no matter how dismal his accompaniment, as his records of the last few years with their generally sorry accompaniments bear witness. Nevertheless, even one who is decidedly lukewarm about the whole 'New Orleans Renaissance' had to record that the Lyttelton band did well at short notice.
>
> The leader's job was particularly unenviable, since Bechet plays a lead much of the time. Lyttelton's conception was righteous, but at times his execution was not deft enough and seldom was his tone pleasing. Wally Fawkes played well and Keith Christie with such daring as to indicate a real future.
>
> The rhythm section, however, was unsatisfactory. A rhythm section should swing and give the front line a lift. In this case Bechet and the horns seemed to be dragging the rhythm section along.
>
> And if it is necessary to employ that anachronism, the banjo, is it necessary to expose the wretched exponent, [Buddy Vallis] dressed as a hill-billy, right in front of the stage? Another time, tuck him away behind the piano, where his plunking may be heard but not seen, please.

In the same issue of *Jazz Journal* Steve Race complained of Webb's piano playing:

> We had an example of the value of some smattering of theoretical knowledge at the Bechet concert when the great man hit upon an ingenious arpeggio device in a chorus of the blues. Poor George Webb was caught completely

on one foot and made a manful attempt to find the elusive chord but time was short, he had 88 notes to choose from, and all was lost. In the meantime the handful of musicians present in the audience were feverishly murmuring 'G9th, George, G9th' but to no avail.

Revivalist groups could do themselves a power of good by learning chord symbols right away. It wouldn't surprise me to learn that Bechet doesn't even know what a chord symbol is but then Bechet is Bechet.

The misalliance between the Musicians' Union and the Ministry of Labour had become an Aunt Sally at which the small magazines and the *Melody Maker* regularly hurled brickbats. In the *Melody Maker*, December 1949, the editor, under the heading 'WHERE ARE THE REPERCUSSIONS?' wrote:

> It has been an epoch-making event and one that, bearing in mind the implications that, according to the MU, would attend such entry into this country, should have had shattering repercussions. One would have imagined, for instance, that the mere sound of Bechet's soprano sax would, like the sound of the biblical trumpet, have brought the walls of Archer Street tumbling down.
>
> But what has happened? Nothing. Stands the Ministry of Labour where it did? Certainly. Is the Musicians' Union all of a totter? Certainly not. Are any musicians unemployed and tramping the streets through the visit of Bechet? Of course not. Has the visit done any harm at all? Not the slightest.

The editor of the *Melody Maker* was rather tempting the fates by enquiring why no official action had been taken only five days after the concert and, sure enough, officialdom eventually acted.

The summons against Wilcox was not served until May 1950, but in the meantime another American artist had played here, again illegally. It was the renowned tenor saxophonist Coleman Hawkins. In the *Melody Maker*, 26 November 1949, the headline ran:

COLEMAN HAWKINS – BANNED!

Two club promoters, Tony Hughes and Bix Curtis, were denied permission to feature Hawkins either at their Music Makers Club in Willesden or at a concert to be held at the Winter Garden Theatre.

Tony Hughes told the *Melody Maker* that the original idea was for Hawkins to come over and act as godfather for his recently born son. 'Then I thought what a thrill it would be if I could get permission for him to appear while he

was on English soil, as guest of honour at a concert in which he would be flanked by some of our leading British musicians.'

More subterfuge to get a musician physically into the country! With Bechet it was accepting a 'social invitation', now Hawkins was to act as a godfather. And neither of the Americans knew either Englishman before these events. That anyone should have to resort to deceptions of this kind with the ultimate hope of their fellow countrymen hearing jazz artists on the public stage is undoubtedly without parallel.

Coleman Hawkins in London, 1949

Hughes advised that he was going ahead with the concert, for which he had booked the Ralph Sharon Quintet, the Music Makers with Canadian tenor saxophonist Bob Burns, and a hand-picked group including Kenny Baker, Johnny Dankworth and Steve Race.

After two weeks of rumour, conjecture, plot and counter-plot, Hawkins appeared not at the Winter Garden, but at the Princess Theatre on Sunday 4 December, accompanied by pioneer bebop drummer Kenny Clarke and two French musicians, pianist Jean Mengeon and bassist Pierre Michelot.

The accompanying contingent was the outcome of a frantic telephone call to Charles Delaunay by Curtis, after the latter had been telephoned by an official of the Musicians' Union informing them that on no account were any British musicians to be allowed to play with or accompany

Hawkins if he appeared. Like Bechet, Hawkins had to be manoeuvred through the immigration officials and, like Wilcox with Bechet, Hughes had to sign a document to the effect that Hawkins would not appear publicly, paid or unpaid, during his visit.

Among those at the airport was Bert Wilcox, who reported the visit in the January 1950 edition of *Jazz Illustrated*. On the night it was uncertain right up to the very last minute whether Hawkins would appear, but when told that his old friend, Fats Waller, would have played in such a situation, he went on. Once again, the law and the Musicians' Union were defied.

'Collector's Corner' (edited by Max Jones and Sinclair Traill) in the *Melody Maker*, 16 December commented:

> Not by any means all of those who turned out for Bechet braved the Hawkins performance (this was no doubt because of the intensely boppish nature of the rest of the bill, but we noticed such 'old-timers' in the theatre as Stanley Dance, Claude Lipscombe, Jimmy Godbolt and Rex Harris).
>
> Indeed when one of us entered the foyer at 9 pm (the bop had begun at 7.30 pm) he stumbled over several fugitives who had come up for air. Every one of them was a familiar figure from the London Jazz Club drawn to the Princess by old jazz associations . . . When Hawkins played, there was at once a feeling of listening to a potent musician – a man of exceptional gifts who possessed instrumental skill above the ordinary.
>
> Last time, in the thirties, when we first heard him in person we were struck by his excessive power and attack and also by his inventive faculty. This time the force of his playing seemed as great as ever, although the tone was harsher and the phrasing more angular. But the creative flair seemed less. Ideas there were in plenty but they sounded well worn. Once or twice a spontaneous note entered his playing and then the old Hawkins spell was momentarily revived . . . One of the things that nobody could help observing was Hawkins' adherence to swing playing. He moved on the beat and swung like no tenor known to bop. Other things were his poise and relaxation, his use of sparsely noted phrases that swung, his penchant for riffs as a jumping-off ground and his obvious disdain for bop clichés.
>
> We believe that many of the progressives present were disappointed in him because, as they argue, his stuff is dated.
>
> We can only repeat the obvious: dates have nothing to do with musical quality and little to do with criticism. We were not disappointed. We had heard his recent recordings and realised he was playing in the modern idiom. His work was about what we expected, and more compelling 'in the flesh' than on shellac.

> A faint hope gleams in the CORNER that his example will help to dis-
> prove the theory that all the best American jazzmen have gone over 100 per
> cent to bop and progressive jazz and that consequently fewer British musi-
> cians will be stampeded into the 'New Noise'.

This notice was as much a commentary on the 'old' versus the 'new'
controversy raging at the time as it was a review of Hawkins' performance, and the writers were obviously uneasy about the 'modern' influence
on the man whose thirties records gave so much joy and the tenor saxophone a prominence in jazz.

Jazz Illustrated concentrated upon the attendant difficulties and ten-
sions from the time he arrived on the morning of the eleventh and on the
interrogations 'reserved for lesser breeds without the law'. The editorial
praised Hughes and Curtis for their courage in bringing Hawkins over
despite overwhelming opposition from the Musicians' Union and the
Ministry of Labour:

> That Hawkins was unable to be given the recognition he deserved at the
> Princess Theatre will be to the everlasting shame of the MU boss, Mr
> Hardie Ratcliffe, whose timidity of approach on lifting the ban is to be
> deplored. That the great tenor man did play to a packed audience is now his-
> tory. Whether or not there will be any repercussions to what the Ministry
> will probably term 'Open defiance of Article 18, Section 1, 2 and 5 Aliens
> order, 1920' is not yet known. But Messrs Hughes and Curtis can be assured
> of the full support of every jazz fan in the country. And there are 100,000 of
> them. Think on that Mr Ratcliffe.

Jazz Illustrated reported on Hawkins being interviewed at London
Airport by several journalists, one of whom, Hector Stewart, asked his
opinions on bop. The grizzly veteran, now apprehensive about the repercussions of his visit, eyed Stewart coldly and after a pause, replied, 'There
ain't no such thing as bop.' This reply was as brief as Bechet's to the same
question: 'Bop! Man, that's deader than Abraham Lincoln!'

These ripostes were reminiscent of Duke Ellington's answer to
reporters' questions in 1933: 'There is no such thing as hot music.'

In the same issue Max Jones reviewed the Bechet/Lyttelton records
which had been released on the Melodisc label and advertised generally.
It had become public knowledge that Bechet had undertaken employment other than his 'generous yielding' to the demand that he play at the
Winter Garden Theatre. The processes of the law were set in motion.

15

Jazz and Justice

The *Melody Maker*, 2 May 1950, reported, in great detail and with much quoting of legal jargon, on the forthcoming arraignment at Bow Street Magistrates Court on 5 June of Bert Wilcox, Bix Curtis and Tony Hughes of the Willesden Music Makers' Club. Summonses were issued concerning alleged false representations to immigration officials and the aiding and abetting of the illegal entries into Britain of Sidney Bechet and Coleman Hawkins, under the provisions of the Aliens Order 1920.

That ass, the law, had to bray. The offenders were put on trial but the jazz aficionado's view was 'Long Live the Accused!' Their lawbreaking had been in a good cause. The deceptions, lies and evasions that led to their being convicted were justifiable means to achieve an honourable end.

When the trial commenced the magistrate, Mr Bertram Reece, was privileged, although it is doubtful if he saw it that way, to preside over a case without precedent in the whole of British legal history. No doubt he pondered on the gallimaufry of individuals who trooped in and out of the dock during the five days of the proceedings; maybe he wondered what it was about jazz music that bound people from such a wide cross-section of society.

He peered at Humphrey Richard Adeane Lyttelton (twenty-eight), bandleader, writer, cartoonist, educated at Eton; Aubrey Rex Vivian St Leger-Harris (forty-four), F.B.O.A., H.D., F.S.M.C., Freeman of the City of London, ophthalmic optician educated at Colfe's School, Purley, Surrey; Anthony Gerald Hughes (thirty-three), jeweller, educated at

Cardinal Vaughan School, Kensington, west London; Thomas George 'Bix' Curtis (twenty-nine), ambulance driver, educated at Central School, Richmond; and Herbert George Wilcox (thirty-three), shopkeeper and jazz-club promoter, educated at Lauriston Road Elementary School, Hackney, east London. A mixed bunch indeed! Perhaps Mr Reece was surprised, if a magistrate is capable of surprise, as to why some of the accused should have gone to such lengths in their defiance of the law, risking contempt of court, merely to get two men from America on to the public stage in Britain.

Early in the trial Hughes and Curtis pleaded guilty, but Wilcox protested his innocence and as he took the stand he must have entertained wry thoughts on the way things had gone against him and on the injustice of being prosecuted for bringing in Coleman Hawkins. He must have reflected on the Bechet recording session and on the manner in which it had been arranged.

He probably hunched his shoulders (a Wilcox characteristic in moments of intense thought), recalling that Emile Shalit, head of Melodisc records, had benefited from his enterprise in bringing Bechet to Britain. To Wilcox's credit he didn't withhold payment to Bechet after the concert when, reasonably, he could have done so. He would have been justified in thinking that some payment was due to him as a gesture for bringing in Bechet, thus providing funds which would help defray the legal expenses he would now assuredly have to face since his cover had been blown. He paid up because he was convinced that Bechet had no idea about the recording session when he, Wilcox, dropped him at his hotel on the Saturday night. He didn't even blame Delaunay who, as Wilcox sees it years later, probably didn't think it untoward that a recording session had been arranged – consistent with the 'permit' to work in this country.

He must have felt particularly chagrined when he heard, at first, that the Ministry of Labour were not going to prosecute him for the Bechet transgression, although they were dissatisfied with the explanation Wilcox gave in a letter. When he heard this he realized how near he had been in his hunch that he wouldn't be charged, but it was equally clear to him that the entry of Hawkins, his reporting the event in *Jazz Illustrated* and the advertising of the Bechet/Lyttelton recordings were the nails that were to pin him to the cross.

Above all Wilcox grimly realized that the recording session, conspiratorially arranged – of this there is no doubt – was nothing short of treachery from those who might have been expected to show appreciation and concern for his delicately poised situation with the authorities.

These and many other thoughts must have passed through his mind during the four days of the hearing, but he probably enjoyed wearing the mantle of martyrdom, aware that he had at least the moral support of the jazz community.

More conspirators: promoters Bix Curtis (*left*) and Tony Hughes (*centre*) with Coleman Hawkins, December 1949

Thousands of words were spoken at the hearing and innumerable piles of depositions were shuffled and examined. Regarding the summons Wilcox referred to his successive applications to obtain a work permit for Bechet, including an application to present him as a 'variety' artist. Prosecuting Counsel Mervyn Griffith-Jones said: 'Apparently the point was that the Musicians' Union are very much opposed to foreign musicians coming to this country.'

He had put his finger on a lunatic aspect of the whole sorry business. A person could not come to the country to play as a musician but might, if he were lucky, appear playing the same music with the same sort of band, as a variety performer. For this the consent of the VAF was required, but official permission had to be given by the Ministry of Labour. It was an artificial distinction which, in the case of Duke Ellington and Benny Goodman, was effective in bypassing the ban.

Proof that the Musicians' Union leaned on the Ministry came when an official of the latter, Charles Henry Hobbs, admitted that his Ministry had no objection to the entry of foreign musicians, and at many stages of the hearing it was obvious that it was the union who were manipulating the statutory powers they themselves did not possess.

Mr Griffith-Jones was insistent that the appearance of Bechet and Hawkins must have increased the sales of *Jazz Illustrated*: 'If you were doing nothing else, you were giving Hughes and Curtis the strongest moral support and offering the congratulations of your paper.'

Jazz Illustrated had a print of two thousand, one thousand of which, month by month, went unsold. Mention of the Hawkins visit was hardly likely to put it in the black.

He read out the *Jazz Illustrated* editorial praising Curtis' and Hughes' action and continued: 'We can leave out the next two pages about "Bopping at the Rose and Crown".' (The Hawkins feature was split by this article.) Up to this point Mr Reece had not indulged in the usual magisterial witticisms; he had not even asked 'What is a saxophone?' but at mention of 'Bopping at the Rose and Crown' he enquired – no doubt in genuine bewilderment – what this meant.

In contrast to the Club Eleven case, there wasn't a 'hip' police inspector to offer an explanation. The jazz experts in the gallery, racked with dissension among themselves, would have been of little help, and the number of available definitions of bop would conceivably have extended the case by several days. The query was passed over and Griffith-Jones continued: 'On page four we find an article entitled "Hawk Comes to Town – by kind permission of HM Immigration officer". Here is stated: "Finally, although your editor was only doing his duty in reporting the event for *Jazz Illustrated* he, oddly enough, came in for some questioning. His Majesty's servants appear to consider him the arch-instigator – for reasons which we cannot possibly conceive!"' He then asked Wilcox: 'What did you mean by that?' Wilcox replied: 'Exactly what it says. Why should I be questioned by people when I had nothing to do with Hawkins being brought in?'

'What is the point of the exclamation mark?'

'To bring home the point.'

'Are you saying, in veiled terms, that you were the arch-instigator?'

'Entirely untrue.'

Wilcox's reply was wholly truthful. The author was working for him at the time – editing *Jazz Illustrated* – and can vouch for the fact that he had no part in this episode except in exercising his editorial prerogative in reporting events of interest to our lamentably few readers.

He was not as truthful in answering questions about his involvement with Bechet. Although Griffith-Jones was on much stronger ground here, even he, with an expensive and prestigious Eton education and a mind that should have been sharpened by study and practice of the law, often fell, bloodied and bemused, after attempting to demolish the sophistry of the obfuscatory Wilcox. As with many a quixotic person, Wilcox's logic and concern for detail was shaky, to say the least, and he compensated with far-out rationalizations in phraseology stiff with non-sequiturs.

A fool can reduce a conversation to his level. Bert Wilcox was no fool, but he could act the bemused peasant and bring a dialogue to utter ruin. His opponents resignedly gave up after battering their heads against the brick wall of Bert Wilcox's 'logic'.

Coming to the subject of Bechet, Griffith-Jones naturally seized on the fact that Wilcox had booked him into a hotel and not, as would have been the usual case with a guest, taken him into his own home. He further asserted that an arrangement had been made on the night of 12 November to record on the following day, a fact of which, he further asserted, Wilcox was aware, but acknowledged that he may not have had any financial interest in this arrangement. He continued: 'You were quite determined from the start that Bechet would play?'

'It was hoped he would play.'

'You knew your application had been refused?'

'Yes.'

'And you went off to Paris knowing you had not got permission?'

'Yes.'

'Did you know that on the morning you went to Paris the Ministry telephoned your office?'

'No.'

'You knew the call was to the effect that permission from the Ministry of Labour had been refused?'

'The story I had was that someone telephoned that Bechet must not play. I thought it was a hoax. We didn't expect a government department to phone.'

'Did you think of checking up?'

'No.'

'Anyway, you went off to Paris, knowing that you had not got permission?'

'Yes.'

'Why did you not say that Bechet would be staying at a hotel?'

'Because the immigration officer made it clear to me I was responsible for him. It would have been just as easy for me to say he was going to stay at a hotel.'

This didn't make sense. It wasn't meant to. Its intention was to confuse this 'Legal Pete'.* Griffith-Jones went on: 'You knew when you left the airport that a condition had been imposed upon his landing that he would not take employment, paid or unpaid?'

Again Wilcox prevaricated: 'I saw the immigration officer stamp his passport. The words were not read out to me.'

'Were you seriously saying that you were not aware of the condition imposed?'

'I did not know.'

'It was quite obvious that you knew when the December issue of *Jazz Illustrated* was published.'

'I knew because that was four weeks later.'

Strangely, Griffith-Jones did not seize upon the fact that a magazine is prepared some weeks before date of publication. This Legal Pete wasn't all that sharp. He continued: 'You say four weeks later, but when you are describing the evening before the actual concert you say "Fully conscious of the ban Sidney Bechet did not sit in with the band." You knew of the ban.'

'Yes, but I was not told by the immigration officer that he should not play.'

'You arranged for Bechet to come to this country for the purpose of playing a concert?'

'For the purpose of appearing,' replied Wilcox, ducking and weaving.

Here, Bertram Reece intervened: 'You knew that permission had been refused.'

'Yes.'

* Jazz musicians' term for member of the legal profession and based on a real character, a solicitor with that Christian name from a town in north-east England. Sandy Brown recorded a tune called 'Legal Pete'.

'Do I understand that you negotiated for him to appear?'

Wilcox countered that question by offering Mr Reece a little-known fact of history of which, no doubt, the magistrate was previously unaware. 'He was last here in 1921. He had travelled the whole of Europe and it was his one desire that he come to London again.'

While Bechet may well have expressed a desire to see London again, he could not have forgotten the circumstances of his departure, nor was he making the visit for the altruistic reason of pleasing a jazz-deprived public. A hard bargainer, he made the trip for primarily financial reasons. He and Delaunay left on the very earliest flight on the morning after the concert, Bechet perhaps fearing he could face charges.

Wilcox told the court that he knew of no arrangements for Bechet to rehearse with Lyttelton's band. He agreed that arrangements had been made for the band to rehearse, claiming they always did before concerts, which was not always true but difficult to refute. He claimed that Bechet just happened to be with him on that occasion. Mr Reece and the lawyers probably didn't see that it was necessary for jazz musicians to rehearse, but no comment was made about that 'mystery'.

Griffith-Jones enquired if it was pure chance that Bechet did some rehearsing with Lyttelton's band that afternoon. Wilcox replied: 'When jazz musicians sit together they always play.'

'Had you discovered by this time that a condition had been imposed on Bechet's landing?'

'No, not from the immigration people. I had no knowledge of the conditions, except through the negotiations which had been going on previously relating to the Musicians' Union and the Ministry of Labour.'

'Do you seriously tell us that Bechet did not tell you a condition had been imposed on his landing?'

'At that time, no.'

'Bechet knew he was not allowed to take up employment in this country. Did he and you discuss the ban which the immigration officer had imposed?'

'No, not a word!'

As Wilcox signed the declaration that Bechet would not play this was really pushing his luck, but counsel obviously hadn't been apprised of Wilcox's signature. The legal machinery works mysteriously, but for prosecuting counsel not to be informed of this vital piece of information was really quite extraordinary and seemingly in Wilcox's favour.

Naïvely, Griffith-Jones commented: 'You could have gone on the stage and told him he was not allowed to play.' Wilcox rose to new heights of sophistry in his reply: 'Yes, had I run after him quick enough.' Fatuously, Griffith-Jones responded to the now comic nature of the dialogue by repeating: 'You could have gone on the stage and told him he was not allowed to play.' Wilcox simply replied: 'Yes,' but could have added that had he done so he might not have been alive to appear in court or anywhere else, simply because in the height of such feverish excitement there were people in the audience who would have certainly done Wilcox a serious injury for making such an attempt. If this author could be howled off the stage at the Hot Club of London for interrupting a *record* of Louis Armstrong, what fate would have befallen Wilcox stopping Bechet *in the flesh* from playing?

These exchanges illustrated that the accused, with his back to the wall and a certain native cunning, was able to fudge the lines of communication and also that learned counsel could ask fatuous questions. Did he really believe that Wilcox would have even considered leading Bechet off the stage?

Rex Harris, described as a leading commentator and talker on the serious aspects of jazz, gave evidence that Wilcox told him that Bechet would be in the theatre and that it would be a very good idea to spotlight Bechet in the box when he was introduced to the audience. He continued: 'The spotlight was played on Mr Bechet. He was received with acclamation and there was an ovation that went on for about five minutes. The audience were shouting: "Play for us Sidney" and in the excitement of the moment I asked him to play and he did so.'

Harris explained that it was such a tremendous thing for British jazz that this virtuoso was actually present. It was a tremendous occasion, comparable to Yehudi Menuhin appearing at serious concerts. Wilcox did not at any time give instructions that Bechet should be allowed to play. 'It was on my own initiative.' This, too, was more than stretching the truth.

Cross-examined by Gilbert Rowntree (counsel for Wilcox), Humphrey Lyttelton said there was no discussion about recording when he saw Bechet on the Saturday evening. There was no idea in their minds then about recording. He did not know who suggested the recording. There was difficulty in fitting in with Bechet's style at the recording session. Rowntree asked the witness if it was true that Bechet, being who he was, would be the one who was not wrong. Lyttelton agreed, amidst laughter from the gallery. Re-examined by Griffith-Jones, Lyttelton said that if no one else had asked Bechet to play he would have asked him himself.

Gilbert Rowntree, apropos Bechet's actions, commented that 'he was a much older man than Wilcox and very much more a public figure and Wilcox was bound to approach him with respect. Wilcox is required by law not to aid and abet, but not to lead him about like a bear on a chain.' He continued: 'I can only say that the only occasion of which we know when exclusive control of Bechet's movements was vested in Mr Wilcox he strictly adhered to the terms upon which he was allowed in the country. When Wilcox's control was divided, when other circumstances intervened, then it may be that the terms upon which he entered the country were broken although I argue they were not.'

Truth and half truth. Certainly the reason for Wilcox's appearance in court was as much the consequence of the activities of others as his own deliberate flouting of the law. The way of the transgressor is indeed hard . . .

Bertram Reece then asked: 'Is it the case then that when distinguished artists come over here they run amok – that no one can control them?'

Rowntree replied: 'No, my client is not charged with letting Bechet run amok but with aiding and abetting.'

That tart rejoinder probably cost Bert Wilcox the points he had scored over Griffith-Jones. Magistrates and judges are not enamoured of counsel who pick them up on points of law or terminology.

The upshot of the case was that Wilcox, Curtis and Hughes were each fined £100 with forty guineas costs.

* * *

The questions have to be asked: would the Ministry of Labour have taken any action, even after the recording session and Hawkins' appearance, had they not been urged to do so by the Musicians' Union? Can that body honestly assert that any one of their members was deprived of work by the appearance of Bechet or Hawkins? Could they deny that some of their members would have gained more employment were it not for their obduracy? It was not only the financial gain they had been denied.

It was the privilege, the publicity and above all the invaluable musical experience. It was dogma the Musicians' Union were defending, not their members' interests.

Bert Wilcox emerged as the principal figure in the drama. To some his action, which inspired Curtis and Hughes to do likewise, was reckless, vainglorious, stupid and carried out for mercenary reasons. To others he had displayed boldness and imagination, rendering a service to the jazz community even if his aim had been financial profit.

Wilcox's counsel persuaded him to appeal on the basis that he had been wrongly charged with bringing in Hawkins, that his reporting the event in *Jazz Illustrated* had been overstressed and that in a free country he had every right to report such an event.

The case was heard by Lord Chief Justice Goddard in the King's Bench Divisional Court on 26 January 1951. Goddard's summing up was in the grand tradition of judicial inanities: incredibly fuddled, factually incorrect and extremely biased. True, it had the merit of being extremely comical, but it also illustrated how erratically the wheels of justice grind.

His Lordship referred to two applications for Bechet's and Hawkins' appearances being refused and asserted that 'directly Bechet arrived he drove him to a recording studio where he made a number of recordings. Whether he was paid or not made no difference – he entered into employment. Wilcox also took a theatre, employed a compère and arranged spotlights for a performance by Bechet. Afterwards he wrote a glowing account in *Jazz Illustrated*, with which he was connected. It was unarguable that he did not aid Bechet in the commission of the offence.'

Goddard's first statement regarding the recording session is entirely untrue and he had either misread the case or was prejudiced. It was in his summing up of the Hawkins affair, however, that he excelled himself.

The noble Lord said: 'Hawkins, who is a celebrated professor of the *trumpet* [my italics] performed on this instrument as well as the saxophone.' He accused Wilcox of 'not standing up in the name of the musicians of England to protest that Hawkins ought not to be playing and competing with them and taking the bread out of their mouths *and the wind out of their instruments* [my italics]. It is not known whether he, Wilcox, actively applauded the performance, but he wrote a most laudatory description, fully illustrated in his magazine *Jazz Illustrated*. Wilcox's presence was not accidental. He went there for the purpose of getting copy for his magazine knowing it was illegal for this man [Hawkins] to play. If he had booed or if he had been a member of the *claque* [again, my italics] that had gone to drown the saxophone [not the trumpet?] he might not have been held for aiding and abetting, but in this case he was there for approving and encouraging what was done and taking advantage of it.'

Lord Goddard hardly seemed the sort of person to be concerned about employment of British musicians. It is almost as if his Lordship, a man of stringent right-wing beliefs, had been in collusion with the extremely left-wing Musicians' Union executive, H. Ratcliffe, T. Anstey, F. W. Turner and F. Whittaker. Strange bedfellows! Wilcox's appeal was accordingly dismissed with costs. He estimated that the total penalty for his involvement in this extraordinary case was £700, no small sum in 1950.

If Bertram Reece had pondered on what strange individuals inhabited the sub-world of jazz, the community also had in the operation of this case an opportunity to observe the sort of Establishment people who practise the law and administer justice; few of us were happy with what we observed.

In addition to the ineffable Goddard, another bright jewel in the legal crown was Mervyn Griffith-Jones, later to make an immortal contribution to the literature of British class relations by asking the jury in the *Lady Chatterley's Lover* 'obscenity' trial in 1959: 'Would you wish your wife or your servants to read this book?' He later achieved further notoriety as a judge.

The Bechet/Hawkins trial was a legalistic charade often reminiscent of a comic opera with the most absurd of plots. It was conducted, at enormous expense, to satisfy the demands of a peeved, blinkered and mulish executive of the Musicians' Union and yet, despite the jolt these diehards got from the Bechet and Hawkins appearances, they dug their heels in for a few more years.

During the trial the NFJO secretary, Sinclair Traill, issued a statement to the *Melody Maker*: 'With regard to the legal action taken by the Public Prosecutor against Messrs Wilcox, Curtis and Hughes, my committee have been asked to inform you that at a recent meeting it was decided that the federation would open a fund for the purpose of defraying the legal costs of the defendants. The federation would like it known that they are fully behind the defendants and will back them to the full limits of their power.'

Wilcox received nothing from the federation. The only contribution was an individual donation of five pounds from Steve Race. The rest of us gave him our moral support.

* * *

The Bechet/Lyttelton records are mementoes of a quite incredible weekend and a unique *cause célèbre*. It must be a matter of some regret to Humphrey Lyttelton that these records are not better than they are, although his band's contribution is nothing to be ashamed of; nor can their failings on these six titles be entirely attributable to those annoying 'men-about-jazz' crowding the studio that historic Sunday, 13 November 1949.

After all, these young musicians had learned what they could from listening to records. From the time they had started on their instruments they had been denied the opportunity to listen at close quarters, and to 'sit in' with, their mentors. Hardie Ratcliffe's sort made sure of that.

I have dealt with the Bechet/Hawkins visits and the resultant trial at length, because these events dramatically brought to public attention the scandal of the Musicians' Union ban on the entry into the UK of American jazz musicians. That such pretexts were employed so as to be able to present two masters of the idiom, and that such a costly trial should have been the outcome, at least helped to establish the idiocy of the union's intransigence.

However, this particular union executive and the readily acquiescent officials at the Ministry of Labour were effective in enforcing this ban, and the trial did take place. So it is on record that they and a handful of Legal Petes played their part in the history of jazz in Britain, a fact that none of them could possibly have envisaged when they entered their particular field. As none of them showed the least knowledge of, interest in, or liking for the music, their participation in its history remains one of the many, many ironies that have permeated the story of jazz in Britain.

In 1977 Griffith-Jones, by this time a Common Serjeant, tried one Thomas Montagu Hickman for two bank robbery offences. He had got away with £17,500 in one bank and clubbed a manager at another, the unfortunate man having to receive fifteen stitches in his head. Griffith-

Jones gave Hickman a two-year suspended sentence, which many, especially the injured manager, thought lenient. It transpired that the accused had not only been to Eton, Griffith-Jones' old school, but had been a major in the Common Serjeant's old regiment, the Life Guards.

Going back to the arraignment of Wilcox, Hughes and Curtis: some uncharitable observers said the fact that Humphrey Lyttelton received only the mildest of questioning was due to the prosecuting counsel having attended the same school as this witness.

Another vagary of the trial was Wilcox's counsel quite irrelevantly drawing the court's attention to his client's exceptional war record. An RAF rear gunner, Bert Wilcox had been on fifty-eight operational flights in Wellington, Halifax and Lancaster bombers, becoming a warrant officer and being awarded the Distinguished Flying Medal. The average 'life' of a bomber crew was five operational flights!

Whoever was on Wilcox's side during this incredible run of good fortune seemed to have deserted him on the morning of 14 November 1949.

16

Britain's First Real
Jazz Age

By 1950 Britain stood on the brink of its first real jazz era, and very different it was to be from the so-called 'Jazz Age' of the twenties.

During the thirties, when jazz appreciation was developing fast, the most optimistic of aficionados could not have foreseen such a widespread interest, such a flood of records, such a degree of media acceptance, and would not have believed that so many musicians would be earning a living playing jazz. The very notion would have been laughed out of any enclave of dedicated head-nodders.

From 1950 all kinds of jazz flourished and became a significant part of the popular music scene. One aspect of this multi-faceted activity had stylistic roots with the ODJB but mainly with the music of black, rather than the white, New Orleanians. Considering its origins and taking into account the fact that it was essentially an emulation of a period style, it proved a truly astonishing happening.

This was the trad boom. In this, literally hundreds of young men assiduously copied and, to a certain extent, absorbed the jazz of the New Orleans pioneers, whose endeavours had been extensively analysed in the small magazines. It is yet another of jazz's many ironies that it was 'old' music that appealed so much to the young. Apart from the musicality of these pioneers, their racial and social background had a particularly romantic appeal. Young white men readily identified with black players three thousand miles distant and living in an entirely different environment.

The roots of this happening were in the Jelly Roll Morton, Clarence Williams and Louis Armstrong records issued in Britain in the twenties. The interest then was limited but accelerated in the thirties when Brunswick issued its *Classic Swing* album with King Oliver's Creole Jazz Band, to be followed by recordings of Sidney Bechet, Jelly Roll Morton and other resuscitated musicians on various labels in the forties.

Few of these British neo-New Orleanians, when they eagerly took up an instrument, would have had the notion that they would become professional, a word with unsavoury associations for many of them when they first started to play. Nor, for one moment, would they ever have believed that this emulation of a music belonging to a different time and culture would have become commercial, another word they spat out in high-minded distaste. But a number of bands, each with the same classic traditional instrumentation of trumpet, clarinet, trombone, banjo, piano, bass and drums, were to become professional and, furthermore, commercial in their presentation of the publicly accepted formula that emerged.

This was the beginning of a Frankenstein's monster, sometimes known as 'traddy-pop', in which exercise the banjo predominated. Stanley Dance's objection to Buddy Vallis' strumming with the Lyttelton band at the Bechet concert was to be echoed many times over by critics, as plectrums rasped against the strings in virtually hundreds of trad bands. The manufacturers of the instrument never had it so good.

The inflexible sound of the banjo – at least as played by local musicians – dominated both the phrasing of the front line and the rhythm section. Other characteristics of a successful and rigidly applied formula were tearaway tempos, hand-clapping on the beat by the front line and throaty vocals, superficially derived from Louis Armstrong but more redolent of the Saturday-night pub performer. Trombonists rasped, clarinettists piped, banjoists strummed and bassists slapped in what they believed to be the style of the originals.

Traditional jazz was to become relatively big business. In the early fifties as many as fifteen bands, hardly distinguishable in appearance or sound, were massed together for infamous, mammoth concerts by opportunistic entrepreneurs. They were paid about fifteen pounds each and then, still glowing with crusading zeal, were compelled to make their impact on the audience with rabble-rousing specialities.

Trad was to become far removed from the original spirit of revivalism

Nat Gonella sartorially impersonating Acker Bilk, watched by Acker in his traditional gear

as personified by Webb's Dixielanders. Three of the bands associated with this phenomenon, led by Acker Bilk, Chris Barber and Kenny Ball, were to achieve hit-parade status, each commanding a tremendous following and earning large sums.

Acker Bilk was billed as 'Mr Acker Bilk' and he and his band dressed in Edwardian apparel: drain-pipe trousers, fancy waistcoats, cravats and curly-brimmed bowler hats, a mode of dress copied by his fans and known as 'rave gear'. The names of Jelly Roll Morton and Sidney Bechet were unknown to the majority of these so-called ravers. Others soon followed this sartorial gimmickry: Bob Wallis and his band were dressed as Mississippi gamblers; Dick Charlesworth and his band as city gents; Bobby Mickleburgh and his band as Confederate soldiers.

Hundreds of clubs, operating in pub back rooms, working men's institutions, drill halls and palais were formed to accommodate the legion of revivalists and their following. Out of all the traditional venues enjoying various degrees of success and duration, 100 Oxford Street has the claim to genuine longevity. From 1942 it has, successively, been the home of the Feldman Swing Club, the London Jazz Club, the Humphrey Lyttelton Club and now the 100 Club. In London the Wood Green Club ran for ten years and in the provinces there were long-running establishments at Nottingham, Redcar, Liverpool and Manchester.

The standards of musicianship increased considerably, especially in the rhythm sections. There were not many British bands in the twenties and thirties in which this vital part of the jazz band, its nerve centre, could be said to have had the least swing. After the fifties the quality of rhythm sections was the most noticeable of the improvements in the traditional bands and it was the influence of the beboppers they had to thank for a welcome advance in techniques and conception.

Running parallel with traditionalism – although not with the same degree of popularity or involving such a large financial turnover – was

Trombonist Chris Barber (*far right*) and his band: Mickey Ashman, bass; Monty Sunshine, clarinet; Ottilie Patterson, vocals; Ron Bowden, drums; Pat Halcox, trumpet; Lonnie Donegan, vocals and banjo

bebop, or modern jazz as it became generally known. Many clubs, particularly in the London area, catered only for those with modern tastes and gave regular employment to the new wave of jazz musicians – saxophonists Johnny Dankworth, Ronnie Scott, Tubby Hayes, Peter King, Art Ellefson, Tony Coe, Ronnie Ross, Joe Harriott, Harry Klein, Don Rendell and Art Themen; trumpeters Hank Shaw, Henry Lowther, Jo Hunter, Harry Beckett, Dickie Hawdon, Les Condon, Ian Carr and Leon Calvert; bassists Sammy Stokes, Kenny Baldock, Kenny Napper, Lennie Bush and Peter Ind; pianists Mike Carr, Colin Purbrook, Michael Garrick and Bill Le Sage; drummers Tony Kinsey, Tony Crombie, Martin Drew and Bobby Gien.

Johnny Dankworth and Ronnie Scott each led highly successful and musically excellent big bands. In 1959 Scott, in partnership with tenor saxophonist Pete King, founded Ronnie Scott's Club, and it is a testimony to their persistence and belief in jazz that it is still running more than four decades later.

* * *

The dichotomy between traditional and modern jazz remained, each camp having its largely separate following, but the senseless acrimony subsided. From each of these factions sprang separate developments that offered two more categories of jazz to the British scene. From traditionalism came 'mainstream'.

Mainstream was a term coined by Stanley Dance to describe the jazz that lay between the two main schools. During the fifties in America he produced records with many of the black musicians who had played with the big bands of the thirties and forties. These players had been rather overlooked in the hoo-ha surrounding the much publicized advent of revivalism and bebop. When Dance's recordings were first issued in Britain they influenced many traditionalists who had become uneasy about trad. To some this became a dirty word. They adopted the characteristics of mainstream – the foremost of the converted being Humphrey Lyttelton, Sandy Brown, Al Fairweather, Wally Fawkes, Bruce Turner and their bands.

The clanking banjo was dropped; saxophones were incorporated in the instrumentation; the over-used traditional themes were replaced by material from a wider repertoire; arrangements, rather than collective improvisation, were employed for the ensemble passages. Players with 'modern' associations came into the rhythm sections.

If, stylistically, mainstream was comfortably middle-of-the-road and to have only limited financial success, 'free-form' was unequivocally experimental and had very little public acceptance. However, from the late 1960s there were many British musicians who believed in its validity, their practice of it adding another dimension to an increasingly varied scene. Free-form was often starkly atonal, the musicians playing in different keys, at different tempos and in different time signatures simultaneously. It could be reasonably described as savagely nihilistic. God knows what George Robey would have made of it. Had he been given the choice it is likely that he would have tearfully pleaded for the Original Dixieland Jazz Band!

The foremost free-form band in Britain was led by the Caribbean alto saxophonist Joe Harriott at the beginning of the 1960s. Others contributing later to this exercise were the saxophonists Lol Coxhill, Mike Osborne and John Surman and the drummers John Stevens, Bryan Spring and South African Louis Moholo. All the percussionists, had they been active in either England or America in the thirties and forties, would have infused genuine rhythmic life into many a *lumpen* dance or 'swing' band, not that any of the leaders, here or in the United States, would have countenanced such a propulsive vitality, with such an inventive shift of accents and markings.

It is perhaps no surprise that from their detached houses in the outer suburbs many of the older bebop musicians threw up their hands in horror at free-form. After the long, fat years in recording and broadcasting studios, the former revolutionaries were characteristically resistant to change.

Clarinettist Sandy Brown with trumpeter Al Fairweather, c. 1950

* * *

Meanwhile, at long last, the Musicians' Union agreed, after lengthy discussions, on a reciprocal deal with the American Federation of Musicians. It was an excellent, if extremely belated arrangement reached in 1956, but in the context of jazz reciprocity, who needed whom the most? The Americans the British? The British the Americans? The answer was obviously the latter, but the agreement also enabled many British bands to tour America: Freddy Randall, Ted Heath and Humphrey Lyttelton among them. Since the lifting of the ban, the

Musicians' Union has shown a better understanding and American musicians have regularly appeared in Britain.

Apart from the self-contained orchestras and bands such as Duke Ellington's, Count Basie's, Woody Herman's, Buddy Rich's, and the smaller bands of Louis Armstrong's All Stars, the Modern Jazz Quartet, Art Blakey's Jazz Messengers, and a host of others of all styles, there came a stream of American soloists. They were accompanied by British musicians, substantiating the claims made for so long that these visits would provide work for Musicians' Union members and would not, as its executive repeatedly asserted, put them out of employment.

The appearance of these foreign visitors enriched the local scene. Besides providing employment for British musicians it gave them the honour, and the invaluable experience, of playing with those who had inspired them in the first place.

*   *   *

At the beginning of the fifties it would have been hard to foresee the extent to which jazz would be accepted in the following decades. It was to gain municipal recognition and to be featured in parks on summer evenings and in local festivals. Summer schools for jazz tuition were to be organized; the Arts Council was to make grants to orchestras and concerts; a society would be set up to create a national jazz centre in Covent Garden (though this came to nothing), and there would be a permanent National Youth Jazz Orchestra, still going strong under Bill Ashton in the new millennium.

A concert devoted to jazz in the thirties and forties had been an occasional experience for aficionados. In the fifties, sixties and seventies they could take their pick of these and during the summer months, choose from a variety of festivals devoted entirely to jazz. As many as twenty thousand people attended the bigger events, the most notable of which in the enthusiast's calendar were the National Federation of Jazz Organizations, Beaulieu and Redcar festivals.

The record companies, in this climate of widespread interest and awareness, profitably launched a flood of releases. With the advent of the long-playing record, whole concert performances were recorded; bebop musicians with a proclivity for lengthy improvisations could fully extend themselves, often beyond the staying power of old collectors, long conditioned to the three minutes' performance on the ten-inch 78rpm recordings by the heroes of their youth. But these old buffs were to have a wide choice of vintage material on compendium LPs and, later, CDs, much of it musically worthless and issued only for its dubious 'historic' value, or the romantic obscurity of the label on which it first appeared.

In pre-war years it would have been inconceivable that there would have been so many specialist jazz-record shops where the buff could make a choice from an extraordinarily large range of albums. One of the first was Dobell's, 77 Charing Cross Road. Doug Dobell took over his father's bookshop on demobilization from the RAF but, in 1947, turned it into a jazz-record shop. Others were to follow his example. Specialist jazz-record distributors were the suppliers.

The Johnny Dankworth Seven. *Back row*: Eddie Harvey, Don Rendell; *middle*: Bill Le Sage, Dankworth, Jimmy Deuchar; *front*: Eric Dawson, Tony Kinsey

Sadly, the little pioneer crusading magazines folded in the early fifties. *Jazz Monthly*, successor to *Jazz Forum*, survived the decade but later ceased publication. Other magazines, such as *Jazz Circle News*, have been founded and failed in the intervening decades leaving *Jazz Journal* (successor to *Pick-Up*) as the only monthly paper surviving from the 1950s. In the new millennium, two further monthlies, *Jazzwise* and *Jazz Review* (now merged with *Jazz Journal*), offered coverage of the whole spectrum of jazz while *JazzUK* focuses on news and features about jazz in Britain. *Jazz Rag* appears bimonthly and other more specialist publications include *Just Jazz* and *Straight No Chaser* while dance-music buffs are catered for in *Memory Lane*, founded in 1968 and edited by Ray Pallett. The house magazine of Ronnie Scott's Club, *Jazz at Ronnie Scott's* reached its twenty-seventh year and contained, apart from club information, articles of broader jazz interest.

Up to 1939 only a handful of books about jazz had been published in this country, but since then there have appeared histories, biographies, autobiographies and discographies, covering every possible aspect of the music. Even in 1977, there was no excuse whatsover for Mrs Thatcher, or her aide, to confuse New Orleans jazz with Duke Ellington.

Many post-war British jazz musicians have become authors on the music that they played, including trumpeters Ian Carr, John Chilton, Digby Fairweather and Humphrey Lyttelton; pianists Brian Priestley and Steve Race; saxophonists Dave Gelly, Harry Gold, Benny Green, Ronnie Scott and Bruce Turner; and bassist Coleridge Goode. Only Spike Hughes of the pre-1939 figures can lay claim to literary endeavour, but his books, two autobiographies and many on classical music, were published after the Second World War.

The popularity of books and magazines about jazz reflects the extent to which an 'alien' musical form has entered the allegedly stolid British psyche; the vast numbers of jazz-record albums issued and purchased provide tangible proof of this interest; the host of musicians practising the craft testifies that the pulse of this music throbs healthily in the Anglo-Saxon.

The hard core of dedicated musicians, writers, record producers and distributors and specialist shops has ensured the survival of jazz, often in the face of much hostility and indifference.

Such a situation, in its manifold aspects, far exceeds the naïve hopes of No. 1 Rhythm Club secretary Bill Elliott in the thirties of the club having its own premises open seven nights a week, and tribute has to be paid to those who in the years between 1919 and 1950 fashioned the events that led to the present healthy situation.

Honours, then, to Bert Firman, Fred Elizalde, Philip Lewis and Spike Hughes for their early 'hot' recordings; to the Archer Street jazzmen who prevailed upon their beaming and bowing bandleaders to allow them the occasional improvised chorus; to the intransigence of George Webb's Dixielanders, Humphrey Lyttelton's band and the Club Eleven musicians that led to their beliefs and practices being so widely accepted; to Leonard Hibbs and Eric Ballard for beginning the tradition of specialist magazines; to Max Jones and Albert McCarthy, especially, for continuing that tradition; to the pre-war record companies, notably Levaphone and Oriole, Parlophone (for their 'Rhythm Style' series), Columbia (for their 'Hot Jazz' releases) and Decca for recording so much British jazz in its formative days; to James Asman and Bill Kinnell for producing and issuing the first post-war British specialist label and inspiring others – Carlo Krahmer particularly – to follow their example.

Praise to the founders of the No. 1 Rhythm Club, especially Bill Elliott and Eric Ballard who, unbelievable as it would seem now, roamed London to seek out supporters of the cause; a bow to those disputative, fractious, prejudiced, pedantic and vitriolic animals called jazz buffs. They are the backbone and the soul of the movement and long may they survive!

In the history of jazz discography, full credit to the indefatigable Brian Rust, whose *Jazz Records 1897–1942* has been regarded as a bible by writers and discographers. The daunting industry and tenacity of purpose required to produce such a tome deserve special mention.

Of all the characters who stalk the pages of jazz history in Britain there will never be another like Edgar Jackson. This all-pervasive and adroitly entrepreneurial maverick was, in his bumbling and often offensive way, the first voice jazz had in Britain and it has not to be forgotten that he founded, and fought for the jazz content of, the *Melody Maker*, which gave jazz in all its aspects so much coverage for over fifty years. The contribution of its sister paper, *Rhythm*, must not be forgotten, either.

The role of the entrepreneur is usually overlooked and although the early impresarios were not concerned with the jazz interests in those early bookings of American bands they nevertheless gave the

British public the opportunity to hear the real thing; special tribute to Jack Hylton for bringing Duke Ellington and his orchestra to British shores, and to Bert Wilcox, Bix Curtis and Tony Hughes whose unlawful activities drew attention to the absurdity of the Musicians' Union's ban on the entry of foreign musicians.

Gathering of jazz authors on 24 July 1984 at Kettner's, London, for the launch of the first edition of this book. *Left to right*: Steve Race, Bruce Turner, James Asman, Roy Plomley, Alun Morgan (hidden behind Plomley), George Melly, Humphrey Lyttelton, Peter Clayton, Jim Godbolt, Eddie Harvey, Rex Harris, Kitty Grime, Charles Clinton, Brian Rust, Max Jones.

From the time the word jazz first entered the national consciousness no one, apart from Ernest Ansermet with his prophetic words in 1919 about Sidney Bechet ('Perhaps his is the road the world will swing down tomorrow'), visualized jazz taking such a grip on the countries outside America.

In the whole history of music it is difficult to identify any other 'alien' form of musical expression so thoroughly researched, passionately appraised and devotedly emulated. There are no parallels to the original development of this art form, springing as it does from a unique combination of racial, social and economic factors in America at the turn of the century, and flowering with the fortuitous invention of the gramophone.

That jazz should have emerged in its own breeding ground is one phenomenon. That it should permeate the musical activity and public consciousness of so many other countries and Britain in particular is another, and is quite incredible in its extent and ramifications. The history of jazz in Britain in its first half century is a remarkable story of missionary zeal, of the propagation of its values right from the early gramophone records, and of the determined assimilation of its essence by successive generations of British musicians.

When those five young men from New Orleans, calling themselves the Original Dixieland Jazz Band, wearing narrow-bottomed trousers, cut-away jackets, stiff collars, bow-ties and button-up boots, whose instruments were trumpet, clarinet, trombone, drums and piano, disembarked from the RMS *Adriatic* at Liverpool on the morning of 1 April 1919 they were to be the catalysts of a revolution in British musical tastes. The echoes of their stomping syncopations, that had the Prime Minister of Mirth, George Robey, rushing to confront producer Albert De Courville at the London Hippodrome on the night of 7 April, are still with us, nearly a century later.

Index

Jazz Books from Northway

Jim Godbolt,
All This and Many a Dog

Ron Brown with Digby Fairweather,
Nat Gonella – a life in Jazz

Digby Fairweather,
Notes from a Jazz Life

Ronnie Scott with Mike Hennessey,
Some of My Best Friends Are Blues

John Chilton,
Hot Jazz, Warm Feet

Peter Vacher,
Soloists and Sidemen: American Jazz Stories

Alan Plater,
Doggin' Around

Vic Ash
I Blew It My Way: bebop, big bands and Sinatra

Leslie Thompson with Jeffrey Green
Swing from a Small Island – the story of Leslie Thompson

Coleridge Goode and Roger Cotterrell,
Bass Lines: a life in Jazz

Alan Robertson
Joe Harriott – Fire in his Soul

Chris Searle,
*Forward Groove: Jazz and the Real World
from Louis Armstrong to Gilad Atzmon.*

Ian Carr,
Music Outside

Mike Hennessey,
The Little Giant – the story of Johnny Griffin

Derek Ansell,
Workout – the music of Hank Mobley

Graham Collier
the jazz composer – moving music off the paper

Peter King,
Flying High: A Jazz Life and Beyond (forthcoming)

Join our mailing list for details of new books,
events and special offers: write to
Northway Books,
39 Tytherton Road, London N19 4PZ
email *info@northwaybooks.com*
www.northwaybooks.com